AF454158

———————

Mondrala Press wishes to thank all its friends, fans, patrons, and
investors for making this book possible, and especially:

Ms. Randa Dumanian
Mr. and Mrs. Karol and Dagmara Maziukiewicz
de domo Sowul

without whose enthusiasm and open hearts this book
could never have happened.

———————

ABOUT THE AUTHOR

Aleksander Krawczuk (1922-2023) was a noted scholar of Greek and Roman antiquity, a professor at the Jagiellonian University, a former minister of culture, and an author of over 30 popular and widely translated books on the subject of the Antique. For fifty years, his books have enjoyed great popularity among a whole army of devoted fans—many of them people who had never taken interest in the Antique until they picked up one of his books.

What other scholar writes scholarly best-sellers? Yet, at one point, the good professor hosted an internationally syndicated TV program on ancient Greece and Rome. Of course, due to Russian cultural policies during the Cold War, Polish books could hardly be published in the West. Thanks to the good USA, EU, and NATO, they now can. Thanks, guys.

This book appears as part of a project to translate all of the works of Aleksander Krawczuk into English. The following titles have appeared already:

Seven Against Thebes: Myth and History
A Meeting in Oea, or Concerning Plato
The Last Olympiad: Twilight of Antiquity
Titus and Berenice: Jews, Romans, War, and a Legendary Love Story

Seven more titles will appear during 2023:

Rome and Jerusalem (a continuation of *Titus and Berenice*)
Constantine the Great: the Thirteenth Apostle
The Sons of Constantine
Julian the Apostate
The Tombs of Chaeronea, or, Concerning the Fall of Greece
The Case of Alcibiades, or, Ambition
Pericles and Apamea
Conversations with Petronius

Follow the series here: https://www.amazon.com/dp/B0BHF7KVTK

TRANSLATOR'S SPECIAL REQUEST
Translating and publishing this series of books has been a labor of
love for me. I grew up reading it, and I have always wanted to be able
to share it with my American friends. And so here it is.
It will not make me rich, but if you liked the book, would you please
recommend it to a friend?
And if you could give it an Amazon review,
you will be helping others find it!
https://www.amazon.com/dp/2919820494

THANK YOU!

HEROD
KING OF THE JEWS

SECOND EDITION

by Aleksander Krawczuk
translated by Tom Pinch

MONDRALA
PRESS

Mondrala Press is an imprint of
Ringel & Esch, S.A.R.L.-S
www.mondrala.com

Originally published in Polish in 1965 as
Herod król Judei

Editing by Mondrala Press
Cover Design by Mondrala Press

ISBN eBook: 978-2-919820-64-1
ISBN paperback: 978-2-919820-65-8
ISBN hardcover: 978-2-919820-66-5

The Illustrations featured in this book are taken from *The Holy Land, Syria, Idumea, Arabia, Egypt, and Nubia*, a travelogue of 19th-century Palestine and the magnum opus of Scottish painter David Roberts. It contains 250 lithographs by Louis Haghe of Roberts's watercolor sketches. It was first published by subscription between 1842 and 1849, in two separate publications: *The Holy Land, Syria, Idumea and Arabia* and *Egypt and Nubia*. William Brockedon and George Croly wrote much of the text, Croly writing the historical, and Brockedon the descriptive portions.

The book has been described as "one of the art-publishing sensations of the mid-Victorian period. It exceeded all other earlier lithographic projects in scale, was one of the most expensive publications of the nineteenth century, and has "proved to be the most pervasive and enduring of the nineteenth-century renderings of the East circulated in the West." Prints from the series continue to be sought after and command very high prices--high three to low four-digits: a very high price for a nineteenth-century print.

Jerusalem viewed from Mount of Olives

Aleksander Krawczuk
THE JEWISH TRILOGY

Herod, King of the Jews
Titus and Berenice
Rome and Jerusalem

TABLE OF CONTENTS

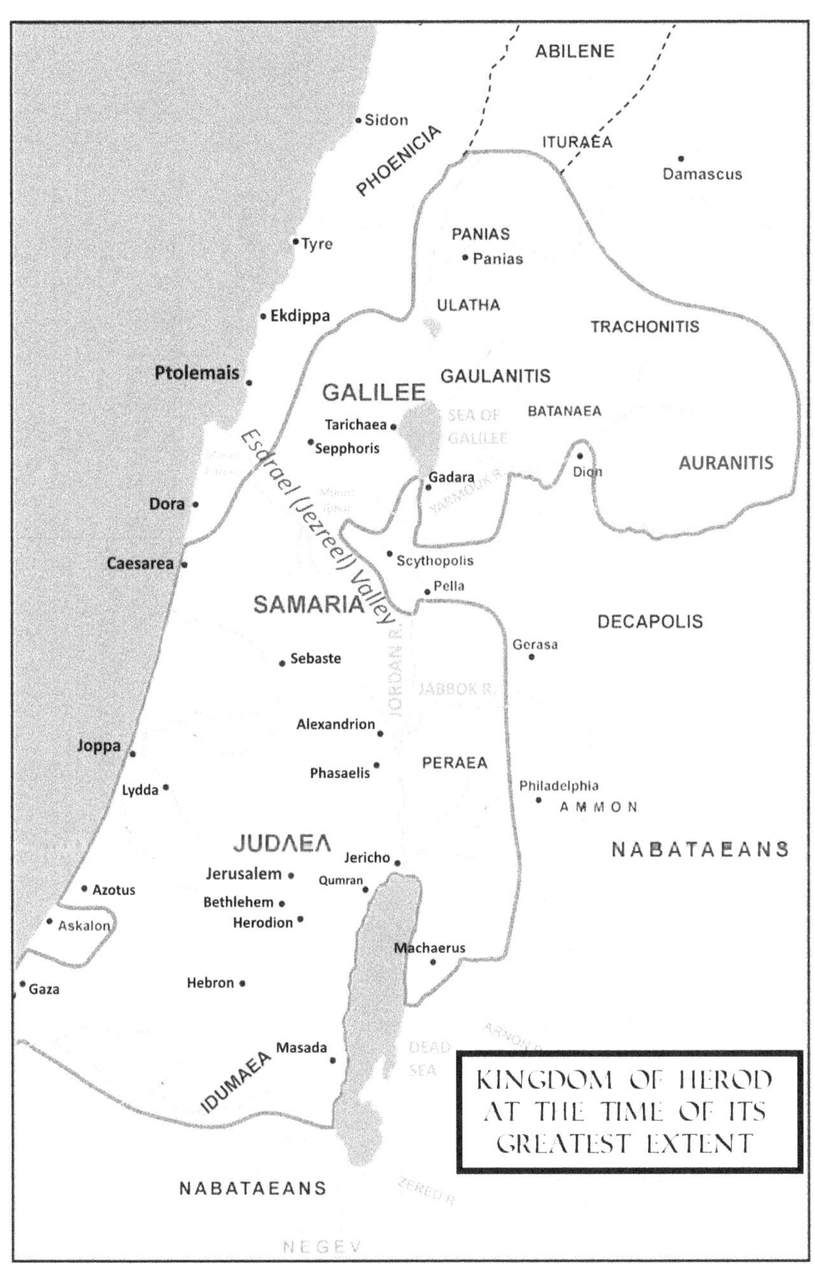

Herod's Kingdom at its apogee

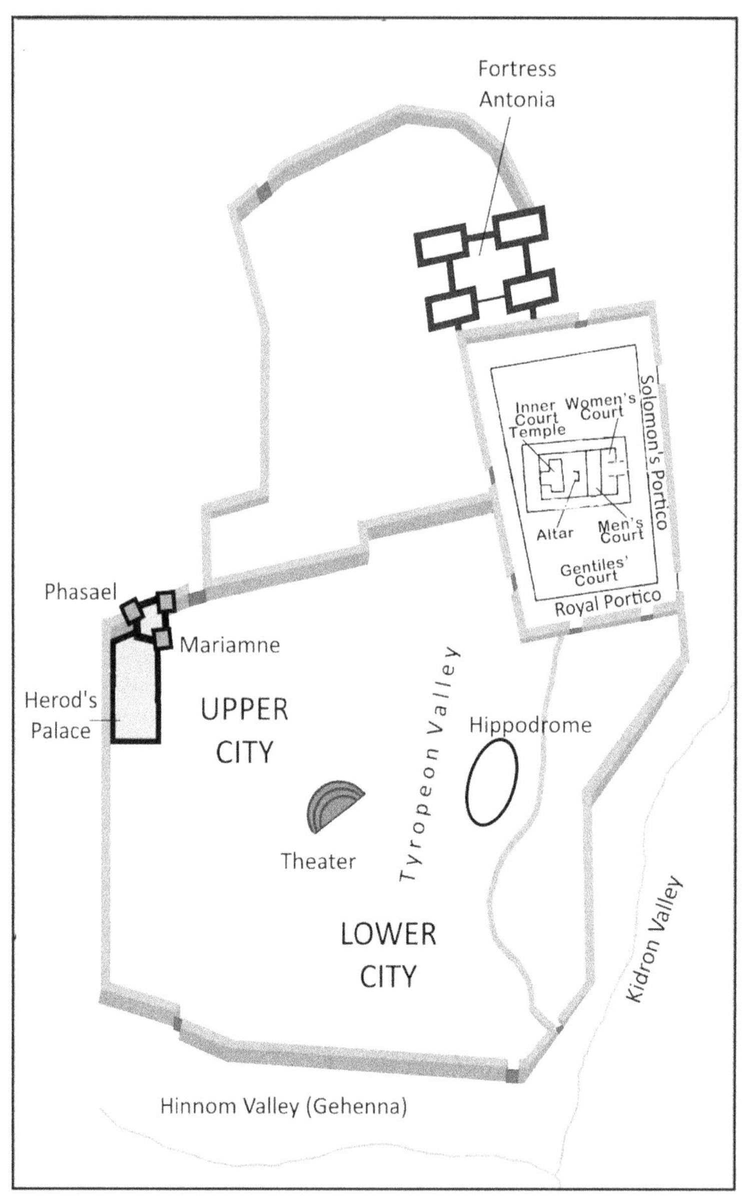

Jerusalem at the time of Herod

Herod's Temple

From your translator
THREE SHORT NOTES
IN THE STYLE OF THE AUTHOR

1. When I set out to translate the two Krawczuk books about the love of Emperor Titus and Queen Berenice (*Titus and Berenice*, 2023, *Rome and Jerusalem*, upcoming), I was unsure whether to translate the first volume of the trilogy as well—the book you are holding in your hand now. While the story of the First Jewish War is relatively little known, Herod the Great has had perhaps two score biographies in English. Why publish another?

But rereading *Herod, King of the Jews* with that question in mind, I realized that Krawczuk brings something unique to the well-known biography. First of all, he brings his highly readable style, of course, which is a joy in itself and which I hope I manage to convey here well enough to motivate you to learn Polish and read him in the original.

Secondly, better than any author I have read, he couches the history of Herod within the parallel history of Rome, laying bare for the modern reader the way in which the two histories intertwine, the limits within which Herod had to work, and the surprising significance of Palestine in Roman imperial politics.

But, above all, Krawczuk allows the reader to sense something that a British or an American reader may not readily intuit: how small nations see their own fate and survival in the shadow of great empires. The fact that the good professor wrote this under Russian occupation, at an ancient institution of learning of a recalcitrant client nation of the Russian Empire, gives his observations vital relevance.

2. While working on the text, I became aware of another dimension of the story. When editing, I read my text aloud to my Japanese friends—who are cultured and cosmopolitan but not necessarily very familiar with minor aspects of the history of the Roman Empire. But as I read my text to them, they suddenly burst out with a surprise of recognition. When, in one of the early chapters, the name of Judah Maccabee came up, they exclaimed: "Do you mean the guy from the Handel oratorio?" "Well, yes," I said. "The very same." Soon enough, we came across Mithridates of Pontus. "*Mitridate Re di Ponto*! Mozart!" my audience exclaimed. Just two lines lower came: "Vivaldi's *Farnace*!" This went on for some time until my friends finally reconciled themselves to the fact that they were reading a story somehow buried very deep in the consciousness of Western Civilization. By the time Aeneus made an appearance in the chapter on Herod saving Troy, my friends said nothing. One got up and put on the Purcell.

3. The back cover of this book features a reproduction of a fragment of Pieter Bruegel the Elder's *The Massacre of the Innocents*. The Bruegel family firm produced many versions of this painting (possibly as many as 14), but only this one, owned by the British Royal Collection, is thought to be by Pieter Senior. One of its previous owners, Rudolph II, the Magician Emperor and a connoisseur of panting, had it overpainted to hide the images of dead and dying children. Contemporary reality delivered enough of that.

Tom Pinch
Ardennes National Park
Luxembourg

HEROD
KING OF THE JEWS

Part One
FOR THE THRONE
OF JUDEA

SABBATH AND WAR

The Maccabees

Is it permissible to fight on the Sabbath?

The Hasidim, or The Pious, said:

"No! Never. Not under any circumstances. Not even when the enemy is about to strike you dead!"

When King Antiochus IV Epiphanes, ruler of Syria and Palestine, banned the celebration of Sabbath, the Hasidim left Jerusalem—a city occupied by the king's troops—and took refuge in caves in the desert The king's men pursued them, saying:

"Return, submit to your ruler's will, and live in peace!"

But the Pious persisted in their stubbornness. Since it was the Sabbath, they did not lift a finger when the others unsheathed their swords. They said to one another:

"We will die in the simplicity of our hearts. Heaven and earth will bear witness that we died without sin."

And all died, all, along with their wives and children—almost a thousand people. When the news of this spread throughout Judea (and an uprising against the oppressor, Antiochus IV, had started that year), the leaders of the uprising said:

"If we act like them, we will all perish. Therefore, from now on, if the enemy threatens us, we will fight even on the Sabbath."

The tiny nation's struggle for freedom continued for nearly

thirty years. The Hasmonean family led the uprising—the priest Mattathias and his five sons. One of Mattathias's sons, Judah,[1] earned the nickname "Maccabee"—the Hammer—because of the way he crushed his enemies. And hence came the name of the entire movement: the Maccabees.

The rebels won. David defeated Goliath, not for the first time in history and not the last. And, in the wake of the death of the thousand Hasidim in the first year of the uprising, everyone had come to accept that to fight on the Sabbath in order to defend one's life did not violate the Law.

But what does it mean "to defend one's life"? What are the limits of self-defense? Does one only defend against a direct blow to the body?

One hundred and five years later, this question returned in all its horror to torment the rebels' descendants. They were defending the most holy of their holy sites—the Temple of Jerusalem—against an enemy a thousand times more powerful than Antiochus had been.

And this is how it came to pass.

Aristobulus and Hyrcanus

Following their final victory over the Seleucids in 141 BC, the Hasmoneans ruled over Judea. They held the titles of High Priest and Prince and later—King. Taking advantage of the weakness of both their powerful neighbors—the Ptolemies of Egypt and the Seleucids of Syria—they seized many cities and provinces of Palestine. Despite this external display of strength, internally, Judea was weak and repeatedly convulsed by civil wars between various pretenders to the throne and different religious factions.

Just such a feud had taken place recently. Queen Alexandra, who had reigned since 76 BC, supported the Pharisee faction, influential among the poor. She understood that opposing the

---

[1] He is referred to in English as either Judah Maccabee or Judas Maccabaeus

Pharisees, as her husband had done, threatened a civil war and the dynasty's downfall. When she died in 67 BC, her throne passed to her elder son, Hyrcanus. Alas, his ambitious younger brother, Aristobulus, gathered armed supporters and took control of important fortresses. He also secured the support of the Sadducees, the priestly aristocracy. He now demanded the throne for himself.

In the third month of his reign, Hyrcanus suffered a defeat in battle near the oasis of Jericho. Besieged in the Temple of Jerusalem, he was forced to accept a compromise: Aristobulus would become king, but Hyrcanus would keep all his personal property. The brothers sealed their agreement with a solemn embrace in front of the Temple in the presence of jubilant crowds.

But, not everyone was satisfied with this arrangement. Soon, a new man emerged, a man who would play a significant role in the subsequent events. He convinced Hyrcanus that it was wrong to trust his brother because Aristobulus would never rest as long as Hyrcanus remained alive.

And thus, one night, Hyrcanus fled from Jerusalem to the city of Petra. Petra was located in the desert, a few days' journey south of the Dead Sea. It was the capital of the Arab kingdom of the Nabateans. By the grace of Rome, Nabateans ruled a large territory east of the Dead Sea, and this made their aid priceless. Hyrcanus's advisor used his good connections with the Nabateans to obtain military aid for the deposed king.

Soon, the king of Petra led tens of thousands of troops against Aristobulus, defeated him in battle, and besieged him at the Temple of Jerusalem. The people of the Judean capital, led by the Pharisees, sided with Hyrcanus. Only the Sadducees remained loyal to Aristobulus.

Fighting was very fierce, and the mood was bloody. Just how bloody illustrates the case of Onias. Hyrcanus's men had great respect for the priest Onias: they said about him that, like Elijah, he had once successfully prayed for rain during a great drought. And now, the crowd demanded that he curse Aristobulus and his supporters. Onias began to pray aloud:

"Lord, those about me are your people. The besieged are your priests. Therefore, I beg you, do not listen to either side!"

He was stoned to death.

It was now 65 BC, and a Roman corps led by Marcus Scaurus, sent by Roman general Pompey, fighting in Armenia, arrived at the border of Judea. Both Hyrcanus and Aristobulus sent envoys to Scaurus asking for his support. He sided with Aristobulus—and not only because he received four hundred talents from him. The Roman officer also assessed the political situation. Putting Hyrcanus on the throne of Judea meant putting the country under the influence of the Nabateans. Why should Rome strengthen the Nabateans?

The prospect of Roman intervention was frightening enough for Hyrcanus's allies to abandon him. Released from siege, Aristobulus pursued the retreating Nabateans, caught up with them, and killed six thousand of them in battle.

But the position of Hyrcanus was not yet entirely hopeless.

The Congress of Damascus

After you cross the mountains, suddenly, a broad vista of the oasis of Damascus opens up before you: a wide valley of lush greenery nourished by a gleaming network of thousands of little canals into which the River Barada splits. This vast stretch of gardens and orchards looks like a great forest from afar. Against its dark vegetation, the white city gleams in the sun like a long and narrow jewel. The air is crystal clear, infused with the blue of the sky and the gold of the sun. The richness of the oasis contrasts sharply with the yellow-and-red, burnt mountains and the vast stretches of desert sand that surround Damascus on all sides.

It was already late spring of 63 BC—the time of the most

beautiful greenery and the mildest air—by the time the supreme commander of the Roman forces of the East, Pompey, arrived here. His troops had captured the city—the ancient heart of Syria—almost two years earlier. And now, in that vast garden, luxurious, abundant, and opulent, the two brothers, Hyrcanus and Aristobulus, presented themselves before Pompey. Hyrcanus had failed to secure the support of Scaurus, but maybe Pompey would be more amenable? Pompey had been to Syria once, in 64 BC, and on that occasion, Hyrcanus and his adviser sent him an embassy with gifts. (Alas, Aristobulus did the same). Now that when Pompey was in Damascus again, both brothers hurried to his feet.

Both brought supporters along to make a good impression. Aristobulus's entourage looked magnificent, almost menacing: a large crowd of young men with long, beautifully coiffed hair, in purple cloaks and gleaming armor. Energetic and decisive, Aristobulus led his procession with dignity and solemnity. He was not a supplicant seeking help but a king calling on his new neighbor. But since he had learned that bribes got nearly anything from Roman officials, he did not arrive empty-handed. He brought a beautifully worked and heavy bunch of grapes made of pure gold, a work of art of immense value.

Hyrcanus had about a thousand men with him, all of them distinguished and respected elders of Judea. Pompey, an experienced politician, immediately noted that Hyrcanus was passive, perhaps even indolent; that while circumstances had forced Hyrcanus to take up the fight, it was clear that he would have preferred to retreat to the seclusion of his own home. He seemed lightweight and inconsequential. However, it did not escape the general's sharp eye that one man stood out among the thousand accompanying Hyrcanus: a man of imposing energy, enterprise, and strength of will.

It was Pompey's first time to deal in depth with the affairs of Judea. From his lofty heights of Imperial politics, spanning the world from the Euphrates to the Atlantic, the internal struggles of the minuscule nation in Palestine seemed both hopelessly tangled and irrelevant. All the same, Pompey was not entirely unfamiliar with the causes and history of the conflict between the two brothers. Their previous embassies and the reports of Roman officers who had visited Palestine gave him some insight into the situation in the country.

The general felt he needed more time to take a position in the matter. The arguments of both sides seemed equally reasonable. While he heard them, a delegation of the Pharisees arrived.

They had supported Hyrcanus in the past, but now they changed their policy and decided to eliminate the House of the Hasmoneans altogether. They accused both brothers of ruling with the help of foreign mercenaries and treating their subjects like abject slaves. Pompey sent the Pharisees away, but their petition had its impact.

There was another factor preventing Pompey from making a quick decision. It was his intended expedition against the Nabateans.

Their lands extended to the east of Judea, from the Sinai Peninsula and the borders of Egypt all the way to the gates of Syria. Their rulers often interfered in the affairs of their neighbors. Since Pompey had annexed Syria as a Roman province, he considered it necessary to secure it from that direction. But if he were to march on Petra, the capital of the Nabateans, his army would have to pass through Palestine—a territory ruled by the Hasmoneans. And once he entered the Nabatean desert, he would face difficulties in supply. It was vital that the ruler of Palestine should be a loyal supporter of Pompey. But which of the two brothers offered a better security guarantee?

Hyrcanus seemed weak. Moreover, his advisor was married—Aristobulus's supporters did not fail to point out—to a woman from a distinguished Nabatean family. On the other hand, the Nabateans had recently attacked Aristobulus; this seemed to make him the natural ally. Yet, the man behaved haughtily. He even managed to offend Scaurus, reminding him point blank of those four hundred talents. His attitude raised doubts as to whether he would ever become a genuinely pliable instrument of Rome.

Therefore, Pompey decided that it would be best to keep the matter open for the moment. He told both brothers that he would consider their case upon his return from his campaign against the

Nabateans, and—he marched out of Damascus. Neither Hyrcanus nor Aristobulus dared to leave the Roman commander's side. They traveled with him, keeping a close eye on each other.

Towards Judea

At first, the army had the rocky Mount Hermon on its right. Snow covered its lofty peaks, and thick forests cloaked its slopes. As the army moved south, it left Mount Hermon behind and entered a vast, rocky plateau with good pastures. Here and there, they encountered Arab nomads. Then, gradually, the road descended into a large, elongated basin called Batanea. To the east, it was closed off by a vast plateau of cracked lava: wild, barren, and sparsely populated. The Greeks called it Trachonitis. Millions of years ago, that lava had flowed from the mouths of great volcanoes, now extinct. Their craters now loomed to the southeast as a massive mountain range. They were called Auranitis. The reddish-brown soil of Batanea was also of volcanic origin and, therefore, very fertile. Wheat yielded splendidly here: the province was the granary of Syria. Only trees were completely absent, and therefore—wood. Houses were built of basalt, which quickly blackened in the sun, giving the towns and villages a gloomy aspect.

To the west rose the hills of Gaulanitis. Beyond them, from north to south, flowed the River Jordan, emptying into the Sea of Galilee. Continuing south, the Romans crossed Batanea and forded the Yarmouk River, a left-hand tributary of the Jordan. It flowed in an arc, east to west, and emptied into the Jordan just below the Sea of Galilee.

The Hasmonean state began here, for they had conquered the lands south of this river and east of the Jordan some decades ago. The Greeks called this land *Decapolis* or Ten Cities. They had begun to settle there shortly after the conquests of Alexander the Great. Later, when Ptolemies and Seleucids ruled over Palestine, Greeks arrived here in even greater numbers. The local Jews did not welcome them warmly since each group maintained its own language and customs. Yet,

Decapolis flourished. This land was not only beautiful but also rich and fertile. Forests covered the slopes of the hills, and vast, succulent meadows fed large herds of cattle. Well-irrigated fields yielded abundant harvests.

In the city of Dion, one of the cities of Decapolis, Aristobulus left the Roman camp. He was in his kingdom and did not think it proper to show himself to his subjects in the role of a Roman courtier. But Hyrcanus and his advisor remained. Of course, they immediately took advantage of their opponent's ill-considered departure. They insinuated to Pompey that this was a hostile act: Aristobulus would ally with the Nabateans and attack the Roman army from behind as it advanced on Petra.

Pompey decided that in view of Aristobulus's haughty independence, he could not delay settling the affairs of Judea anymore. He started with his entire army in pursuit of Aristobulus, marched through the hills of Decapolis, and quickly reached the city of Pella. Its Greek settlers had named it after the capital of Macedonia, where Alexander the Great had been born. It perched on a natural terrace overlooking the Valley of the Jordan. And now, Pompey and his men saw this famous river for the first time. It wound its way with capricious meanders through a wide valley; a belt of lush vegetation grew along its banks, above which rose the plumes of magnificent palm trees, but the valley itself was sparsely cultivated. At this time of year, crossing the Jordan presented no difficulty—the river, depleted by the dry season, was only several paces wide in most places. On the other—western—side of the river, the Romans found themselves in the province of the city of Scythopolis, where many Greeks lived. It was the only city of Decapolis west of the Jordan. The lands around Scythopolis were well-watered and produced abundant crops, but the city owed its wealth and importance to its excellent location on the main tract from Decapolis to the sea, through the Jezreel Valley, and from Galilee to the south, towards Jerusalem.

The Romans took this latter road. They marched along the right edge of the valley, crossing a narrow strip of the province of Samaria, which reached down to the river here. The slopes of its hills, cultivated in places, rose to the right of the marching column. After several hours, the army entered the town of Coreae. It was the first town located in the province of Judea. Here, the army had to stop because, slightly south of town, on the top of a high, steep hill, there rose the walls of a mighty fortress. It was called Alexandrion, and Aristobulus was waiting for them there.

Pompey Marches on Jerusalem

The Roman commander summoned the Jewish king to appear before him. Aristobulus considered ignoring the order, but the prevailing opinion among his advisors was that such a demonstration of independence would be too dangerous. Everyone was impressed by Pompey's recent victories in Asia Minor, Armenia, and Syria. Aristobulus reluctantly yielded to persuasion, swallowed his pride, and descended to the Roman camp to argue in defense of his right to the throne. Immediately after his meeting with Pompey, however, he returned to his eagle's nest. Thus, he hoped to show that he was an independent player and an equal partner of Rome.

He repeated this errand two or three more times to argue against his brother and to persuade Pompey of the righteousness of his cause. No one stopped him from returning to his fortress because the Roman commander had not yet decided whom to support in Judea.

Finally, Pompey demanded that Aristobulus issue an order instructing all fortresses in his kingdom to surrender to the Romans. The king could not refuse this proof of peaceful intentions. But, after signing the order, he hurried to Jerusalem, and this raised suspicion among his enemies that he would gather his forces there and put up armed resistance. Hyrcanus and his advisor fueled this suspicion in every possible way. Pompey eventually decided it would be wisest to call on Jerusalem in order to assess the situation on the spot.

The road now led down the Jordan Valley. The landscape became wilder, desert-like. Bare, rocky slopes rose steeply on the right, and a similar range stretched on the other, eastern side of the Jordan.

Only a narrow strip of trees and bushes grew along the river. Other than that, everything was fawn, parched, and lifeless. And no wonder: it was already the height of summer, and it never rains in Palestine at this time of year. After a day's march through the scorching desert, the soldiers's eyes were suddenly dazzled one evening by the sight of a beautiful oasis. The steep slopes opened to the west, creating an amphitheater-like valley covered by a vast grove of palms, cypresses, olive trees, and sycamores. Here and there grew plantations of fragrant balsam. Cheerful streams flowed from a powerful spring at the foot of the mountains, playfully winding among trees and bushes. In the distance, to the south, lay the vast, dark-blue expanse of the Dead Sea.

On a low hill above the oasis rose the white walls of a city. This was Jericho. The soldiers immediately set up camp and constructed fortifications to protect it against a surprise attack—a practice always followed by the Roman army, even on friendly territory.

Pompey went out of the camp to enjoy a ride. At that moment, his men spotted military messengers approaching from the direction of Coreae. They were waving spears wrapped in branches of laurel, a sign that they were bringing good news. Pompey returned to camp, and a crowd of legionaries gathered around their leader. The couriers delivered a letter.

The letter had come from very far away, from the northern shores of the Black Sea, from a peninsula known at that time as the Tauric Chersonese—today's Crimea. Its author, Pharnaces, reported that his father, King Mithridates, had died and that he, his son, took power and recognized himself as a servant of Pompey and of the Roman people.

Mithridates had been king of Pontus, a land in the northeast of Asia Minor, and of the Tauric Chersonese, and an implacable enemy of Rome. He fought three bloody wars against her legions—all of which he lost. Two years ago, Pompey defeated him in the Third Pontic War, driving him out of Pontus and Armenia and pursuing him as far as the Caucasus. Mithridates fled to his possessions on the Tauric Chersonese, hoping to gather forces for a fourth war against Rome, but now everyone abandoned him, even his son Pharnaces.

Betrayed, the old king committed suicide.

Now Pompey's hands were free. Nothing threatened him from the north, and he could concentrate on the business of Judea. The following day, the army broke camp and set out for Jerusalem. The road led westward, steeply up from the Jordan Valley. The landscape was bleak: everywhere rose bare, chalky cliffs, and there was not a trace of greenery.

Suddenly, the Roman vanguard spotted a group of horsemen galloping from the direction of Jerusalem. It was Aristobulus and his entourage. He had come to clear up the misunderstanding, insisting that he harbored no hostile intentions. As proof, he offered Pompey a significant sum of money and free entry into the city. This time, the Roman general kept Aristobulus with him and sent one of his officers, Aulus Gabinius, ahead to fetch the promised gifts and assess the situation.

Jerusalem was not far away, but Gabinius returned surprisingly quickly. He reported that he had not been allowed into the city, that the gates were closed, and armed men occupied the walls. Aristobulus himself was surprised by this turn of events. He was blameless, he said. If only Pompey had allowed him to return to his people immediately, as he had done at Alexandrion, no one would have prevented the Romans from entering the city. But since the Roman officer arrived alone, the king's supporters and soldiers, thinking Aristobulus had been captured or killed, felt it was their duty to defend the city.

Pompey saw a sign of treachery in this. He decided that the king had been preparing an ambush. Hyrcanus and his adviser did their best to confirm the general in this conclusion. Aristobulus was put under arrest.

The Fall of the City

Meanwhile, the army approached the city. As it passed by the charming oasis of Bethany, the road began to ascend the slope of Mount of Olives, so called because of its countless olive trees.

From its summit, a magnificent panorama unfolded before Pompey and his men. As far as the eye could see, the gray hills of Judea rose and fell like frozen waves. Densely scattered white stones covered the hills of Judea, creating from a distance the impression that the land was strewn with ruins or with desiccated bones of giants. This land was very poor, but at its heart lay a great city: Jerusalem. Those gazing from Mount of Olives had it before them on a slightly lower hill on the other side of a deep valley. To their southeast, the Dead Sea shone in the distance. Beyond it, the horizon was closed off by the blue range of a mighty mountain range—the land of the Nabateans. The clarity of the air made the sea appear within the reach of a hand, even though one had to walk for a day to reach its shores. To the east, where they had come from, stretched the vast Jordan Valley. The dark green stripe running down its center was the vegetation growing along the river.

But the commander had not come to Mount of Olives to revel in the majesty of the sights. He observed the city and listened to the explanations of the Jews accompanying him. He quickly understood the city plan and its defenses and familiarized himself with its history.

Jerusalem lay on a wide, undulating promontory extending southwards from the Judean plateau. This promontory was difficult to access as it sloped steeply down on three sides into two rocky gorges. On the east, between Mount of Olives and Jerusalem, ran the Kidron (Cedron) Valley. Some people called it the Valley of Jehoshaphat and believed that the Last Judgment would take place there, perhaps because every step of the valley was filled with tombs and gravestones. The equally gloomy Hinnom Valley (Gehenna) surrounded the city from the west and south. It also served as a cemetery as well as a massive garbage dump. In both valleys, streams flowed only in winter and spring; nothing grew there, and they were uninhabited. The general immediately realized that Jerusalem's location permitted an attack from one direction only: from the north, where the promontory on which the city stood connected with the hills of Judea.

Across the entire city ran, from north to south, a steep valley called Tyropoeon, dividing Jerusalem into two parts. The western side, between the Hinnom Valley and Tyropoeon, was the more extensive part. The city's business center and its most populous districts had been here for centuries. The eastern part, on the other hand, between Tyropoeon and the Kidron, though smaller and slightly lower, was older and more venerable. On a narrow ridge at the junction of the two promontories, the earliest inhabitants of this land, the Jebusites,[2] had built their settlement. Then, almost a thousand years before the arrival of Pompey, King David conquered it and established the capital of his kingdom here. This was the famous Zion of David praised in the Book of Psalms.

David's son and successor, Solomon, moved to the northern, slightly higher, and broader part of the ridge between Tyropoeon and Kidron. There, he built a palace and a temple. He brought cedars from Mount Lebanon for their construction. The enormous quadrangle of walls opposite the Mount of Olives was that Temple.

True, it was not Solomon's Temple. The Babylonians had conquered and destroyed Jerusalem five centuries earlier, driving its inhabitants into captivity beyond the Euphrates. Half a century later, King Cyrus of Persia captured Babylon and allowed the Jews to return to their homeland. They rebuilt the city and the temple, though on a far less magnificent scale. It was then, after returning from Babylonian captivity, that Jews settled on the ridge between Tyropoeon and the Hinnom Valley. Finally, a hundred years ago, Judas Maccabeus

---

[2] The Jebusites were, according to the books of Joshua and Samuel from the Tanakh, a Canaanite tribe that inhabited Jerusalem, then called Jebus prior to the conquest of Joshua. Although a majority of scholars agree that the *Book of Joshua* holds little historical value for early Israel and most likely reflects a much later period, The Books of Kings as well as *1 Chronicles* state that Jerusalem was known as Jebus prior to this event (*1 Chronicles* 11:4). The identification of Jebus with Jerusalem is sometimes disputed by scholars.

fortified the Temple walls. It became a fortress within a fortress: it could continue to defend itself even after the city fell.

Pompey listened, observed, and analyzed. Days passed, and he could not make a decision. The siege promised to be brutal and bloody.

And then, the inhabitants of the city decided to help Pompey.

The Desecration of the Temple

The inhabitants of Jerusalem observed the Roman legions with fear and admiration as they deployed on the hills surrounding the city. Each Roman soldier knew his place on the march, in camp, and in battle. Iron discipline and constant practice made this army into a formidable, ruthlessly efficient fighting machine.

The name of Pompey also struck terror into people's hearts. Five years ago, within a few short months, Pompey had cleared the Mediterranean Sea of pirates. Two years ago, he defeated Mithridates and carried the Roman eagles all the way to the Caucasus. Last year, he took Syria and dethroned the last Seleucid king—the descendant of the persecutor of the Jews from a century ago.

Calls to surrender the city echoed in Jerusalem even before any fighting began. Those connected to Hyrcanus fervently advocated it, believing that Pompey would restore him to power. The city was in turmoil.

Finally, the followers of Aristobulus realized that they could not hold the whole city. They locked themselves within the temple complex, burning the bridge over the Tyropoeon Valley, and prepared to fight to the death. The rest of the inhabitants opened the city gates.

Thus, the Romans captured Jerusalem without drawing their swords. No harm befell the inhabitants: the scenario of two years ago replayed itself: motivated by their hatred for the Sadducees, the Pharisees sided with the besiegers against the defenders. But, locked up in the Temple, Aristobulus rejected all Roman proposals for negotiations.

Access to the Temple was difficult because of its deep moat and massive towers. The legionaries attempted to fill in the moat to bring their siege engines to the Temple walls. Despite their best efforts, however, progress was slow. The besieged fought with desperate courage and pelted Roman engineers with missiles. Weeks passed, and a general assault was still impossible.

And then, at some point, the Romans noticed a peculiar pattern in the behavior of their adversaries. Every seventh day, they ceased all activities as if withdrawing into themselves. On such days, anyone could approach the walls, and no one even threw a stone at him from above. Curious, the soldiers inquired of the Jews about this oddity and learned that the seventh day of the week was the Sabbath, when fighting was allowed only in self-defense.

Pompey immediately seized the opportunity. Every seventh day, the legionaries filled the moat and built ramps for the war machines but were strictly ordered not to attack the Jews under any circumstances. Several consecutive Sabbaths allowed the Romans to fill in the moat and bring their siege towers and engines to the foot of the walls. From the towers, Roman catapults and ballistas rained a hail of missiles on the defenders while battering rams pounded the walls from below.

From the neighboring hills and from the platforms of their siege towers, the Romans had a clear view of the inside of the Temple. The Temple itself was not a large building. It faced east, and on the spacious courtyard before the main entrance stood a massive altar made of unhewn stones, where a sacrificial fire burned day and night.

The Romans were struck by the priests' calm performance of sacrifices and prayers at the altar, according to the elaborate ancient ritual. They observed that the priests sacrificed a one-year-old lamb, flour, oil, and wine every morning and evening. During the Sabbath, they doubled the offering and sang psalms during the ritual. Silver trumpets resounded at the end of each stanza, and everyone within the temple grounds bowed down to the ground. All of this continued unfalteringly, even as the horror of death drew nearer with each passing day.

After three months of siege, the final Roman assault took place on a Sabbath day. Battered by the Roman siege engines, the highest tower of the Temple came crashing down. Legionaries poured in through the breach in the wall and quickly encircled the vast courtyard. The followers of Hyrcanus rushed in after them. Some defenders continued to fight, believing that now was the time to fight for their lives. Others threw themselves from the walls into the abyss of the Kidron Valley. Many perished in the flames of a fire they had set to the wooden sheds surrounding the courtyard.

Almost all the defenders of the temple perished—around twelve thousand men. Jews—the supporters of Hyrcanus—and not Romans—killed most of them: such unrelenting hatred divided the Jewish society. While blood flowed in the courtyard and conflagration raged, the priests never interrupted their sacrifice. They performed it with complete concentration, just as they did in times of peace. The words of their psalm mingled with the clash of weapons and the cries of the dying.

Pompey and his entourage entered the Temple. There, he beheld the inner altar where the priests offered incense twice a day, the seven-branched golden candlestick, and the equally precious offering table on which, on the Sabbath, the priests placed twelve loaves of bread. Stacks of coins and crates of valuable incense filled the chambers adjacent to the main temple building.

The general left these treasures untouched. However, he took a step that was to shake all Jews across the world: he lifted the veil and entered the second part of the temple, the Holy of Holies, where only the high priest could enter, and only once a year, on the Day of Atonement.

Pompey later recounted with some surprise:

"There was nothing there! The chamber was empty. And you would have expected a treasure or a statue. Or *something*."

Filled with admiration for the courage of the Jews, the conqueror ordered a ritual cleansing of the temple and the resumption of sacrifices on the following day.

The memory of those bloody days and of the desecration of

the Holy of Holies was to endure for centuries. A few years after Pompey's capture of the Temple, a book of psalms was composed in Palestine, later called the *Psalms of Solomon*.[3] The book has survived to our times, but only in its Greek translation. In it, the author, with sorrow and horror, speaks of the invasion of unbelievers and the desecration of the Holy of Holies, lamenting the indifference of the Lord:

> The proud conqueror's battering ram broke the mighty walls, and You did not prevent it. Foreign nations entered your altar and scornfully trampled it with their boots. (...) Our sons and daughters suffered harsh slavery, and their captors branded them. [4]

The temple was captured in the autumn of 63 BC when the Roman consuls were Marcus Tullius Cicero and Gaius Antony. In September of that year, a boy was born in Rome who, thirty-three years later, would become the ruler of the world.

And the memories of the war, the massacre in the Temple, and the dreadful magnificence of the Roman legions would leave an indelible impression on the mind of a certain boy from Judea. That boy, then ten years old, was interested in everything happening around him, mainly because his father was among the leading figures of the great drama in Judea.

He was the son of Hyrcanus' advisor. And his name was Herod.

---

[3] One of the apocryphal books, the Psalms *of Solomon* is a group of eighteen psalms (religious songs or poems) written in the first or second centuries BC that are not part of any current scriptural canon.

[4] *Psalms of Solomon*, 2: 1-2, 6

JUDEA DIVIDED

Winners and Losers

At the end of September 61 BC, Pompey made his triumphant entry into Rome. Kings and chieftains of conquered nations—three hundred and twenty-four men, along with their families—walked before his chariot. Among the captives was Aristobulus Hasmoneus, King of Judea, who had once ruled Jerusalem but now faced humiliation and ridicule before the Roman crowd.

They led him up the Via Sacra[5] to the Capitol. There, triumphant Pompey offered a thanksgiving sacrifice to Jupiter Best and Greatest, the guardian deity of the Roman state, for helping him defeat so many princes and granting such glory, wealth, and territory to Rome. And as a votive offering to the Capitoline temple, the victorious general hung inside it that bunch of golden grapes he had once received from Aristobulus in Damascus.

Pompey now named Syria and Judea among the newly conquered territories, the former kingdoms of the Seleucids and the Hasmoneans. And thus, metaphorically speaking, the mighty conqueror reconciled the former mortal enemies as subjects of Rome, equal in status and humiliation.

In Rome, there was no mercy for the defeated, only contempt and mockery. Two years after Pompey's grand triumph, Cicero, one of his contemporaries, insulted the unfortunate people of Judea:

Each city, O Laelius, has its own peculiar religion, just as we have ours. Yet, even when Jerusalem flourished and Jews lived in peace, their religious ceremonies and observances were very far from the splendor of this empire and from the dignity of our name and the

---

[5] Via Sacra was the main street of ancient Rome and part of the traditional route of the Roman Triumph that began on the outskirts of the city and proceeded through the Roman Forum and up to the Capitoline Hill

institutions of our ancestors. And those ceremonies are all the more odious to us now because that nation has demonstrated with its arms that it hates our Republic. How dear that nation was to the immortal gods was proved by it having been defeated, by its revenues having been farmed out to our contractors, and by its reduction to a state of subjection.[6]

Following the conclusion of the Maccabean wars, Judea had enjoyed eighty years of independence. However, with Pompey's capture of the Temple, foreign rule once again descended on the hills and plains of the beautiful land.

The land had no natural frontiers, and it was easy for invading armies to penetrate the heart of this small country. Over the centuries, the people living between the rocky desert near the Dead Sea and the forested mountains of northern Galilee had had to bow repeatedly before superior hostile forces. Egyptians, Assyrians, Babylonians, Persians, Ptolemies of Egypt, and Seleucids of Syria successively imposed their rule upon them. But the Jews always rose again, proud and unyielding. Nearly every generation of Jews engaged in battles with enemies far more powerful than they and endured bloody reprisals. The conquerors razed their cities and villages, took thousands of inhabitants away to distant lands, or sold them into slavery. Hunger and poverty drove others away from this small, poor, and overcrowded land. Its people could be found in every land of the known world, still turning their eyes in fond memory towards their distant, unfortunate homeland.[7]

And now, all the great empires of the East had fallen. The erstwhile haughty masters of the universe, who had once set their proud feet on the necks of the rebellious people of Judea, crumbled into dust. The Romans were the new overlords. How would they govern their new acquisition?

––––––––––––––––––––

[6] M. Tullius Cicero, *Pro Flacco*, 69.

[7] A Polish reader of these words written in 1965 would no doubt have noticed how much the fate of Poland 1688-1945 resembled the history of ancient Israel described in this paragraph.

Usually, Romans incorporated conquered lands into the Empire and organized them as provinces, with the population paying high taxes and living under the direct rule of governors appointed from Rome. In the case of Judea, Ptolemy made different arrangements for the time being, perhaps because the country was so small. He indeed subjected it to the supervision of a Roman governor—not its own, but the governor of the neighboring Roman province of Syria. He also levied a heavy tax, but he left intact certain vestiges of Judea's former statehood in order to reward Hyrcanus for his loyal service to Pompey.

And now Hyrcanus, the brother of the dethroned Aristobulus, ruled Jerusalem by the grace of Rome: the prolonged struggle for the throne had ended in his victory. But what a high price he had had to pay for the victory—he and his people!

Ptolemy denied Hyrcanus the royal title: he was only allowed the title of *ethnarch*, meaning "the ruler of the people." He held the office of High Priest, which, from a political perspective, was perhaps the more powerful, but the conquerors ordered the demolition of the walls of Jerusalem to prevent future attempts at independence. Even more significantly, they took from Hyrcanus several significant and wealthy cities that his ancestors had incorporated into their kingdom: the entire Decapolis and all the coastal towns. These cities, inhabited mainly by Greeks, were declared "free." In practice, this only meant internal autonomy, as they had to obey the will and directives of the governor of the province of Syria: the same official who oversaw Hyrcanus and his greatly diminished possessions.

What, then, remained for the descendant of the illustrious Hasmonean dynasty? Only three regions: Judea proper, meaning Jerusalem and its surroundings, with the adjoining Idumea to the south and a small sliver of Samaria to the north (the rest of Samaria had also received "freedom" from the Romans); Galilee, minus a few districts incorporated into the province of Syria; and Perea: a narrow strip of land to the east of the lower Jordan and the Dead Sea.

The economy of all these regions had suffered greatly from the prolonged wars fought by the generations of Hasmonean contenders for the throne. Nevertheless, Romans burdened them with high taxes.

The rulers of the world did not spare painful humiliations to the rebellious people of Palestine. It was an age-old custom that every Jew, whether in the country or abroad, who reached the age of twenty had to pay a small annual tribute for the temple's upkeep, amounting to two drachmas. But now, the Roman Senate and the governors of individual provinces repeatedly forbade sending such funds to Jerusalem. Supposedly, the measure was designed to prevent the outflow of specie from the Empire. However, more often than not, the confiscated Jewish funds ended up not in the state treasury but in the governors' private pockets.

Thus, the weak Hyrcanus had to meet challenges that even a ruler of great talent and energy would have found difficult. How could he heal the wounds inflicted by the wars and simultaneously satisfy the ever-hungry Romans? How could he sustain the economy of a small country whose organism had suffered such brutal quartering, was cut off from the sea, and deprived of many of its cities? And, above all, how did one stay in power when part of the population still saw Aristobulus as their rightful king, another part scorned both brothers, and everyone was full of hatred for the Romans?

If Hyrcanus did not succumb immediately to the burden of these tasks, it was thanks to both the efforts of his highly gifted adviser and the deep internal conflict within the nation he ruled: social, religious, and ethnic. These internal divisions weakened the nation's ability to fight the common enemy and allowed one group to rule over the others.

The Land and its Inhabitants

Palestine had never been a land flowing with milk and honey; it might have appeared that way only to those arriving from the desert. There are a few lush areas in it, like the oasis of Jericho, but most of the land is rocky and parched. Its fertility depends on winter rains, which bring heavy showers and, to the highlands, snow. Dry riverbeds then fill with rushing water, and fields and pastures turn fresh green and bloom with colorful flowers. However, by May, the hot and dry east wind from the desert causes the vegetation to wither. Rain is very rare in the summer.

Constant labor is needed to retain some of the water that would otherwise escape to the sea in winter, carrying fertile soil with it. Since ancient times, the inhabitants of Palestine have carved rock cisterns, built levies, and patiently carved terraces on mountain slopes. They established settlements around the few year-round springs. But winter rainfall varied across the country, decreasing sharply south of Jerusalem. Eastern slopes of the Judean plateau and the Jordan Valley received very little rain, making those areas either desert or, at best, meager pasture for goats and sheep.

The ancient Palestinian farmer cultivated every piece of land he could, hoping for rather than expecting a harvest. His main crops were wheat and barley, and the harvest, depending on the region and type of grain, took place between April and June. The grape harvest occurred in September and October, coinciding with the ripening of olives and pomegranates. Figs were harvested at the height of summer.

If winter rains failed, if violent winds raged in spring or autumn, or a locust plague hit during the summer, the country faced starvation.

Palestine had little in the way of wealth except for what the land provided. There were no metal ores or extensive forests. Important land routes passed through Palestine, connecting Egypt with Syria and Mesopotamia, but the most profitable of these routes were controlled not by Jews but by Greeks, who predominated along the coast, and Nabateans, who ruled the cities east of Jordan.

Nevertheless, trade enriched many Jewish families in larger towns. In Jerusalem itself, the influx of vast numbers of pilgrims during holidays brought significant revenues, especially for priests, shopkeepers, and bankers. Pilgrims came not only from all over Palestine but also from many lands around the Mediterranean Sea.

Of the various crafts, weaving prospered most in Palestine. Linen and wool were the source of fiber. In Jerusalem, weavers occupied a whole separate quarter. There were plenty of potters, blacksmiths, and stonemasons in Judea. Due to the scarcity of wood, people constructed mostly with stone.

No branch of industry could reach economies of scale in a small, poor country like Palestine. However, during years of good harvest, the people were able to feed themselves. In part, this was because their needs were relatively modest: they consumed meat only on special occasions; even dried fish was considered a delicacy. The staple diet consisted of barley or wheat cakes, olive oil, wine, and dates.

The wealth of the upper class starkly contrasted with the poverty of the masses. Of course, this relative wealth could not compare with the enormous fortunes of the Roman senators in Italy. Nevertheless, considering the size and income levels of the two regions, social conflicts were just as sharp in both countries.

It is difficult to determine precisely how the large estates had emerged in Palestine, but it is clear that in the times of Hyrcanus, enormous landed estates coexisted with small farms. Usually, the large landowners did not reside on the land. Most of the year, they lived in Jerusalem, occupied with the business of the Temple, courts, politics, and trade while leasing their land to sharecroppers or leaving their estates to overseers.

Like in all of the Mediterranean, slavery existed also in Palestine. However, it was far less common compared to Italy or Greece. The inflow of slaves into Italy resulted primarily from Rome's wars of conquest. There, slaves served as cheap labor and were in high demand due to the depopulation caused by the demands of military service. Additionally, many regions of the peninsula depopulated because their inhabitants migrated to the capital or to newly conquered provinces, where fertile land was readily available, and cunning and ruthless individuals could amass considerable wealth through trade or the exploitation of the vanquished.

In Palestine, the situation was different. Even during their heyday, the Hasmoneans fought mainly in border conflicts, and there was no hope of acquiring large numbers of slaves through conquest. Furthermore, there was not much internal demand for such labor either. Despite its poverty, the land was densely populated, and there was no labor shortage. So why spend money on an enslaved person, maintaining and clothing them for many years, when one could easily hire people for meager day wages? At any time of year, whole squads of young people could be found on the towns' squares and streets, waiting for a chance to earn a penny.

As a result, slavery in Palestine was limited. Slaves, such as there were, served mainly in the households of the great lords. Or else, the ruling elite employed them for the heaviest tasks requiring great physical effort.

Due to the low supply of slaves, the class conflict between the rich and the masses of poor farmers and landless poor was more pronounced in Palestine than elsewhere. These conflicts erupted in frequent bouts of spontaneous unrest, and such developments will be seen throughout the story of Herod's life. Class antagonisms often found expression in conflicts between religious sects. Throughout the period, numerous sects arose within the Jewish community, and we will discuss some of them in the following pages. But two sects should be characterized immediately, as their social background is most apparent and as they played an especially significant political role in the country.

The Sadducees and The Pharisees

Once upon a time, in the days of King David, a notable priest named Zadok lived in Jerusalem. In later centuries, a whole priestly lineage claimed descent from him. Many believe that the term "Sadducee" was derived from his name. It originally described the political supporters of the priestly aristocracy. However, during the Maccabean Revolt, the Sadducees emerge as a distinct political and religious group.

The Sadducees possessed vast land holdings, held high religious and secular offices, and were part of the council known as the Sanhedrin. All of this defined and shaped their beliefs. They were staunchly conservative, favoring regimes that upheld the privileged status of the aristocracy and generally supported rulers from the Hasmonean dynasty. They mistrusted the lower classes and showed open disdain for wealthy Jews from neighboring regions like Idumea and Galilee, who, in their eyes, were not really pure Jews.

The Sadducees regarded religion primarily as a tool of power and political influence, tried and tested over the centuries. *The Torah*—the first five books of the Bible attributed to Moses—sufficiently elevated and buttressed the position of priests, and therefore, the Sadducees saw no reason to supplement or update the laws outlined in it. Consequently, they rejected religious views that had arisen among the Jewish people over the centuries or filtered in from foreign religions, especially those of Iranian and Syrian origin. Since *The Torah* did not mention the immortality of the soul, the Last Judgment, or the resurrection of the body, the Sadducees did not accept such notions.

Ironically, such beliefs had become prevalent among the general population of the faithful. And no wonder: they stoked the imagination, offering simple and weary people the hope of a better future—even if only after death. These beliefs became deeply rooted in popular religion and found expression in the later books of the Bible. The Hasidim—the Pious who had played such a significant role in the Maccabean Revolt—came from the people and, therefore, shared those beliefs.

The Hasidim movement gave rise to many other groups and sects, including the Pharisees. Like the rest of the people and like the Hasidim, but unlike the Sadducees, the Pharisees accepted the authority of the oral tradition and the authority of ancient teachers alongside the authority of the Torah. They developed a subtle art of interpreting the scripture to demonstrate that *The Torah* only seemingly remained silent about the beliefs so dear to them but really spelled them out in a veiled or secret manner.

They also insisted on meticulous adherence to the holy texts and traditions. Of course, only a few could meet the demanding requirements of formal orthodoxy. These individuals distanced themselves from ordinary people to avoid tainting their purity with the lax and sinful ignorance of the many. Hence, the proud name *Perushim*—the separated ones—emerged, and the Greek term "Pharisees" is derived from it. The Pharisees were not numerous; their number most likely ranged from six to eight thousand. They formed closed communities and called themselves *chaverim*, or "companions." They mainly came from the middle and lower social strata, which inherently fueled their hostility toward the priestly faction and the grand aristocracy.

The significance of the Pharisees cannot be measured solely by their numbers. Their lofty separation, demonstrative display, reputation for unyielding piety, and meticulous observance of the Law earned them extraordinary respect among the ordinary people. Typically associated with the Pharisees were the *soferim*, the scriptural scholars. They constituted a numerous and highly respected group of teachers and expounders of the Law and were found in all the synagogues of Palestine and the diaspora.

The rift between the Sadducees and Pharisees deepened from generation to generation. The Pharisees, growing increasingly zealous, accused the aristocrats of deviating from the strict requirements of the Law and succumbing to Greek cultural influences. They considered Sadducee support for the Hasmoneans disastrous and reprehensible. They preached a return to an idealized past when, allegedly, Jews had no king but were ruled by the revealed Law alone.

The conflict's religious garb concealed the fundamental antagonism between different social strata—though the participants in the conflict had to be fully aware of it. Nevertheless, with each passing decade, the disputes became more intense. Periodically, they escalated into violence, especially when they overlapped with the Hasmoneans' internecine struggle for the throne.

Up to a certain moment, the Pharisees had been favorably disposed toward Hyrcanus and his advisors, perhaps because they shared a common enemy: Aristobulus, supported by the Sadducees. However, in time, the Pharisee faction attempted to eliminate both Aristobulus and Hyrcanus. They sent envoys to Pompey in Damascus, requesting "restoration of the old system." And they contributed to the fall of the city when the Roman army arrived at Jerusalem. They did not take part in the massacre of the defenders of the Temple, but many of their sympathizers did.

THE SONS OF EDOM

Prophecy

> And its streams shall be turned into pitch, and its dust into brimstone, and the land itself shall become burning pitch. And the burning shall not be quenched, neither night nor day; its smoke shall go up for ever: from generation to generation, it shall lie waste; none shall pass through it for ever and ever. But the cormorant and the bittern shall possess it; the owl and the raven shall dwell in it: and a rope shall be drawn for it, the epitome of punishment. They shall call the nobles of the kingdom but find none, and for the king but find him not. Thorns shall come up in their palaces, nettles and brambles in their fortresses: and it shall be the habitation of jackals and a pasture for ostriches. [8]

In these ancient words, the prophet Isaiah depicted the fate that awaited the land of Edom. Who in Judea didn't know this ominous prophecy?

Edomites were related to Israelites; both belonged to the Hebrew Semitic lineage. Yet, for a thousand years—since the times of Saul and David—the two nations lived apart and waged bloody wars. Jews attacked Edom because it lay south of the Dead Sea, along the vital routes connecting Palestine with Egypt and the Red Sea. Edomites raided Judea because Judea was more fertile than their homeland; they were always ready to join any enemy of their northern neighbor. Their mutual hatred only grew fiercer with each generation. By the time of the prophet Isaiah—the 8th century BC—the hate was as unrelenting and ravenous as his grim visions of fire and destruction.

Only a part of the prophecy was fulfilled, for it certainly did not unfold as the prophet had envisioned. Edomites did abandon their homeland. However, it did not become a burning desert. Arab Nabateans settled that land, building a magnificent kingdom there. As

---

[8] *Isaiah* 34:9-13

for Edomites—if only Isaiah could have foreseen where to and why Edomites would migrate! Because they settled in… the southern part of Judea, the hills between the Dead Sea and the coastal plain from Hebron southwards. This migration happened in the 6th century BC, shortly after Isaiah's time. It happened because the Babylonians had conquered Jerusalem and driven thousands of Jews from Judea to Mesopotamia. And thus, Edomites were free to occupy a significant part of their age-old enemy's land without any resistance.

After several decades, Judean exiles returned from Babylonian captivity thanks to the new rulers of the East—the Persians. Quarrels between Jews and Edomites rekindled immediately, even stronger this time since the Edomites didn't want to, and to be fair, couldn't abandon their current settlements. But since both nations were now subject to the same overlords—first Persians, then Ptolemies of Egypt, then Seleucids of Syria—they didn't engage in wholesale open warfare.

At length, thanks to the Maccabees, Judea regained its political independence in 141 BC. Just fifteen years later, it conquered the Edomites and imposed the Hasmonean rule on them. That happened sixty-three years before Pompey captured the Temple of Jerusalem— a span of two generations. During that time, the Jewish conquerors imposed their customs and religious practices on the defeated Edomites yet continued to treat them with contempt. The age-old hatred still smoldered in human hearts.

Antipater

The advisor to Hyrcanus, an enterprising and influential man, was an Edomite. During his time, the region was often called by its Greek name—Idumea; hence, we shall refer to its inhabitants as Idumeans. Yet, fundamentally, this is just another version of the old name of Edom.

Antipater, the Idumean minister of Hyrcanus, bore a Greek name. At the time, the practice of adopting Greek names was quite common in Palestine, especially among the upper classes. Antipater hailed from one of the most prominent families of his land. His father had served the new Hasmonean rulers faithfully and secured for himself the post of the governor of Idumea. Later, Antipater also held that post.

Although Antipater's family adhered to the Jewish Law, the priestly aristocracy of Judea scorned them openly. As Antipater rose to prominence in Jerusalem, his supporters tried to spread the rumor that he was descended from the illustrious ancient priestly lineage that had brought Jews back from Babylonian captivity five centuries earlier. But his opponents claimed that Antipater's father had been a slave and—oh, horror of horrors!—in the temple of the pagan god Apollo, too, in Ashkelon, a gentile city on the coast of Palestine. Allegedly, he was then, still as a child, abducted from the temple by brigands from the neighboring Idumea. And only then did his rise to prominence begin.

Thus, Antipater's origins alone were enough to estrange many Jews from him. Yet, in his youth, he took a step that made things even worse: he married an Arab woman—though a woman from a distinguished Nabatean family. Her name was Kufra, a variant of Kypros in Greek. She bore him four sons: Phasael, Herod, Joseph, and Pheroras, and a daughter, Salome. Interestingly, among these five children, only one took a Greek name—Herod, derived from the Greek word *heros*, signifying "hero." It is probable that Antipater's father had also borne the same name.

Forging connections with the Nabateans was worth enduring all manner of insults. It was a wealthy and populous nation, and Antipater proved adept at leveraging the connections gained through his wife's family in Petra, the Nabatean capital.

Who knows if grand political designs were not already germinating in his mind? Perhaps he pondered the unification of the whole of Palestine, divided as it was between Jewish and Nabatean polities? The significance of Idumea in such a united Palestine, due to its location and affiliations with both sides, was self-evident.

What the Idumean noble really intended remains uncertain. One thing is certain: Antipater's ambitions were audacious and driven by admirable energy.

Antipater, Hasmoneans, Romans

Only naturally, Antipater sought to exploit the conflict between Aristobulus and Hyrcanus to bolster his own position. He foresaw that if Aristobulus were to emerge victorious, Idumea's significance would diminish. Aristobulus' ability to chart an independent political course and his alignment with the Sadducees were the main reasons for this assumption: the priestly aristocracy disdained those who didn't come from pure Jewish stock.

Antipater, therefore, believed it was imperative to rekindle the rivalry between the brothers, which had somewhat subsided following the settlement of 67 BC. Seeing that Hyrcanus would likely be a pliant tool in his hands, he induced him to leave Jerusalem and secured military assistance from the Nabateans. When Hyrcanus, Antipater, and the king of the Nabatean converged outside the walls of Jerusalem in 65 BC, many Jews joined their cause, particularly the Pharisees.

Yet, just as the stars appeared to be aligning favorably for Antipater, an unexpected element emerged: the Romans.

From that point on, an avalanche of events was set in motion, inexorably drawing Antipater into a trajectory he had likely never foreseen. If Aristobulus solicited Roman support, Antipater and Hyrcanus could not afford not to do the same. And later, when Aristobulus antagonized Pompey, they would have been remiss not to seize the moment and stoke the general's suspicions. Ultimately, owing to Pompey's missteps and the zeal of Aristobulus' adherents, the siege of Jerusalem and the capture of the Temple followed. Once they breached the sanctuary and killed its defenders, Hyrcanus and Antipater reached the point of no return: they were now inevitably bound to Rome, come what may. From that point on, Antipater emerged as Rome's most steadfast ally and her unwavering bulwark in Palestine.

Scaurus and the Nabateans

Pompey departed Judea shortly after the fall of the Temple. Matters in Rome demanded his attention: he had been away from the capital for too long. As a result, he did not have the time to carry out his original design, which had brought him to Palestine in the first place: to attack Petra.

His deputy, Marcus Scaurus, left in charge of the province of Syria, undertook this task in the following year, 62 BC. The road to Petra traversed the desert, making the supply of provisions a significant problem. And, since Petra was quite inaccessible, Scaurus's forces did not manage to reach the city in the time frame foreseen. Ultimately, the Roman commander had to limit himself to plundering Petra's surroundings, but as the land was poor, hunger soon affected his army.

A clear defeat of the expedition would have been lampooned in Rome and would undoubtedly have affected his future political prospects. Therefore, Scaurus was determined to withdraw from Petra only after securing at least a semblance of victory.

And now, Antipater's diplomatic talents shone in all their glory. As a new ally of Rome, he was part of the expedition, though its targets were his friends and kinsmen. Observing Scaurus's helplessness, he now offered a compromise. He journeyed to Petra as an envoy and a mediator. In a short time, he facilitated an agreement favorable to both parties. The Nabatean king agreed to pay three hundred talents to the Romans, while Scaurus withdrew his troops and pledged not to attack Petra again. Thus, one received money and preserved his honor; the other kept his kingdom; and Antipater gained a reputation as a friend of both and a man of peace. In fact, his relations with Petra became so good that a few years later, during yet another war in Judea, he sent his family to the Nabatean capital for safety.

What was that city like—that city that hosted young Herod, his mother, and his siblings for two years? It lay in the heart of ancient Edom, the original homeland of the Idumeans, the land that Isaiah had threatened with fire and brimstone, desolation, and wilderness for eternity.

Petra

A stream had carved a narrow gorge through massive reddish rock. A road ran along its bed. As one advanced, the canyon became narrower, its walls taller. At some points, the passage was so narrow that only two horses could walk side by side. Smooth rocks rose up almost perpendicularly. In places, they nearly met at the top, creating a dark tunnel within the gorge. However, in those places where sunlight did reach, the rocks shimmered with glorious colors: reds, greens, and purples.

Then, abruptly, the gorge took a sharp turn, and straight ahead, against the backdrop of gray rock, a vibrant yellow facade of a two-story temple appeared. Graceful columns, arches, pediments, statues, and urns in niches adorned the structure. The temple's inner chamber was carved deep into the rock.

The gorge, now slightly wider, curved gently to the left. Both sides of its rocky walls featured a multitude of tombs arranged in many rows, one above the other. The entrances to these tombs bore intricate carvings and statuary.

Finally, the gorge opened into a wide valley. On its opposite, western side, rose a rugged mass of rocks, closing it off, resembling the formation the traveler had just traversed. To the south and north, the valley seemed to open as far as the horizon, but in reality, its sides sloped steeply downward, forming an inaccessible plateau.

Within this space lay a grand, densely built-up city. Two parallel defensive walls protected it. A stream flowed out of the gorge, passing through the city's center and flowing towards the opposing rock, where it had carved another, even narrower passage. The city's main street ran alongside the stream. In the southern district, to the left of the stream, stood impressive temples and grand buildings. This area also contained caravan inns and warehouses.

To the north, on the other hand, was the densely packed residential district. At the foot of the western rock, atop a hill, rose the walls of a mighty fortress.

Steep mountain walls enclosed the city from the east and west. These walls were covered with tomb facades to almost half their height. These facades appeared like a haphazardly stacked, perpetually frozen stone decoration, born from a fairy tale dream. Steep and treacherous paths led to the highest nearby peaks. On those peaks, altars and objects of worship—symbols of the sun and celestial bodies—stood carved into rock or constructed with enormous boulders.

All colors here were intense and vivid. The green of the trees and gardens of the city and its immediate surroundings stood out against the golden and red rocks. The stream's waters, led through a network of canals, generously irrigated the vegetation.

The city pulsed with rich, loud, colorful life. Caravan routes from southern Arabia, Syria, Palestine, Phoenicia, and Egypt converged here. This oasis, nestled defensively among rocks and deserts, served as a center for transshipment and exchange of goods from distant lands. As a result, Arabs of various tribes, Greeks, Syrians, Phoenicians, and Jews lived here, as did recent arrivals from distant Italy—Roman merchants. However, the Greek element predominated, evident in the architecture of temples, palaces, and tombs; everywhere, Hellenic motifs could be seen, albeit strangely interwoven with elements borrowed from Egypt and even Assyria.

The city was like a grand desert port. Here, Herod and his brothers learned the rich and intricate business of global trade and the languages and customs of diverse peoples. However, Petra was not a haven of peace: Judea lay too close. Echoes of events in Jerusalem, just a few days' journey away, reached here swiftly and found a lively resonance, especially in the home of Antipater's family.

And dreadful things began to unfold in Judea in 58 BC.

JUDEA AT WAR

The Uprising of Alexander

Former King Aristobulus, taken to Rome as Pompey's trophy, had two sons: Alexander and Antigonus. Pompey imprisoned both of them. However, the elder, Alexander, escaped captivity before Pompey's army left the East. For several years, he lived in hiding, but in 58 BC, he decided to initiate an armed uprising. He organized armed forces in Palestine, consisting of his father's loyalists and those embittered by Judea's loss of independence, Roman taxation, and the rule of the Idumeans. Young Alexander quickly rallied ten thousand infantry and fifteen hundred cavalry around him. He also managed to seize three mighty fortresses: Alexandrion,[9] near river Kore, Hyrcania,[10] on the northern shores of the Dead Sea, and Machaerus,[11] to the east of the same sea. Their commanders had turned out loyal to the defeated king and his sons.

Hyrcanus and Antipater were powerless against him. Although Alexander did not dare attack Jerusalem, he freely roamed the entire country, posing as the true king. Even his supporters in the city started to rebuild the walls of Jerusalem, which Pompey had demolished five years earlier.

The Romans decided to intervene only in 57 BC. Aulus Gabinius, the then-governor of Syria, marched south with his army. Nevertheless, he advanced slowly and sent ahead a corps composed mainly of cavalry, led by a young officer named... Mark Antony.

The choice proved excellent. Although Antony was only twenty-five, he had already displayed exceptional military talents. Jews loyal to Hyrcanus joined him—internal divisions persisted among the inhabitants of Judea, and the prospect of a new war fanned old

---

[9] Today's Qarn Sartabe
[10] About 5 km west of Qumran, and 16 km east of Jerusalem.
[11] Mukawir in modern-day Jordan.

hatreds.

After suffering a defeat at the hands of Mark Antony in a battle near Jerusalem, Alexander withdrew to his strongest fortress, Alexandrion. It perched atop a steep mountain and was difficult to take, but it could only accommodate a part of his forces. Some had to camp outside the walls, at the foot of the mountain. Although their position was untenable, they refused to surrender to the Romans. They were cut down to a man.

The fortress itself put up a staunch resistance. When Gabinius arrived, he realized that the siege would last long, and to avoid unnecessary delays, he left only some of his forces at the siege and proceeded to Palestine with the rest. He wanted to get firsthand information about the situation in its various regions. He mainly focused his attention on the cities that had "gained freedom" thanks to Pompey a few years earlier. He found that most of them were ruined, and some even partially depopulated. Their decay was due to both the recent wars and the Hasmonean policies, which were generally unfavorable to the Greeks. Gabinius now made various efforts to revitalize these once-thriving towns and create a sense of stability. In gratitude, the residents of one of them—the city of Samaria—adopted a Latin epithet: "Gabiniani." Decades later, they would change it to an even more prestigious name, also derived from the name of a living person.

Finally, Gabinius returned to Alexandrion. He found the situation unfavorable to both sides. The besieged lacked food and had no hope of relief; for the besiegers, the remote location of Alexandrion caused problems with supply. Now, both sides accepted the mediation of the prince's mother. Although her husband, former King Aristobulus, was a prisoner in Italy, she and her two daughters lived free in Palestine and enjoyed Roman confidence.

The negotiations were crowned with success: Alexander and his people laid down their weapons but retained personal freedom; the prince had to hand over all his fortresses, which the Romans now destroyed.

Immediately after suppressing the uprising, Gabinius showed

with full brutality the true feelings of the Romans towards Judea. He stripped Hyrcanus of all political authority; from then on, the heir of the royal Hasmonean lineage would only hold the position of High Priest. The entire country, formerly under his rule, was now divided into five districts governed by councils of local magnates ("the five Sanhedrin"). Jerusalem lost its privileged position and henceforth became merely the administrative center of one of these five districts.

Gabinius did not invent this administrative technique. Romans applied such principles in all conquered territories. They dismantled former power centers, dividing larger political entities into smaller administrative units with little historical basis but some internal autonomy. They made alliances with the upper classes of those regions, entrusting local offices to their representatives. However, this access to power came at a cost: local dignitaries and affluent individuals became responsible for maintaining tranquility in their region and ensuring consistent tax flows. The risk of tax collection was passed on to Roman entrepreneurs who personally guaranteed the revenues but committed all kinds of abuses in the collection of taxes. Another burden on the local elites was the obligation to supply Roman troops in their winter quarters.

Thus, Gabinius finally abolished the last remnants of Judea's independence and political unity. These "reforms," he explained, were a "liberation" because they "liberated" the Jews from the rule of their *ethnarch*.

The Return of Aristobulus

With these developments, Hyrcanus's power and popularity reached a new nadir. He appeared weak and indecisive, easily manipulated by his Idumean adviser and yielding to the Romans at every step. Nevertheless, he still retained loyal supporters due to his status as the High Priest and his affiliation with the Hasmonean lineage. However, among the masses of Jews, the popularity of his brother Aristobulus was infinitely greater: they saw him as a brave champion of Jewish independence.

This became apparent only a year after the "liberation." Aristobulus fled Italy accompanied by his younger son, Antigonus. As soon as he set foot on Palestinian soil, he became the rallying point for masses of men eager to fight—so many, in fact, that there were not enough weapons for all the volunteers.

Aristobulus's primary objective was to recover and reconstruct the recently demolished fortress of Alexandrion, a stronghold guarding the northern approaches to the heart of Judea—to Jericho and Jerusalem. However, a Roman pacification force was already advancing from Syria, among whose commanders was—once again—Mark Antony. Upon receiving this news, Aristobulus dismissed those of his followers who lacked weapons. With merely eight thousand men, he retreated to the east, crossing the Jordan.

The two armies met on the eastern shores of the Dead Sea. Reportedly, the Jewish army displayed unprecedented heroism. Nevertheless, five thousand perished on the battlefield. Leading only a handful of survivors, Aristobulus broke through the Roman encirclement and fortified himself in the ruins of Machaerus, which the Romans had razed the previous year. This resolute and courageous man did not surrender to despair even in the new, extreme circumstances. He firmly believed that sooner or later, a widespread uprising would ignite in Judea—as long as he could keep the conflict going. However, reality revealed that his small detachment could not hold the ruins of the fortress. After a desperate two-day fight, Aristobulus surrendered. He was taken back to Rome in chains. His two sons shared his fate.

And yet, their freedom was soon restored, chiefly due to the intervention of Gabinius. He contended that during the negotiations at Alexandrion, he had given their mother his personal assurance that no harm would ever come to her sons. It was said that a generous gift aided his memory.

Mount Tabor

In the spring of the following year, 55 BC, Gabinius embarked on a military expedition to Egypt. His purpose was to reinstate the exiled King Ptolemy XII to the throne. The people of Alexandria had bestowed upon that ruler the rather undignified nickname "Auletes"—The Flute Player—given his preference for the instrument over the affairs of state. Unsurprisingly, the monarch enamored with music was eventually deposed from his throne. Gabinius, driven by a fondness for Egyptian gifts, provided generous armed assistance, expecting even more lavish rewards to follow victory.

Antipater played a pivotal role in the expedition. He marched alongside the Roman units, ensured the provision of arms and victuals, and negotiated the surrender of the Egyptian frontier fortress Pelusium, largely garrisoned by Jews.

Gabinius achieved his objectives. Auletes again played the flute in the royal palace, and Gabinius left for Syria carrying immense wealth. However, the absence of both Antipater and the Roman governor—busy in Alexandria—had been seized upon by Prince Alexander. He again rallied thousands and again ranged through Palestine. He expelled or slew Romans—many of whom had already been present in the country, often amassing wealth through questionable means. Those who managed to evade the massacre took refuge on the flat, expansive peak of Mount Gerizim in Samaria, a mountain sacred to Samaritans. There, they valiantly resisted the besieging hordes of Alexander.

Antipater's forces were insufficient to confront the insurgents. While he managed to entice many of Alexander's followers to lay down their arms, the prince still retained nearly thirty thousand men. At their head, he decided to oppose Gabinius and the Roman legions advancing from the north.

The dome-shaped Mount Tabor rises directly from the Jezreel Valley at the borders of Galilee. More than a millennium ago, on this very mountain, leaders of Israelite tribes had defeated Canaanite forces. Now, the same mountain witnessed a dire massacre of Jews. Ten thousand insurgents perished on the battlefield. How could they, poorly armed and even more poorly trained, withstand the might of the Roman legions?

Once again, Gabinius spared Alexander's life, likely not solely due to his mother's influence but also to that of his uncle, Hyrcanus, as the prince had recently married Hyrcanus's daughter, Alexandra.

By marrying Alexandra, Alexander had married his first cousin. Marriages between close kin were not uncommon during that era in the East, particularly among ruling families; such unions hoped to resolve disputes over succession, and this was also the objective of the marriage between Aristobulus' son and Hyrcanus' daughter.

From this union, a daughter named Mariamne was born, followed by a son named after his grandfather—Aristobulus. The siblings resided at Hyrcanus' court along with their mother.

Marcus Licinius Crassus

The chief cause of the annual uprisings in Judea was Roman misrule. The governor himself provided an example of how to exploit and plunder this recently subjugated land. Gabinius's ruthlessness and abuses provoked outrage even in Rome, where, in general, people tended to overlook governors' irregularities.

After Gabinius, Mark Crassus assumed control of Syria in 54 BC. While the man changed, the methods did not. Crassus was preparing a grand expedition against the Parthians. The Parthian empire encompassed the entire area of present-day Iraq and Iran. The middle course of the Euphrates served as the border between the Roman and Parthian territories. Crassus prepared for war with total premeditation. He was the wealthiest man in Rome, but those who possess much desire even more. He dreamed of the fabulous treasures of the East, heaps of gold, diamonds, and pearls.

Even more, Crassus coveted military glory. He envied Caesar, who was at that time completing his conquest of Gaul, taking control of areas between the Atlantic and the Rhine, and even twice leading expeditions across the sea to Britain. In 60 BC, Crassus, Pompey, and Caesar had entered into a secret agreement called the *triumvirate*. They united their influence and agreed on a joint political program. Thus, they became the de facto rulers of political life in Rome. However, cooperation did not eliminate mutual envy and competition.

Now, war is an expensive business, and Crassus needed to rake in as much money as possible. One of the victims of his undertaking was Judea. The governor did not spare even the Temple. He took the money deposited in it—untouched by Pompey—and almost all the more valuable objects. One of the priests, a man responsible for the carpets and curtains, wishing to preserve at least the sacred utensils, revealed to Crassus a secret: that the massive beam from which the precious curtain of the Holy of Holies hung, dividing the central nave of the sanctuary into two parts, was hollow and contained a rod of solid gold.

The Roman solemnly promised that the rod would satisfy him and that he would not touch any sacred vessels. But in the end, he took both the rod and everything else he deemed valuable.

The following year, pursued by the Parthians, Crassus found himself fleeing with the remnants of his magnificent army through the wastelands of northern Mesopotamia—thousands of legionaries had paid with death or slavery for their leader's incompetence and misplaced ambition. At last, surrounded by enemy forces, Crassus had to negotiate. He went to meet the Parthian envoys, only to be murdered. His severed head was taken to the royal court in Ctesiphon and used as a theatre prop.

Lake Gennesaret

After the news reached Judea, a rebellion erupted there again. The moment seemed opportune. There was no Roman army in the Middle

East. But since neither Aristobulus nor his sons, imprisoned by the Romans, could assume command, the rebels heeded the call of Peitholaos, a man who had gained fame in previous uprisings.

However, the defeat of one army was not the defeat of Rome. After Crassus's death, his officer, Gaius Cassius Longinus, took command of the few units left along the Euphrates. He acted energetically and decisively. Despite his limited forces, he prevented Parthians from entering Syria. He secured the border and unexpectedly quickly arrived at the heart of the Jewish rebellion—on the shores of Lake Gennesaret.

This beautiful, vast lake is also known as the Sea of Galilee. Its waters are clear and abundant in fish. Along its eastern shores, the hills descend steeply, there are occasional rocky cliffs, and greenery is sparse. On the western—Galilean—side, the hills slope gently, occasionally opening up into bucolic plains. The name of the entire lake comes from one of these plains, the land of Gennesaret.

The vegetation here was lush and succulent. This was a densely populated and affluent territory. Traveling from the north, from the sources of the Jordan, one encountered towns like Bethsaida, Capernaum, and Magdala. The Greeks called the latter Tarichaea because it was a center for drying and salting fish, which in Greek is *taricheuein*. From here, fish were exported all over Palestine.

The bands of Peitholaos gathered in that city. They were mainly composed of local peasants and fishermen, brave and strong, yet almost defenseless. Longinus quickly took Magdala by storm. The captured insurgents—there were thirty thousand of them!—were sold into slavery. However, he could not decide what to do with Peitholaos himself. Ultimately, on the advice of Antipater, he condemned him to death.

The death toll exceeded thirty thousand, and the Romans enslaved over thirty thousand more. And how many suffered injuries, and how many became disabled? How many widows and orphans? How many ruined towns and abandoned, once thriving farms?

Such was the toll on the Jews during ten years of heroic struggles against Roman oppression, terrifying bloodshed for the local population, and grievous losses for the whole wretched country. The blows were all the more painful since each uprising brought even heavier bondage on Judea. Many Jews must have looked with horror at the streams of spilled blood and must have asked themselves in despair: Were these sufferings necessary? Will they serve any purpose? What will be the ultimate end of these struggles? Where can we seek help?

The War of the Sons of Light against the Sons of Darkness

Wild, rocky hills slope steeply towards the western shores of the Dead Sea. The shores are barren, devoid of vegetation, torn apart by ravines and gorges, yet also captivatingly beautiful in their majestic terror and contrast of colors: the sea and the sky are dark blue, the rocks vivid yellow, red, and black. At the northern stretch of the coast, thin streams of water trickle from rocky crevices. Around these springs, greenery thrives—small islands of life amidst the lifelessness of burning stones.

The Essenes, the true heirs of the spirit of the Hasidim from the time of the Maccabees, favored these surroundings. They constructed their communal dwellings on rocky platforms high above the sea to avoid its fumes and the overwhelming heat of the valley. Men of various professions and classes from all over Judea came here, fatigued by the apparent senselessness of world affairs and its vexations. They faithfully adhered to the Law and delved into the mysteries of the Scriptures with all their hearts. They lived a communal life, following strict rules of poverty and purity, earning their livelihood through hard physical labor. In addition to the Scriptures revered by all Jews, they had their own commentaries on the words of the prophets, their teachings, and their guidelines for conduct.

They believed that the ancient prophecies contained hidden wisdom but in a coded form. They sought to uncover that hidden meaning and to understand the current events in the land of Judea in its light. Though the wars and ravages of recent years had not reached these distant, desolate, and impoverished areas, the Essenes were pained by the suffering of their nation. They also questioned why such calamities should befall villages and towns from Galilee to Jerusalem.

A book provided them with answers. This book had emerged recently and immediately found many readers because, unlike any before it, it offered the promise of ultimate victory. Because of its opening line, it was known as *The Rule of War of the Sons of Light against the Sons of Darkness*. It spoke of a great struggle that would last for forty years between the priests and Levites and the sons of Judah and Benjamin on the one hand and their mortal enemies on the other. Leading the latter would be the eternal foe of Israel, the nation of Kittim; they would also be joined by the Edomites, Moabites, Philistines, and all the others who had always opposed the cause of righteousness. In this battle, not only humans but also the forces of heaven and hell—angels and demons—would fight. The Sons of Light would triumph three times, as would their enemies. However, the final victory would belong to the righteous, who would exterminate all their adversaries, and the Kittim people would fall and vanish forever.

But in order to win, the Sons of Light had to fulfill certain conditions. They had to adhere to the prescribed order and battle formation, recite prayers, and perform designated ceremonies. The book provided detailed instructions on all these matters. It also indicated how the nation of Kittim would engage in battle and described their weaponry and their battle formation. Remarkably, they were the same as those of the Romans.

With what fervent desire must the Essenes have read the prayers presented in the *Rule of War*! They were to recite these prayers before every battle against the Kittim—the Romans:

The Hero of War is in our assembly, and the army of His Spirits accompanies our footsteps. Our horsemen are like clouds. Like the clouds that cover the earth and like heavy rain that showers all of its creatures.

Arise, O Warrior! Seize Your captives, O Man of Glory, and take Your spoils, O Valiant One!

Lay Your hand upon the necks of Your enemies and Your foot upon the pile of the slain. Shatter the nations of Your enemies, and let Your sword consume their sinful flesh.

Fill Your earth with Your praise and Your heritage with blessings. Let animals be abundant in Your fields, silver and gold, and precious stones in Your palaces.

Rejoice, O Zion, and amidst joyful cries, reveal yourself, O Jerusalem, and let all the cities of Judah rejoice! Forever open your gates, that you may receive the wealth of nations. Their kings will serve you, and all those who oppressed you will bow before you, and they will lick the dust of your feet. [12]

Herod and the Essenes

Many, many years later, stories circulated in Judea about a certain Essene who once saw a boy walking down the street in Jerusalem on his way to school and greeted him:

"Welcome, king of the Jews!"

The boy took offense at this jest. However, the Essene, a man named Manahem, smiled, patted him on the back, and said:

"You will be king and a lucky king at that. Remember then that Manahem touched you, and learn from it how fickle the turns of fate can be. Even you will face sad days at the end of your life: you will bear punishment for your impiety and unjust deeds."

Someone invented this tale to explain the seemingly astonishing fact that Herod—for he was the boy in the story—displayed much goodwill towards the Essenes after coming to power.

---

[12] Based on a translation in W. Tyloch, *Rękopisy z Qumran nad Morzem Martwym* [The Manuscripts from Qumran on the Dead Sea], Warsaw, 1963, p. 226-227

The real reasons for this benevolence were, of course, different—and political. But it is possible that one cause of Herod's favorable disposition towards the Essenes might have been the broadly held fear of the sect known for its piety and the gift of prophecy commonly attributed to its members.

But Herod never shared the Essene's view of the meaning of the drama unfolding in Judea. He was twenty when tens of thousands of rebels were taken into captivity on the shores of Lake Genezaret. The entire second decade of his life, when the mind is most pliable and the memory most faithful, was filled with bloody wars and uprisings—fanatical and frenzied, but all doomed to failure from the start. Like any thinking individual in Judea of that time, he must have pondered where his people had gone wrong and how to avert a future catastrophe. But he did not seek solace in mystical books and prophecies. A clear, calculating mind and the instinct of a born politician pointed him towards a path of salvation other than waiting for the help of the Sons of Light. And he followed that path consistently. He owed his greatness to it; and Judea—three decades of peace. But he also paid for walking down that path with infamy—both in his lifetime and after his death

Descent into the Valley of the Jordan

CEASAR AND THE JEWS

The Joys and Sorrows of Antipater

While these events unfolded in Judea, Rome, the world's capital, stood on the precipice of a major civil war: the inevitable showdown between Caesar and Pompey. Armed conflict began in the opening days of 49 BC: Caesar led his troops into Italy, and Pompey and the Senate fled to Macedonia.

Immediately after entering Rome, Caesar freed Aristobulus. He intended to send him to Palestine at the head of two legions. He knew that a large number of Jews would side with the former king and, therefore, against Pompey's men in Syria. After all, Pompey was widely despised in Judea as the man who had desecrated the Holy of Holies. Thus, a significant armed rebellion would erupt in Palestine and tie up at least a part of Pompey's forces.

However, the opposition did not remain idle. Friends of Pompey—and despite Caesar's successes, there was no shortage of them in Rome—secretly poisoned Aristobulus. The body of the king was turned over to Roman Jews, who embalmed it in honey and, several years later, buried it in the homeland.

The sudden death of Aristobulus squashed in its infancy a plan that may have steered the fate of Judea in a new direction. And it was a warning for Hyrcanus and Antipater that they dared not remain neutral in the Roman civil war. They had to choose sides, or the torrent of events might lead them and their country to ruin.

Caesar's plot led to the death of Aristobulus's older son, Alexander. The Romans had imprisoned this prince—well remembered for his two uprisings—in Antioch, the capital of Syria. On Pompey's orders, the then-governor of the province prosecuted Alexander on the charges of hostility towards the Empire—which was indeed hard to deny—and sentenced him to death by beheading. He also decided to place Alexander's younger brother, Antigonus, and his two sisters under the supervision of Ptolemy, the ruler of the tiny client principality of Chalcis in the mountains of Lebanon.

Antigonus was staying with his mother and sisters in the coastal city of Ashkelon. Ptolemy sent his son Philip to collect them. He snatched the children from their mother's arms and led them to Chalcis under escort. On the way, he fell in love with one of the princesses, Alexandra, and—married her. (Brides-to-be were usually not consulted in the matter). Unfortunately for Philip, soon after they arrived in Chalcis, Alexandra caught the eye of her father-in-law, Ptolemy, who, without too much scruple, murdered his son and married her.

Thus, tragic fate continued to hound Aristobulus and his family: they experienced defeat, captivity, and death. Meanwhile, Hyrcanus and Antipater had reasons to breathe a sigh of relief: their two most dangerous potential adversaries were dead, and the third and last, Antigonus, was kept under guard in Chalcis.

However, their joy did not last long. The Roman civil war was evolving quickly, and now doom hung over Pompey's friends. In August 48 BC, Caesar defeated Pompey at Pharsalus in northern Greece. Although Pompey managed to escape, it was only to meet his death on the shores of Egypt. As he disembarked, men sent by King Ptolemy XIII—supposedly to welcome the general—murdered him: the young king was hoping to secure Caesar's favor. He needed his help because he was involved in a domestic struggle himself—against his sister Cleopatra.

Pursuing Ptolemy, Caesar arrived in Alexandria in early October. When messengers brought him the head of Pompey, the conqueror's eyes filled with tears of sorrow. Meanwhile, the people of Judea received with joy the news of the death of the man who had defiled the temple, drenched the whole country in a sea of blood, and stripped it of many of its cities and independence.

The author of the Psalms of Solomon wrote about the death of the conqueror of Jerusalem:

> I did not wait long, and behold, God showed me his shame. He was

stabbed at the borders of Egypt and murdered like the lowest of men, between land and sea. The waves contemptuously cast away his corpse, and there was no one to bury this body. Thus, God took the life of the one who forgot he was merely human and did not think of the future and said: I will be the master of land and sea![13]

While the enemies of Hyrcanus and Antipater no longer had the strength or the leadership to initiate a new uprising at this moment, there was widespread anticipation of significant changes in Judea. The political calculus seemed obvious: Caesar had clearly sided with Aristobulus, for he planned to send him to Palestine at the head of two legions. And now that Caesar was victorious, he would not suffer in power in Judea men placed there by Pompey. He would surely hand the country over to Antigonus, the legitimate heir of Aristobulus.

And no doubt, things would have turned out just that way if not for an unexpected development: Caesar fell in love with Cleopatra.

War in Alexandria

Advisors to the young Egyptian monarch, Ptolemy XIII, reasoned as follows:

Caesar has only four thousand men with him in Alexandria. We can oppose him with an army five times as large. We are still trying to determine how Cleopatra has managed to slip into the royal palace and join Caesar, but since they are together, we can capture both at once. Capturing the palace will be straightforward; its edifices connect directly to the city's residential district. Even if the assault fails, the siege will not last long. There are no Roman forces loyal to Caesar anywhere near Egypt, so he can't count on any outside help. The civil war in the Empire is not yet over. Despite the defeat and death of Pompey, forces loyal to him and the Senate are gathering in various regions. How eagerly those people will welcome Caesar's downfall! As

---

a reward, they will name Ptolemy XIII a friend of the Roman people, confirm him in his rule, and reject and condemn Cleopatra, who has aligned her fate with Caesar.

But if we do not act, Caesar will do everything he can for Cleopatra, and she is ruthless, cunning, vindictive, and, above all, power-hungry. Caesar will probably recommend that Cleopatra and Ptolemy, the two siblings, rule together. He does not understand that there cannot be an amicable resolution to the conflict and that any attempt at co-rule will be tantamount to a death sentence for the young king and all his advisors—if not immediately, then immediately after Caesar's departure.

So logic dictates that both must die: both the Roman general and the Egyptian princess.

The logic of the argument was solid. It only overlooked two minor points: Caesar's energy and military experience and the perseverance of his soldiers. The surprise attack on the palace failed. Trapped inside, attacked from land and sea, and deprived of food and fresh water, the Romans nevertheless doggedly repelled all attacks. Sometimes, they even launched counterattacks. Of course, Caesar immediately realized the situation was dire because his forces were too small. Therefore, in the early days of the fighting, in October 48 BC, he sent appeals for help to all corners of the world. Among others, he dispatched his ally, Mithridates of Pergamon,[14] to Cilicia and Syria to assemble troops and bring them to Egypt via Palestine.

Antipater Brings Relief

Mithridates performed his assignment well. By February 47 BC, he stood at the gates of Egypt at the head of a substantial army. However,

---

[14] Mithridates II of the Bosporus, also known as Mithridates of Pergamon, was one of the sons born to King Mithridates VI of Pontus from his mistress, the Galatian Princess Adobogiona the Elder. For his services in Egypt, Caesar nominated him king of Bosporus (Crimea).

he encountered an obstacle: the fortress of Pelusium, which blocked the entrance to Egypt from the east. Mithridates withdrew from the walls of Pelusium to Ashkalon—and waited. Meanwhile, the situation of those besieged in Alexandria worsened by the day.

And then Antipater appeared in Ashkalon. He brought a contingent of fifteen hundred Jews and troops drawn from friendly princes on the Syrian border. Some Nabateans also arrived—they still harbored a bad memory of Pompey because he had threatened them with an invasion fifteen years earlier.

So reinforced, Mithridates launched an attack on Pelusium, Antipater was the first to breach the walls of the fortress, and the way to Egypt stood open. It was impossible to march directly on Alexandria through the Nile Delta, divided by all the river's branches and canals as it was. So, they opted for a longer but safer roundabout route. They marched along the eastern arm of the delta to the apex of the triangle, where the vast river's branches diverge. There, they crossed to the western bank near the city of Memphis, the ancient capital of the pharaohs.

Throughout the journey, Antipater rendered invaluable services to Mithridates. He secured the support of local Jews, many of whom lived in the cities of Egypt. He persuaded them to support Caesar's cause and give generous assistance. He showed them letters from Hyrcanus, calling on all Jews to support the cause of Caesar. And the Jews listened to him not only because Hyrcanus was the High Priest but also because Antipater was the nominal commander of the Jewish army. The Egyptians tried to block Mithridates's further advance in the vicinity of Memphis. They were defeated. Antipater contributed significantly to the victory, distinguishing himself with great courage in battle, and fought again just outside Alexandria after Mithridates's corps joined Caesar.

The defeat of the Egyptians was complete. Ptolemy drowned while fleeing. His overcrowded boat capsized, and his heavy, golden armor dragged the young king underwater. At the end of March, Caesar triumphantly re-entered Alexandria, where he had faced annihilation only a few days earlier. Cleopatra was to be the mistress of both the city and the whole of Egypt from now on. The victor quickly showed that he remembered well to whom he owed his salvation.

In Antioch

After many days of festivities, leisure, and love, Caesar departed from Alexandria. At the end of June, he arrived in Antioch, the capital of Syria. This city, situated on the Orontes River, had a population of half a million, which made it one of the largest cities in the ancient world. It was also one of the most magnificent in terms of its riches and splendid architecture. It had been founded in 300 BC by King Seleucus and named after his father, Antiochus. The city attracted Greeks, Macedonians, Syrians, and Jews. Antioch grew due to the might of the Seleucids, who once ruled over Syria, Mesopotamia, and Iran, and its excellent location.

The Orontes River originates in the mountains of Lebanon. It initially flows north but then turns westward and southwestward, cutting a passage between the Amanus Mountains to the north and the Kasion Mountains to the southeast. Between the two lay Antioch.

The city sat on a plain on the left bank of the river and extended to the slopes of the rocky Mount Silpius, part of the Kasion Range. The meandering Orontes flowed toward the sea—just a few hours' journey away from Antioch in a straight line. A boat sailing upstream, against the current, could reach the capital from the river's mouth in just a day. Seleucia, known as Seleucia Pieria—that is, Seleucia by the Sea—served as the port of Antioch and maintained trade connections with many countries along the Mediterranean Sea.

The Orontes Valley and a network of land routes connected Antioch with all of Syria and all the major caravan routes from Mesopotamia to Arabia. The surrounding areas of the city were fertile, and the climate was mild, with numerous sources of delicious fresh water flowing from the slopes of Mount Kasion.

Like all cities founded in the Hellenistic era, Antioch had been carefully planned. A regular grid of streets intersected at right angles. A central grand artery traversed the city, running east to west. Part of Antioch stood on a large island within the river's bend, where the royal palace was situated. The city boasted many magnificent temples, theaters, gymnasiums, and beautifully decorated public squares.

Caesar remained here for nine days. In order to win the favor of the people of Antioch, he granted the city significant privileges. (Nevertheless, the city remained the residence of the Roman governor of Syria). Caesar also inaugurated the construction of several grand public buildings: a theater, a basilica, and an aqueduct.

Immediately upon his arrival in Antioch, the commander rewarded Antipater's courageous service. He and his family received a special honor—Roman citizenship. It was customary for new citizens to adopt the name of the patron to whom they owed this honor while retaining their original name as a nickname. Therefore, one of Antipater's sons would henceforth be officially known as a Roman: Gaius Julius Herod.

Thus, the son of an Idumean and a Nabatean, a Jew by upbringing and religious conviction, now became a Roman. The future would reveal one more identity important to him: his sense of belonging to the Greek civilization.

Cesar's Decree

Almost immediately after the splendid citizenship ceremony, Antipater's mortal enemy, Prince Antigonus, the son of Aristobulus, presented himself before Caesar. Antigonus requested justice, which, in his view, required punishing Hyrcanus and Antipater and granting him control over Judea. He argued that, as the son of a king, he was the rightful heir to the throne. He reminded Caesar that his father, Aristobulus, who had allegedly been poisoned in Rome, had once been intended by Caesar to rule over Judea. Antigonus also brought up the execution of his older brother, Alexander, in Antioch two years earlier. Antigonus argued these events were clear evidence of his family's opposition to Pompey and loyalty to Caesar and requested a favorable consideration of his request.

Antigonus spoke passionately, accusing Hyrcanus and Antipater of ruthless exploitation of the people of Judea. He suggested their support for Caesar in Egypt came not out of loyalty but out of the desire to erase the memory of their past friendship with Pompey.

In response, Antipater, who was standing nearby, dramatically tore his garments, revealing his scar-covered body. He passionately defended himself, arguing that his scars were proof of his loyalty to Caesar. He accused Antigonus of being the son of a rebel who had twice escaped Roman captivity and twice incited anti-Roman unrest. Antipater said that Antigonus should be grateful to be spared and questioned why he demanded power and privileges.

Caesar rejected Antigonus's appeal. He carefully considered the current situation: while Antipater had indeed been a valuable ally in Egypt and had shown unwavering loyalty to Rome for the past fifteen years, Caesar was also aware of the complexities of Judea. Appointing Antigonus as ruler could lead to a civil war in Palestine and require repeat Roman interventions, as both the High Priest and the Idumean had loyal supporters willing to fight for their cause.

Meanwhile, pressing matters in Asia Minor demanded Caesar's attention. Alarming news arrived from Pontus, where Pharnaces, the son of Mithridates, made a bid to reclaim his father's kingdom. He was taking advantage of the Roman civil war and of Caesar's stay in Alexandria. Therefore, Caesar made a swift decision.

I, Gaius Julius Caesar, imperator and high priest, dictator for the second time, decree based on the advice of my advisory council:

That Hyrcanus, the son of Alexander, a Jew, has shown unwavering loyalty and zeal for our cause, many commanders have confirmed. Recently, during the Alexandrian War, he came to our aid, bringing a thousand five hundred men who displayed exceptional valor in battle. Therefore, I decree that Hyrcanus, the son of Alexander, and his descendants will hold the office of *ethnarchs* of the Jews in perpetuity, according to their ancestral laws. They will also be our allies and counted among the friends of the Roman people.

I also order that he and his descendants enjoy all the privileges granted to high priests according to their laws. If any disputes arise among the Jews regarding their customs, I recommend that he be the arbiter. I prohibit the establishment of winter camps for our legions in Judea and the collection of monetary tribute from this land.[15]

These decrees were inscribed on bronze tablets in Latin and Greek and publicly displayed in Rome on the Capitol and in cities such as Sidon, Tyre, and Ashkelon. The decree was also communicated to the authorities of many other cities and allied states.

Antipater Rules

The decree mentioned Hyrcanus but said nothing about Antipater, which was understandable as Antipater did not represent Judea in any official capacity. Everything he did was ostensibly in fulfillment of Hyrcanus' will. However, Antipater had made a significant contribution and constituted the best assurance of a pro-Roman policy of the High Priest—and this was clear to everyone.

Therefore, Caesar granted Antipater a position of substantial authority, though one not strictly defined. Antipater received the Greek title *epitropos*, equivalent to the Latin term *procurator*. In later times, procurators served as governors of minor provinces and regions. Of course, Antipater was not and could not be a governor. Judea did not formally constitute a province, nor was it a part of the Empire—only a dependent territory. The head of the Jewish state was Hyrcanus, the *ethnarch* and High Priest, and Caesar's decree abolished the division of the country into five districts imposed ten years earlier by Gabinius.

So, what were Antipater's functions, and what was the scope

---

[15] Josephus Flavius, *Antiquities*, XIV, 10, 12

of his authority? In theory they were quite broad: to assist Hyrcanus as his advisor and, as a Roman citizen, represent the interests of the Empire in Judea. In reality, he ruled the whole country.

Immediately upon his return from Syria, Antipater embarked on a vigorous campaign of reconstruction. With Caesar's approval, he initiated the reconstruction of Jerusalem's walls, which Pompey had demolished. He appointed his eldest son, Phasael, as the governor of the capital and his younger son, Herod, as governor of Galilee; both held the title of *strategos*. Antipater toured the entire country, resolving long-standing disputes on the spot. In a firm yet candid manner, he explained the current situation to the nation:

"Judea is a small, impoverished country ravaged by wars. Its strength is as nothing against the might of Rome—recent years have demonstrated this abundantly. The most crucial task, therefore, is to ensure peace and revive agriculture, crafts, and trade. We must avoid any conflicts with our powerful "ally." Instead, we must, by all means, gain his trust and gradually, step by step, secure concessions and privileges."

Antipater was straightforward in his declarations:

"Those who stand loyally with Hyrcanus can expect a peaceful life, prosperity, and the blessings of general peace. However, woe to those who harbor hopes of revolt! For them, I will not be a master but a despot; Hyrcanus will not be a ruler but a tyrant; and Caesar and the Romans—not allies but enemies!"

Despite the deep-seated resentments of the past and the continuing opposition of the nobility, who continued to sow discord between him and Hyrcanus, Antipater gradually gained considerable popularity among the people. It increased as he achieved his clearly stated political goals and negotiated further privileges from Caesar.

And thus, prohibitions were put in place, preventing Roman officials and commanders from conducting conscription of auxiliary units within the borders of Judea. Joppa, an important port city, was returned to Judea, as were parts of the fertile plain of Esdraelon[16] and

---

[16] Jezreel Valley

some towns on the Syrian-Phoenician border that had once belonged to the Hasmoneans. The entire population of Judea was to pay tithe to Hyrcanus, just as the Hasmonean kings had received it in the past. Most importantly, Jews residing in Roman territory outside of Palestine, numbering in the hundreds of thousands, were granted the right to govern their internal affairs according to their religious principles and customs.

Yet, just as the situation seemed to be developing favorably at last, a sudden dispute erupted. This dispute, connected with Herod's early political career, shed light on the enduring internal divisions within Judean society and played a significant role in his life.

THE HISKIAS AFFAIR

Galilee

Galilee was green, rich, and beautiful. Herod had grown up in the south of Palestine, where the desolate wilderness of the rocky desert dominated the landscape. How delighted he must have been to see this colorful and smiling land. Its gentle hills rose beyond the vast, green Jezreel Valley and the dome-shaped Mount Tabor, extending north right up to the high mountain ranges of Lebanon. Everywhere one looked, there was lush and vibrant vegetation. Date palms, fig trees, and olive trees grew densely in the valleys, golden wheat fields stretched out to the horizon, and vineyards flourished on the hillsides.

Further up, there were rich pastures and, above them—oak forests. To the east, the hills sloped down to the crystal-clear waters of the Sea of Galilee, teeming with fish. This land was abundant in life, and there was never a shortage of water. Many springs gushed year-round here, and voluminous streams flowed down the valleys in winter and summer.

Numerous villages and towns were scattered throughout the region. The hardworking and resilient people of Galilee, well aware of their distinctiveness, lived surrounded by strangers on all sides: Syrians and Phoenicians to the north, Greeks on the coastal plain to the west, Samaritans and Greeks from Scythopolis to the south, and Syrians, Nabateans, and Greeks from the cities of Hippos and Gadara to the east, beyond the Upper Jordan and the Sea of Galilee.

Galileans held steadfastly to Judaism. They made pilgrimages to the Temple of Jerusalem for every holiday, regardless of the cost, hardship, and dangers this entailed. They meticulously observed all the commandments and rituals. And they defended their land with admirable courage. Despite this, the Jews of Judea looked down on them, mocking the rustic simplicity of their customs and their distinctive accent. This did not diminish the pious fervor of the

Galileans.

When Herod took over the governorship of Galilee, he was twenty-five years old. He brimmed with energy and enterprise, matched by his physical prowess. He was strong and agile, excelled in horsemanship, spear-throwing, and archery. He longed for a worthy adversary.

He soon found one.

The Zealots

There is a story in the *Book of Numbers,* the fourth book of *The Torah*:

On their long journey from Egypt to the Promised Land, Israelites eventually arrived at the Plains of Moab: a plateau that stretched east of the lower Jordan Valley, almost exactly opposite Jericho. It was their last encampment before crossing the river and entering the Promised Land—the land of milk and honey. However, their stay on the Plains of Moab extended, and the Moabite women captivated many Jews. They enticed many to offer sacrifices to foreign gods, especially Baal Peor. As a result, a plague broke out. When deaths did not abate, Moses commanded the judges and elders of the Israelite tribes to kill all those who had consorted with foreign women and worshipped foreign gods. Even though Moses declared that it was the command of the Lord and that the plague would only cease when they carried out his command, no one dared to do so.

Then, a young man, emboldened by impunity, openly brought a Midianite woman into his tent before Moses and the whole assembly. Tears overcame those who should have stopped him. Seeing this, Phinehas, the son of Eleazar, rose from among the assembled. He held no office. He was neither a judge nor an elder. Taking his spear, he followed the two into their tent and killed both the Israelite and the woman.

Whereupon the Lord spoke to Moses:

"Pinehas, son of Eleazar, has turned my anger away from the

Israelites, for he was zealous for my honor among his people. On his account, I shall not put an end to them."[17]

This story inspired many throughout the ages. Almost every generation had its own Pinehas, who imitated his fervent zeal. They desired, just like him, to punish mercilessly and immediately those they considered blasphemers and sinners. They wanted to administer justice in place of the judges and officials they believed to be negligent and weak-willed. They wished to fulfill this sacred, bloody duty, believing that otherwise, the sins of the wicked would bring calamities upon the entire people. Only exemplary punishment of all those who violated the Law could avert disaster. This zealous defense of purity required self-sacrifices and courage on the part of the faithful. They had to take up arms even against foes a hundred times more powerful. They had to be ready for martyrdom. And those who died as martyrs for the love of the Lord would gain eternal life.

The Zealot movement began to take shape only when the internal disputes and cultural deviations of the later Hasmoneans became apparent and when, obviously as punishment for those sins, Rome invaded Judea, conquering the land and desecrating the temple and when the blood of Aristobulus and Alexander flowed in streams. The most fanatical defenders of the country's freedom and of the purity of the Law probably adopted the name *kana'im*—Zealots—at that time. This term became widely accepted two generations later, after the death of Herod, when the movement became broader and better organized. The English word comes from the Greek translation of *kana'im*: *zelotai*.

Over time, the Zealots became the fourth largest sect within Judaism, alongside Sadducees, Pharisees, and Essenes. Some feared them, while others found in them an inspiration for action. To achieve their goals and punish the guilty, Zealots were ready to resort to any means, including assassination.

When Herod assumed the governorship of Galilee, Zealots were still few and far between. They lacked leadership and a fully

---

[17] *Numbers,* XXV

developed ideology. They were most numerous in Galilee, the northern bastion of Judaism. Various supporters of the movement from other regions, even from Judea proper, congregated here. In Jerusalem, most residents looked at these fanatics with fear, for they were hostile to all compromises and cultural novelties and dealt ruthlessly with anyone who they believed violated the Law. But, the brave and straightforward Galilean population wholeheartedly supported the courage and iron resolve of the Zealots. They believed that whoever violated the law harmed the nation and, therefore, deserved death. Such reasoning resonated with the simple fishermen from the shores of the Sea of Galilee and the peasants from Cana to Sepphoris.

However, even in Galilee, Zealots were only a small group. Therefore, they sought a remote refuge as a base of operations. They found it in the steep, wooded mountains of northern Galilee. To sustain themselves, they conducted raiding expeditions—of course, not into Jewish territory but rather into the borderlands of Syria. Their leader was named Hiskias, and his name and deeds became famous throughout Palestine.

Even though Hiskias left his province untouched, Herod saw it as his duty to deal with these "bandits" (as he always called Zealots) and decided to confront Hiskias. The decision was reasonable, given the political situation at the time. The lands that Hiskias targeted in his raids were part of the Roman province. While the governor of Syria of the moment, one Sextus Caesar, showed little interest in the welfare of the population under his care and ignored numerous complaints, the situation could change at the drop of the hat—especially if the matter became suddenly profitable to Sextus. By conducting raids from the Galilean territory into Syria, Hiskias risked providing a pretext for any Roman commander to invade Galilee and plunder the entire region under the guise of "suppressing banditry."

Herod's campaign against Hiskias was successful. All the Zealots hiding in the mountains, including their leaders, were captured and executed. This relieved the population of Syria, and the

Roman governor expressed his pleasure.

It was late 47 BC.

Herod before the Sanhedrin

And now a summons came from Jerusalem: the Sanhedrin demanded that Herod stand before it because by executing Hiskias and his men, he had committed a crime.

Indeed, all major legal cases, especially those involving capital punishment, fell under the jurisdiction of the Sanhedrin. This council comprised seventy or seventy-one members, including representatives from the priestly and secular aristocracy and the most eminent scholars versed in Scripture. The latter were usually Pharisees, but the Sadducees always held sway in the council. The High Priest presided over the proceedings.

The case of Hiskias was really just a pretext. The aim was to censure Herod, undermine the influence of his entire family, and sow discord between the family and Hyrcanus. Those in power exerted every conceivable form of pressure on the High Priest and used every means to incite the appropriate sentiments among the masses. Mothers of the slain appeared in the temple courtyard, weeping and wailing, pleading for justice. Who could possibly not have felt both pity and anger seeing the tears of these wretched women? Who was not ready to demand the punishment of the cruel murderer?

However, Herod was yet to yield. Although he heeded the summons and came to Jerusalem, he was prudent enough to bring a contingent of armed men. Of course, it was merely a show, for in the event of a skirmish in the city, neither this detachment nor the bodyguard of Antipater and Phasael would be a match for their adversaries. Still, a threat of violence was worth its weight in gold.

At the session of the venerable council, Herod appeared not as an accused begging for mercy but as a victor—clad in royal purple, finely coiffed, and surrounded by armed men. He acted in such a way guided by the audacity of youth. And yet, at first, it seemed he had acted wisely: at the sight of the weapons, the distinguished members of the Sanhedrin fell silent. It was a close call; the audacious youth very nearly escaped uncharged.

However, just as Herod seemed to win the day, the venerable and stern old Shemaiah rose to speak. He was a scholar of scripture and in authority and fame, second only to his friend Abtalion, who also sat in the Sanhedrin. Their fame would outlive them as that of the two greatest scriptural scholars of their time. Indeed, they did much to deepen the interpretation of the Law, teaching how to adapt its requirements to new life situations. Most Jews considered the opinions of the two scholars binding. They flocked to their schools, even though the two charged high tuition. In general, Shemaiah leaned more towards a strict interpretation of the scriptural mandates. And now he rose to speak against Herod.

Shemaiah shunned politics. He generally preached the principle: dedicate yourself to study, resist all temptation of power, and never associate with the mighty. But he knew no compromises regarding obedience to the Law. He now clearly and unconditionally condemned both the arrogance of Herod and the cowardice of those assembled. He threatened them with divine retribution if they disregarded the holy ancestral laws and allowed the murderer to go unpunished.

The bold speech of the older man, so influential among the people, convinced the others. The mood changed: now, all of a sudden, there were many valiant councilmen, courageous defenders of justice. A torrent of condemnations rained down on Herod. A verdict against him seemed inevitable.

Who knows, perhaps even more than Herod himself, the president of the council, Hyrcanus, feared this turn of events. True, he was under the intense pressure of its members—and the Sadducees in general—who had long been inciting him against the Idumeans. On the other hand, he feared a rupture with Antipater and trembled at the thought of new bloodshed. To make matters worse, he had received a letter from the governor of Syria, Sextus Caesar, concerning Herod's case, in which he demanded the cessation of the proceedings. And the governor had every right to intervene since, after all, Herod was a Roman citizen.

Terrified by this turn of events, the High Priest found only one way out. He postponed the session until the following day.

That night, Herod fled from Jerusalem.

Herod's March on Jerusalem

The humiliated and wrathful prince hastened to meet the governor of Syria, Sextus Caesar, in Damascus. And soon (allegedly for a sum of money), he received an appointment as procurator over southern Syria and Samaria. The latter province, although seemingly "free" since the time of Pompey, was subject to Roman rule. As a Roman citizen, Herod had every right to hold such an office.

When leaving for Jerusalem to stand trial before the Sanhedrin, Herod had wisely left his men in Galilee in charge of all the principal strongholds. Thus, he remained the master of the land, and now, thanks to Sextus Caesar, he became master of new territories bordering his province from the north and the south. In other words, since his humiliating escape from Jerusalem, he became even more powerful. And he gained considerable popularity among the common folk as the exterminator of bandits and a daring youth who scoffed at the priestly aristocracy.

Herod was in a good position and knew how to use it. He conceived a plan that beautifully showcased his political talent.

And now, one day, grave news struck Jerusalem: Herod was leading an army against the city! Terrified dignitaries immediately summoned Antipater and Phasael and sent them out to meet Herod, begging them to find a way to turn him back. They awaited the return of the Idumeans with anxiety. Everyone still remembered the bloody scenes of fifteen years ago, when, after Pompey captured the Temple, Jews slaughtered Jews. Would there be another fratricidal massacre now?

The envoys returned with good news. Although deeply

offended, Herod had allowed himself to be persuaded and relented at the entreaties of his father and brother. He withdrew to Samaria, generously restraining his righteous anger for the sake of amity and peace.

In truth, it was all political theater. Herod could never have dreamed of attacking Jerusalem. Even Pompey, with all his legions, had had to siege the temple for over three months; and Herod would have had to wage war against the aristocracy *and* Hyrcanus *and* most of the inhabitants of Judea.

But threatened with Herod's bluff, the Sanhedrin folded, and Herod won the confrontation. He washed away the humiliation and satisfied his self-love and ambition. No one could boast of having humiliated Herod.

HEROD AND
THE DEATH OF CAESAR

Gaius Cassius

On the 15th of March 44 BC, news from Rome shook the Mediterranean world: a group of conspirators in the Senate had murdered Caesar. At the Forum, where the people cremated the dictator's body on a pyre, the Jews of Rome wept the longest and perhaps the most sincerely. After all, he had been their friend and protector—not only theirs but of all Jews in all the provinces of the Empire. But Caesar's death was particularly ominous for the Palestinian Jews. Thanks to Antipater's sensible policy, Judea had enjoyed almost two decades of uninterrupted peace. But now, there was no room for naïve self-deception: the murder of Caesar would lead to a civil war in Rome, and that war would draw Palestine into its dangerous vortex.

Other small states and peoples dependent on the Empire could still afford to sit on the fence, watching how the situation developed. But the Jews in Judea could not afford delay or hesitation. For two years already, battles had raged among the Romans in neighboring Syria: some supported Caesar, while others were his enemies. After the dictator's death, these battles gained new momentum and—a deeper significance. A former officer of Pompey, one Cecilius Bassus, initiated the newest round of fighting. Following Pompey's defeat at Pharsalus, Bassus had hid for some time in Phoenicia. Later, emboldened by the prolonged civil war, he gathered a band of former supporters of Pompey and even recruited some soldiers of the governor of Syria, Sextus Caesar, to his side. Sextus paid dearly for his inaction: he was murdered by his own men acting on Bassus's instigation.

This happened shortly after the events involving Herod in the matter of Hiskias in 46 BC. Bassus chose the perfect moment to start his revolt, for in that year, Caesar was engaged in a difficult campaign in Africa against a strong army of Senate supporters.[18] The campaign initially went badly, and rumors of Caesar's defeat and death circulated widely. Even though the news was soon disproven, it spurred Bassus to take action and helped him seize power in Syria. Caesar promptly sent one of his generals to the province. His forces besieged Bassus in Apamea, a city in southern Syria. The fighting dragged on, even though Antipater, Caesar's faithful ally, supported the besiegers with his own forces and even sent his sons to Apamea. The siege continued even after the dictator's death, even though, in the new situation, no one was quite sure who was fighting whom and why.

Finally, at the end of 44 BC, one of Caesar's assassins, Gaius Cassius, arrived in Syria to take over the governorship. He came because the dictator had appointed him governor of the province several months before his death. Think about it: Cassius had conspired against Caesar because he saw him as a tyrant, but he now happily went to Syria as the tyrant's appointee! Obviously, those of the tyrant's decisions that benefited the defenders of liberty had to be respected.

Cassius knew Syria and the neighboring regions well. He had been in charge of the defense of the eastern provinces nine years earlier when, after Crassus's defeat, the invasion of the Parthians seemed imminent. Now, he skillfully exploited old relationships, his reputation as Caesar's assassin, the authority of the Senate, and his formal appointment as governor. Soon, he swayed to his side both those besieging Apamea and those besieged in it. And thus, he became the master of the East.

Thanks to Pompey, Hyrcanus and Antipater had gained power over Judea nearly twenty years ago. Fifteen years later, when Pompey suffered defeat, they wisely switched sides to support Caesar, his vanquisher, for which he generously rewarded them. Now, to stay in power and ensure peace for their country, they had to find a way to make a deal with the man responsible for Caesar's death.

---

[18] For a moving account of the finale of the African campaign, see Jacek Bocheński, *Divine Julius* "Epilogue: After Plutarch," p. 175

The Tribute

The situation in Italy was still confused, but a war had already begun. While the Senate supported Caesar's assassins, Mark Antony, one of the closest collaborators of the murdered dictator, finally declared himself after some months of dithering. He broke with the Senate and tried to seize northern Italy (then called Transalpine Gaul) by force. This province was administered by Decimus Brutus, one of the leaders of the assassins, alongside Marcus Brutus and Cassius. An army loyal to the Senate marched to Decimus's aid, and Octavian, a twenty-year-old youth, came with them at the head of a privately raised force.

Octavian's loyalty seemed suspect to the assassins and the Senate. He was Caesar's grand-nephew and had been adopted by the dictator in his will. Thus, legally, he was Caesar's son and heir. Yes, he despised Antony, who had seized almost the entire private estate of Julius Caesar, but everyone asked themselves: would Octavian not become a danger to the Republic someday? Would he not reach for the power his adoptive father had once held? The assassins were certain about one thing: they had to organize a powerful army as soon as possible to keep all the Caesarias at bay.

Creating an army required money. A lot of it.

Therefore, one of Cassius's first moves in Syria was to impose a high tribute on the cities of Syria and Palestine to finance a war that was entirely indifferent to their inhabitants. Provinces under Hyrcanus's rule were required to pay the vast sum of seven hundred talents. Cassius toured the districts and oversaw the smooth progress of the operation.

Facing this challenge, Antipater deemed it expedient to divide the country into districts, each of which was to contribute a specified amount proportional to the number and wealth of its inhabitants. And he appointed in each men responsible for collecting the money. Some were his supporters, including his sons, but others were his outspoken opponents from the high aristocracy. One of the latter was a certain Malichus.

Antipater's reasoning was wise. Why should the general resentment for this painful operation fall only on him and his faction? He decided to share the public odium with his enemies.

Herod was responsible for the tribute imposed on Galilee. His district was the first to pay its designated sum of a hundred talents. Cassius expressed his satisfaction. Although many accused Herod of servility and overzealousness, most realized that he had acted wisely and in the interest of the population. The Romans were certainly not lambs when money and taxes were at stake.

It quickly became apparent what awaited anyone attempting resistance or procrastination. When Malichus failed to deliver in full and in time from his district, Cassius demanded his head. Antipater saved Malichus by covering the shortfall out of his own pocket. But when the inhabitants of four small towns in Judea were late in paying the tribute, Cassius sold the lot into slavery.

Among these towns was Emmaus, located on the road from Jerusalem to Joppa, a day's March from the capital, just where the hills descend to the coastal plain. Emmaus had gained fame in the history of Judea when, over a hundred and twenty years earlier, Judas Maccabeus unexpectedly surprised a large army of King Antiochus there. He won an astonishing victory even though he had only three thousand poorly armed men. He acquired an enormous booty, purple robes, and many gold and silver coins. Some of these treasures belonged to the merchants, whose swarms had followed Antiochus's armies to buy the captured Jews; they had even brought the chains with which to bind the slaves.

That was a few generations ago, in the time of the Maccabees. Now, Roman merchants led away the inhabitants of Emmaus.

The Death of Antipater

If only Antipater could have known whom he was saving by covering the shortfall for Malichus! His beautiful gesture proved misplaced. Malichus had been and remained Antipater's enemy. As soon as

Cassius left Judea, Malichus began to show this openly. He had so many friends and supporters among the Judean aristocracy that Antipater began to gather troops beyond the Jordan—just in case. This worried Malichus. He changed tactics. He ostentatiously assured Antipater that he harbored no hostile intentions towards him. He even managed to convince his sons, Phasael and Herod, of this. They reached an agreement. To seal it, Antipater once again interceded for Malichus with the Romans, for upon hearing about the disturbances in Judea, they had threatened him with death.

Of course, Antipater did not support Malichus out of love but in the hope that through him, he could reconcile with the Judean aristocracy. Faced with the civil war in Rome, the outcome of which was unpredictable, the country needed internal unity. And now, Antipater—an old and experienced politician—blundered. For Malichus only postponed the implementation of his grand plan. He was awaiting a suitable moment.

It came in 43 BC. Cassius, a faithful supporter of Antipater, had his hands tied by Dolabella, one of the Caesarians, who invaded Syria. Although Cassius managed to besiege him in Laodicea, the siege dragged on. It immobilized all the Roman forces in the East.

And then Antipater the Idumean perished.

He died suddenly, right after leaving a feast at Hyrcanus's. All circumstances indicated that Malichus had bribed a deputy high priest to poison Antipater. Even Antipater's greatest opponents admitted that a politician of great stature and a man loyal to Hyrcanus had passed away.

Phasael, present in Jerusalem, warned Herod that immediate revenge for his father's death was impossible, for their enemies had the upper hand in the capital. Herod agreed. The brothers accepted Malichus's explanations and pretended to believe him fully when he solemnly swore: "I am entirely innocent in this matter. The accusations repeated in the city are slander aimed at deceiving the naive and sowing unrest! Everything the witnesses say is false!"

However, it was clear that Malichus was responsible and that he had removed Antipater to take his place. He counted on the support of the aristocracy and the Sadducees. The Romans were not able to intervene in Judean affairs for the time being, and once the dust settled, they would have to come to terms with facts on the ground.

After his father's splendid funeral, Herod left Jerusalem. He attended to some administrative matters in Samaria, where conflicts erupted among various ethnic groups. He did not forget his duty of vengeance but bided his time; he had learned that from Malichus. Therefore, contrary to Phasaels' fears, he did not make a sudden move, even when he found himself in Jerusalem again during the holidays. Hyrcanus, fearing bloodshed, forbade Herod to enter the city. Incensed by this, the prince and his men ignored the order and entered the city at night. But once inside, Herod remained calm. He appeared to accept Malichus's assurances once again and participated in the religious ceremonies like the most devout of pilgrims. In this way, he showed publicly that Malichus had nothing to fear from him.

Finally, in the summer of 43 BC, he received the long-awaited news: Laodicea had fallen.

The Causeway of Tyre

From all the lands of the Roman East, notables now hurried to offer congratulations and magnificent gifts to the victorious Cassius. Of course, had Dolabella triumphed, they would have expressed their joy to him just as sincerely. Hyrcanus, Herod, and Malichus departed for Syria with the same mission, stopping in Tyre on their way.

This ancient city lay on a small rocky island just offshore. Due to its limited space, the streets were extraordinarily narrow, and the houses were several stories high. However, the residents tolerated this overcrowding because the island offered the advantages of two small but excellent ports and a superb defensive position. For centuries, in part due to its location, Tyre had held primacy among the cities of Phoenicia. Its ships visited nearly all the lands of the Mediterranean. It was said that "its merchants were like princes and held silver for clay and gold for street dirt." The Assyrian king Sennacherib, who conquered the entire Near East, failed to take Tyre, despite a five-year siege. The Babylonian king Nebuchadnezzar, who captured Jerusalem in 586 BC, had to besiege the "jewel of the sea" for thirteen years. It was said that Tyre had scoffed at its sister city, saying:

"The city that bustled within its gates (Jerusalem) now lies in ruin! Now, I will enrich myself and prosper because the other has been laid low!"

The prophet Ezekiel thundered against Tyre, seeing in the Babylonian invasion a punishment for its joy at the tragedy of Jerusalem. He expressed his anger by putting these words in the mouth of the Lord:

> For thus saith the Lord God: Behold, I will bring upon Tyre Nebuchadrezzar king of Babylon, king of kings, from the north, with horses, and with chariots, and with horsemen, and companies, and much people. He shall slay with the sword thy daughters in the field: and he shall make a fort against thee, and cast a mount against thee, and lift up the buckler against thee. And he shall set engines of war against thy walls, and with his axes, he shall break down thy towers. By reason of the abundance of his horses, their dust shall cover thee: thy walls shall shake at the noise of the horsemen, and of the wheels, and of the chariots, when he shall enter into thy gates, as men enter into a city wherein is made a breach. With the hoofs of his horses shall he tread down all thy streets: he shall slay thy people by the sword, and thy strong garrisons shall go down to the ground. And they shall make a spoil of thy riches, and make a prey of thy merchandise: and they shall break down thy walls, and destroy thy pleasant houses: and they shall lay thy stones and thy timber and thy dust in the midst of the water. And I will cause the noise of thy songs to cease; and the sound of thy harps shall be heard no more. And I will make thee like the top of a rock: thou shalt be a place to hang nets upon; thou shalt be built no more: for I the Lord have spoken it, saith the Lord God. [19]

But the prophecy did not materialize. The Babylonians did not destroy

____

[19] *Ezekiel*, 26:7-14

Tyre. The prophet, though regretful, was compelled to say later:

> Son of man, Nebuchadrezzar, king of Babylon, caused his army to serve a great service against Tyre: every head was made bald, and every shoulder was peeled: yet had he no wages from Tyre, nor his army, for the service that he had served against it. [20]

Like all of Phoenicia and the entire East, Tyre then fell under Persian rule, but this did not diminish its wealth or importance. On the contrary, the vast extent of the Persian monarchy gave great impetus to trade. That was perhaps why proud Tyre refused to accept the troops of Alexander the Great, the conqueror of the Persians, in 333 BC. The king had to conduct a siege. It lasted eight months and cost Alexander's soldiers more effort and blood than all his previous battles combined. He took the city by building an enormous causeway connecting the island to the mainland. Then, along this causeway, he brought up siege engines and battering rams directly against the city walls. Even then, the defenders fought on—the battle raged in every street and every house. The Tyreans fought to the death. The victor sold almost thirty thousand captives into slavery and crucified two thousand on the beach by the causeway.

Over the years, Tyreans returned to their homeland; the city was rebuilt and prospered once more, occasionally even enjoying relative independence. However, it never regained its former glory, in part because it was no longer an island. Alexander's causeway remained and, over the decades and centuries, became broader and stronger as the sea reinforced it with deposited sand.

In 63 BC, Pompey declared Tyre a "free city." For all that, Roman military units often stationed there. The Romans also used Tyre as a prison to house hostages, usually members of influential families from neighboring regions, thereby ensuring the loyalty of their subject peoples.

Among the hostages held in Tyre was Malichus's son. His

---

[20] *Ezekiel*, 29:18

father intended to seize the opportunity of passing through to free his son and spirit him off to Judea, where he had already prepared a palace coup. It was not an irrational plan; on the contrary, it had a good chance of success. Everyone in the East knew that after capturing Laodicea, Cassius would lead his army out of Syria to unite with the army of Marcus Brutus, governor of Macedonia and Greece. They also knew that both commanders would then focus on the events unfolding in the West and leave the East and its peoples to their own devices.

And in the spring and summer of 43 BC, significant new developments did take place in Italy. Defeated by Octavian and the Senate army on the banks of the Po—the chief river of North Italy—Antony fled beyond the Alps to what is now southern France, where he secured the support of the governor of that province, Lepidus.

Since both consuls had died in the course of the operations against Antony—an odd coincidence—Octavian, despite his very young age, assumed the post of the supreme commander of all forces in Northern Italy. It soon became evident that he intended to seize political control over the Senate. He coerced it to grant him the consulship, although, due to his age, he had no right to hold the highest state office. The question was on everyone's mind: would a war now break out between Octavian on the one hand and Antony and Lepidus on the other? And if so, should Cassius and Brutus's armies strike into Italy now, or should they await to see the results of that war?

Whatever the future course of events, Malichus rightly reasoned that he would not find a better opportunity to achieve his ambitious goals. Antipater was no longer around. The Roman army would leave Syria in what might well be the first convulsions of a terminal disease, perhaps even agony, of the Roman Colossus. The time to become the master of Judea was now or never.

But Malichus was not the only one to assess the situation in this way. Others did, too.

During their meeting in Tyre, Herod invited Hyrcanus and Malichus to a feast. Malichus's quarters were on the mainland, so he had to walk across the causeway to reach the city. Herod and Hyrcanus, who stayed in Tyre, went out to meet him. Suddenly, they saw several Roman officers blocking Malichus's path and drawing their swords. Hyrcanus fainted. When he came to, he saw Malichus's bloody corpse on the beach. The officers approached them. Hyrcanus asked:

"Who gave the order to kill him?"

"Cassius, of course," replied one of the officers.

Wisely, he did not add that his instructions from Cassius were: "In the matter of Malichus, do whatever Herod orders."

The High Priest exclaimed:

"Cassius saved me and the entire country!"

These were the words of fear. Why was Hyrcanus afraid?

Herod The Defender of Judea

As was widely anticipated, Cassius left Syria at the beginning of 42 BC. He met Marcus Brutus in Asia Minor. Together, they began preparations for a decisive confrontation with Antony and his two new allies, Lepidus and Octavian.

Yes. Octavian. Those three, instead of fighting each other, as had been widely expected, had formed an alliance and now ruled Italy and the western provinces together. The terrorized Senate in Rome granted them an extraordinary office with unlimited powers—the *Triumvirate*.[21] One of its first actions was to outlaw all of Caesar's assassins and put many of their political enemies to death.

After the departure of Cassius' legions, Syria and the bordering regions plunged into total anarchy. The rulers of small states, princes and nobles, raced to settle old scores and grab whatever they could at the expense of their weaker neighbors. It was a war of all against all.

---

[21] Formally recognized by the Roman Senate in the *Lex Titia* (November 43 BC). It and lasted *de facto* until the fall of Lepidus in 36 BC, *de jure* until 32 BC.

Cassius had foreseen just such an outcome, and because he trusted Herod, he appointed him governor of southern Syria and assigned him a certain number of armed men. However, shortly after the Roman general's departure, Herod fell seriously ill in Damascus.

Meanwhile, clouds gathered over Judea. A certain Helix, taking advantage of Herod's absence, rose to present himself as the avenger of Malichus. Hyrcanus had, in fact, been in secret collusion with Malichus: that is why he fainted with fear on the causeway of Tyre. That was the meaning of his cryptic remark: he wanted to distance himself from even the slightest suspicion of sympathy for the man.

Relying solely on his own forces, Phasael quickly dealt with Helix and routed his men in Jerusalem. Meanwhile, Malichus's brother, again with Hyrcanus's knowledge, seized several fortresses, including Masada, on the western shores of the Dead Sea. Marion, the ruler of Tyre, occupied parts of Galilee, and Ptolemy, the prince of Chalcis, conceived an even more ambitious plan: he was, after all, married to Antigonus's sister, the legitimate heir of King Aristobulus. He now decided to place his brother-in-law on the throne of Judea.

A man who had not hesitated to murder his son in order to marry his widow certainly did not offer his support disinterestedly. He calculated that as a Hasmonean and the heir of Aristobulus, Antigonus would find many supporters in the country. Later, however, Ptolemy himself would assume power—Antigonus was to be but a stepping stool. The Prince of Chalcis spared no effort to carry out this plan, for it promised to give him dominion over almost all of Palestine. By bribery, he managed to secure the friendly neutrality of the Roman commander of the small garrison left by Cassius in Syria.

And now, internal strife rocked Judea while an invasion threatened it from the outside. It was beyond Phasael's abilities to deal with all the enemies at once.

But Herod recovered in time and came to Phasael's aid. He expelled Malichus's brother from all fortresses he had taken, including the powerful Masada, but he set him free. He dealt with the Tyreans equally generously. He expelled them from many towns in Galilee but allowed them to leave unmolested, and many of them received gifts: Herod wanted to win over the inhabitants of the Phoenician city, and he knew well that they despised their tyrant, Marion. Finally, right on the borders of Judea, Herod crushed the approaching armies of Antigonus and Ptolemy. The people of Jerusalem enthusiastically welcomed the victorious commander. According to Greek custom, they crowned him with a wreath—a symbol of triumph.

Mariamne

Hyrcanus, who, following the death of Antipater, had tried to scheme against his sons, now finally understood that he could never hold onto power without the help of Herod and Phasael. After all, Antigonus, though defeated, was still around and still enjoyed Ptolemy's support. It was perfectly foreseeable that he would someday reassert his claim. Therefore, the high priest changed his policy towards the brothers. The victor of Antigonus, Herod, now became the object of his special love. He promised him the hand of his very young granddaughter, Mariamne.

Let us recall: Mariamne's mother was Hyrcanus' daughter, but her father was Alexander, the elder son of King Aristobulus, the same Alexander who had been beheaded six years earlier in Antioch—and the brother of Antigonus now in Chalcis. So, Mariamne was a Hasmonean on both her father's and her mother's side. In her veins flowed the blood of both Hyrcanus and Aristobulus—whose feud had so tragically affected the fate of Judea for twenty years. In her person, as it were, the two opposing claims united.

"Mariamne" is the Greek form of a name once common in Palestine. It used to be "Miriam," later "Mariam." It lives on today as "Mary." Therefore, it would be quite correct to refer to Hyrcanus' granddaughter as "Mary." But let us continue the established tradition and call her, like everyone else, "Mariamne."

The offer of her hand opened up fantastic prospects before Herod. By marrying Mariamne, he, an Idumean, a man despised by

Judea's proud aristocracy, referred to by many as "only a half-Jew," would enter into family ties with the royal Hasmonean lineage—and both of its lines at once.

Mariamne was still very young, so the wedding would have to be delayed. However, engagements contracted according to the prevailing customs had legal force in Jewish society. By tradition, the fiancé presented the girl's father with valuable gifts—a symbol and, at the same time, a relic of the ancient custom of bride money—and said to her: "You are promised to me according to the laws of Moses and Israel." Then, the couple received the blessings of both sets of parents. If the girl, like Mariamne, was not yet of age, she remained in her family home until the wedding day.

Herod now divorced his first wife. Her name was Doris, and she was probably an Idumean. For a man, divorce was not a complicated procedure; it was enough for him to send a divorce letter to his wife. Even in slightly later times, scholars of the Law were not unanimous about what constituted sufficient grounds for ending a marriage. The strict school of Shamaiah maintained that divorce was justified only in the case of some moral lapse by the wife; others argued that even burning a dish could constitute sufficient cause, as it showed that the wife did not look after her husband.

Of course, these were legal disputes. In practice, divorces were rare, and the reasons used were very diverse. Polygamy was also a common practice, and people regarded it as permitted by the Law, so Herod could have chosen not to divorce Doris. But by divorcing her, he made a clear gesture towards Hyrcanus and Mariamne: he demonstrated to them how much he valued their future relationship.

But Doris had already given Herod a son. He was named after his grandfather—Antipater. Now, the mother took him with her. They lived away from Jerusalem for many years, probably in Doris' ancestral home in Idumea. The future held an hour of triumph in store for both of them—as if to compensate them for the extended period of humiliation and abandonment that now followed.

And thus, the year 42 BC, after a difficult beginning, brought

Triumphal Arch at Petra

Herod many successes. Nevertheless, this smile of fortune was short-lived. In late autumn, Antony and Octavian's legions defeated Brutus and Cassius's legions in the battle of Philippi in Macedonia. The defeated generals committed suicide. The victors divided the spoils. Octavian returned to Italy, while Antony went east. The entire Jewish people—all factions of Judea—now faced a great unknown: how would the new ruler act? Whom would he see as his friend, and whom—as his enemy?

HEROD AND ANTONY

Daphne

It was said that the nymph Daphne, fleeing from the god Apollo, was transformed into a laurel tree here, in this charming place. Hence, it was named after her.

Numerous springs gushed on the slopes of its hills, and streams cascaded down into the valley in long, pearly waterfalls. Among its lush, dark-green groves stood scattered marble palaces and temples. From their terraces stretched extensive views of the vast, fertile valley through which the silvery stream of the Orontes stately wound its way. On the opposite side of the valley, the horizon was closed off by the blue massif of immense mountains.

Daphne lay only a few miles away from the capital of Syria, Antioch. The road to it was beautiful and led along the slopes of hills amid magnificent gardens and elegant villas of the wealthy.

In the autumn of 41 BC, Antony decided the future of Judea here. One hundred Sadducee elders presented themselves before the *triumvir*. However, the opposing party also arrived—Hyrcanus and Herod, along with their friends.

The most eloquent of the one hundred brought heavy accusations against the sons of Antipater: of having favored the murderer of Caesar, Cassius; of seizing Roman territory unlawfully; and of committing many crimes and abuses against the civilian population.

The wealthy elites of Judea, mortal enemies of the Idumeans, had reached out to Antony several months earlier, right after the battle of Philippi, when he was still in Asia Minor. Nevertheless, Herod had beaten them to it. He had hastened to Asia Minor himself, quickly contacted influential people in Antony's entourage, spared no gold, and won over, among others, one Valerius Messalla.

Messalla was one of the most prominent politicians in Rome; he was also interested in poetry and history, was a good writer and an excellent orator.[22] Herod found it relatively easy to come to terms with him because, until the battle of Philippi, Valerius Messalla had been in the camp of Cassius and Brutus; in the first phase of the battle, he vigorously attacked Octavian's positions. However, immediately after the battle, he accepted the amnesty offered by the victors.

Now, he served Antony.

Through vigorous efforts, Herod managed to prevent his opponents from coming before the ruler of the East in Asia Minor. He also cultivated Antony's favorable disposition towards Jews in general. This became apparent later when the official delegation of Hyrcanus presented gifts and congratulations to Antony in Ephesus. On that occasion, the *triumvir* issued two decrees. The first ordered the people of Tyre to disgorge those Galilean territories which Herod had not managed to recover. The second restored the freedom to all those Jews who were sold into slavery by Cassius two years ago to settle arrears of the war tribute.

Herod's defense in Daphne was all the easier because Antony was already familiar with both Jews and Palestine. He had fought there twice two decades earlier, helping to put down the rebellions of Alexander and Aristobulus. He met Antipater and admired his energy, political adroitness, and loyalty to Rome. It is also possible that Antony met Phasael during those campaigns (Herod, still a child, was in Petra with his mother).

Antony realized that handing power to the Judean aristocracy would lead to more civil war in Palestine because the current leadership—Hyrcanus and Herod—would never give up power without a fight. And why should Antony risk a civil war in Palestine when the two men were known to him as loyal and trustworthy? It was obvious that both Phasael and Herod intended to continue their father's policy of serving whichever faction was in power in Rome.

---

[22] For a brilliant appearance of Marcus Valerius Messalla Corvinus (64 BC–AD 8 or 12) see "The concert at Messalla's," in Jacek Bocheński's *Naso the Poet* (Mondrala Press, 2022), p. 39-50, a scene in which Ovidius reads his poetry to the patron of the arts.

They have shown that they knew how to keep the reigns of power, that they had numerous supporters, and that the authority of the Hasmonean inheritance and of the office of the High Priest reached far beyond the borders of Judea.

Did Antony reason correctly? The future was to show that he did. For all their faults, Romans had always been politically pragmatic—this is how they built their empire. If the sons of Antipater had had little to offer other than their loyalty to Rome, Antony would never have supported them. But he knew that they were both loyal *and* powerful. Their cooperation with Cassius had stemmed from political necessity: Antony understood that and did not hold it against them. A political operator himself, he appreciated that others had to make temporary arrangements, too.

The sons of Antipater had two great supporters in Daphne: Valerius Messalla and Hyrcanus. When Antony asked the latter about his opinion, the High Priest begged him to retain Phasael and Herod in their current posts. Since the invasion of Antigonus and Ptolemy, Hyrcanus had lived in constant fear. He suspected the Sadducees of playing a double game: they accused the sons of Antipater of having usurped the powers of the High Priest only to get rid of them, but secretly, they sided with Antigonus and Ptolemy. The whole point of getting rid of the Antipatrids was to get rid of Hyrcanus later.

At length, after all the presentations and debates, Antony announced his decision:

Hyrcanus was to retain the office of High Priest and the powers of the *ethnarch* of the Jews within those borders of Judea which Pompey had defined: Judea, Idumea, part of Samaria, Galilee, and Petrea. Phasael and Herod were to retain their powers within their regions and use the title of *tetrarch*. This last title had come to mean "a ruler of a part of the land" and carried a princely rank with it.

The Causeway of Tyre Again

As was to be expected, the Sadduccee delegation protested vehemently against this decision. However, Antony was not of a gentle disposition, and he was in a hurry. Therefore, without any further niceties, he ordered the imprisonment of the fifteen most vocal members of the delegation.

Later, Herod spread the rumor that they were going to be put to death and owed their survival only to Herod's intercession. However, the matter did not end there. A few weeks later, Antony, continuing his inspection of Syria and Phoenicia, arrived in Tyre. Here, a second delegation of the anti-Idumean faction awaited him, hastily dispatched from Jerusalem upon the news of the unfavorable decision handed down in Daphne. To demonstrate their influence to the *triumvir*, a thousand people came to Tyre. They were all dignified and prominent men.

This numerous and unexpected delegation infuriated Antony. He saw it as an attempt to threaten him, which he would not tolerate. He immediately ordered his officers to "restore order" and support the authority of the current rulers of Judea by "any means necessary."

Meanwhile, the crowd of envoys and those accompanying them gathered on the sandy shore in front of the causeway connecting the city to the mainland. They had gathered there because they were not allowed into the city. They decided to plead their cause by staging a loud demonstration.

Upon hearing about Antony's order and the demonstration on the coast, Hyrcanus and Herod, who were in the city with the Romans, immediately went outside the city walls and onto the causeway. They understood well what the command to "restore order" meant. Therefore, as they walked, they called loudly on their opponents to relent and not to endanger themselves and the whole country. Antony would not, they said, under any circumstances, rescind the orders he had already issued.

However, their words aroused even more protests. The crowd

began to surge, and the slogans became increasingly menacing.

That was when the Romans struck. The compact cohorts marched down the causeway and pounced on the defenseless and disorderly crowd on the coast. Most were allowed to escape, but many were injured, and dozens of bloodied bodies remained on the beach.

Shortly thereafter, the news came that some who had survived the massacre had gone to Judea to incite the people against the Romans. This was all the more significant because Hyrcanus had done as much as he could to placate his opponents: he paid for the cost of the funerals of those killed on the Tyrean coast and provided medical care for the wounded.

Upon hearing about the new disturbances in Judea, Antony ordered the execution of the fifteen delegates imprisoned in Daphne.

Cleopatra

The *triumvir* was in a hurry. Many pressing matters in Syria and Palestine urgently required attention, but the Roman commander postponed most of them and disregarded others. If anything slowed his haste, it was one thing: the need to extract as much money as possible from the cities and regions he passed through.

And thus, he organized an expedition against Palmyra solely to enrich his coffers. Palmyra was an oasis in the Syrian desert northeast of Damascus. Due to its location, it was an essential transit point on the caravan trail between Syria, Mesopotamia, and Arabia. Its riches were famous. The expedition failed for the simple reason that the population of the oasis, forewarned of the approach of the Romans, abandoned Palmyra with all their movable property and fled beyond the Euphrates into the territory of the Parthians.

Unphased, by the onset of the winter rains, Antony was already in Egypt, in Alexandria. Cleopatra had been waiting for him there. She had been the reason for his haste.

Antony had met Cleopatra long ago, some fifteen years earlier, when, as a young officer, he participated in Gabinius's Egyptian expedition. That expedition restored Cleopatra's father, Ptolemy Auletes, to the throne. But the princess was too young at that time for a grown man to pay her much attention. Ten years later, Antony met Cleopatra again, this time in Rome, where she stayed as Caesar's guest. On that occasion, he had to treat her with the utmost respect, as she was not only Caesar's beloved but also, as was commonly said, destined to be the dictator's wife and the co-ruler of the Empire.

And then, a few months ago, he met her again as the queen of Egypt in Tarsus, a city on the southern coast of Asia Minor, where both she and he assumed mythical disguises for the occasion.

Cleopatra had come to Tarsus as an accused. She was supposed to clear herself of the allegation of having supported Cassius. In fact, during the conflict between the *triumvirs* and Caesar's assassins, she had taken a wait-and-see attitude. Who, in her place, would have acted differently? Regardless of her relationship with Caesar, she was a queen: she was responsible for her country and for her dynasty. Antony understood this perfectly well. Besides, a man like him could never have harshly judged a beautiful woman.

With what skill had Cleopatra arranged their meeting in Tarsus! She arrived on a magnificent ship, dressed as the goddess of love, Aphrodite; her attendants, dressed as nymphs, scattered flowers before her. She never mentioned the actual reason for her arrival in Tarsus at all. The *triumvir*, enchanted by the intelligence and charm of the lovely woman, never mentioned it either and eagerly accepted her invitation to visit her in Alexandria.

In this most prominent and wealthiest city of the East, the winter months of 41/40 BC passed amid magnificent entertainments and sumptuous feasts. Antony immersed himself in the pleasures of love.

The romance had an extraordinary backdrop: the splendor and excess of the royal court, the refinement of Greek culture, the feverish pulse of the great million-strong metropolis, and the mystery and wonder of the ancient land of the pharaohs. How could a forty-year-old man, who had spent half his life enduring the hardships of warfare in remote barbarian lands and the rigors of military camp life, resist such splendors?

The infatuated commander completely forgot about the affairs of the Empire.

Yet, there was a lot to bear in mind. After the battle of Philippi, Octavian had returned to Rome to rule over Italy and the West. Antony and Octavian no longer considered Lepidus their equal. They had discovered that he had engaged in intrigues with Cassius and Brutus. He was now granted the governorship of Africa—present-day Tunisia and Algeria—as a "get-lost" gift.

But young Octavian now faced serious challenges in Italy. Above all, he had to distribute land to the soldiers who had won the war for him. There were over a hundred thousand men, and they clamored for their rights. In order to satisfy them, Octavian had to expropriate and displace the population of several cities in Italy. This caused immense turmoil throughout the province. Two individuals who should have aided Octavian exploited the wave of discontent against him instead: Antony's wife, Fulvia, and Antony's brother, Lucius. They tried to incite an open rebellion in Italy in order to destroy Octavian and open the way for Antony to seize the whole of the Empire. Some said that Fulvia hoped to spark another civil war in order to divert her husband's attention away from Cleopatra.

And thus, in the autumn of 41 BC, a war broke out in Italy. Both Octavian and his opponents repeatedly sent envoys to Alexandria, asking Antony to take their side and intervene, but he did not respond.

While Antony indulged in every pleasure that winter in Alexandria, his brother Lucius's troops suffered from hunger. Octavian besieged them in Perusia, a city in central Italy. The desperate summons for help did not manage to tear his *triumvir* brother away from Cleopatra's arms. Antony only left the capital of Egypt in the spring of 40 BC. By then, the starved Perusia had surrendered to Octavian, and the threat of a new war hung over Syria and Palestine.

ANTIGONUS AND THE PARTHIANS

The Invasion from Across the Euphrates

The rulers of Iran and Mesopotamia, the Parthians, had an excellent political advisor. He was a Roman named Quintus Labienus.[23] Even before the battle of Philippi, Cassius and Brutus had sent Labienus to King Orodes of the Parthians with a mission to request his assistance. After the defeat of the two commanders, their envoy had nowhere to turn to. He remained at the Parthian court and entered the service of Orodes. Familiar with Roman affairs, he quickly realized that the current situation of the Empire presented an exceptional opportunity for Parthia to achieve easy success in the East. He presented this to the king and his advisors as follows:

"Octavian is occupied in Italy with the war against Antony's brother. He will probably defeat him, but inevitably, a conflict between the two *triumvirs* will follow. Furthermore, the issue of land distribution in Italy is still open. If the soldiers receive all the land promised to them, it will lead to mass riots among the dispossessed Italians. On the other hand, if Octavian does not fully satisfy his veterans, they will feel aggrieved, and some may take up arms against him. Thus, deep internal conflicts will continue to rend Italy, the center of the Empire, making it impossible for Rome to shift any forces to the East.

"Meanwhile, Antony is totally consumed by his love affair with the Queen of Egypt. He abandoned the business of the regions under his control to their natural course. Meanwhile, the population of Syria and Asia Minor has seethed with hatred against Roman rule. Cassius plundered those provinces two years ago; Antony did it just as ruthlessly last year.

"Yet, Roman forces in these lands are few and weak. There are

---

[23] Son of Caesar's best commander in Gaul, Titus Labienus, who took the side of Pompey in the Caesar-Pompey War.

only two legions in Syria—and they are composed of the former soldiers of Cassius. They are entirely demoralized and only think about their pay, which they have not received in months. It is highly doubtful whether they would bother to resist us.

"Thus, all circumstances are aligning as favorably as never before. We can easily seize the Roman East and restore the boundaries of Persia of five centuries ago."

These arguments convinced the king and his advisors. And thus, in the spring of 40 BC, the splendid Parthian cavalry crossed the Euphrates. Three commanders led them: Prince Pacorus, the king's son, Satrap Barsapharnes, and Labienus himself.

Everything unfolded precisely as Labienus had foreseen. The Syrian legions betrayed their commanders appointed by Antony and went over to Labienus. They had known him well from the time when they fought together under Cassius' command. When capturing the major cities of Syria, including Antioch, the Parthians encountered almost no resistance. The population welcomed the new rulers with joy and relief. They had had enough of Roman oppression and civil wars. There was a widespread expectation that the Parthians would bring moderation and stability.

Moreover, the invaders from across the Euphrates and the inhabitants of Syria quickly found common ground, for both sides owed much to Greek culture. Many Greeks, mainly from the cities of Mesopotamia, served in the administration of the Parthian state. They had settled there in large numbers after the conquest of Alexander the Great when Mesopotamia and Syria were united under the rule of the Seleucid monarchy for almost two centuries. The Parthians favored Greeks, and Greek culture thrived at the Parthian court. They now granted the newly conquered cities considerable internal freedom. The invasion seemed to offer the hope of a better future for Syria and the entire East.

Labienus and his corps moved westward into Asia Minor, while Pacorus and Barsapharnes headed south. The principal cities of Phoenicia surrendered without a fight, but precisely for this reason, the inhabitants of Tyre, who had always taken a position contrary to their brethren, decided to defend themselves. Many Romans took refuge in the city.

The ruler of the principality of Chalcis in southern Syria, Lysanias, switched sides to the Parthians. (He was the son and successor of that Ptolemy, who, nine years ago, had married the sister of Antigonus and two years ago had tried to install him on the throne of Jerusalem).

It soon became apparent that even the Nabateans favored the Parthians. The cities and peoples in the East, which had hitherto remained faithful to Rome, eagerly awaited news from Alexandria. When would Antony break free from Cleopatra's embrace? When would he appear at the head of his legions to repel the invasion or at least protect what had remained? To their horror, they soon learned that Antony had indeed left Egypt, but having stopped in Tyre only briefly and determined that the city, due to its location, could defend itself for a long time, he—sailed away.

To Italy.

He was returning to Italy not only because a war was raging there. What mattered more to him was that he needed more troops for the East. Only the metropolis could supply him with the legionaries he needed.

And now the Parthians arrived at the borders of Judea. All of Palestine pondered the question: how should the Jews act in this new situation? What would Hyrcanus do? How would the sons of Antipater, deprived of Roman assistance, act?

Mount Carmel

That spring, Antigonus' supporters gathered at the foot of Mount Carmel, a sacred site revered for centuries. Its long ridge extended far into the sea, forming a bay where the city of Haifa now lies. A magnificent tapestry of gardens and vineyards covered its extensive slopes. This gave the entire area its name, since "Carmel" means "garden." Even in the 19th century, when a dark forest had overgrown the mountain, travelers did not stint in their words of praise:

> In all its abandonment, Carmel looks beautiful: the air is pure and healthy, and the climate is mild because breezes from the sea moderate the heat. Fragrant herbs grow in the shade of oaks, olive trees, laurels, and beautiful carob trees, and wild vines, as if remnants of ancient gardens, pleasantly pamper the traveler with their strong scent.[24]

The mountain had its own ancient legend, still vivid in the time of Antigonus:

During the reign of King Ahab of Israel eight centuries ago, a devastating drought afflicted the land. Not a drop of rain fell from the sky; not even dew refreshed the parched land. The drought was said to be a divine punishment brought about by the king and his wife Jezebel, who hailed from Sidon: the royal couple worshipped the Phoenician god Baal and his prophets and persecuted the prophets of the Jewish God. Only Elijah had escaped, but he lived in hiding.

Finally, when the animals had no grass left to eat, the desperate king agreed to a trial of strength between the prophets of Baal and Elijah. It took place on Mount Carmel. There were four hundred and fifty prophets of Baal. They quartered a bull and laid it on the sacrificial pyre. From morning till evening, they cried, danced, and inflicted bloody wounds on themselves in ecstasy, hoping that Baal would descend and ignite the fire, but all was in vain. Then Elijah raised his altar and doused it with water four times. When he called on Yahweh, and fire immediately descended from heaven and consumed his offering, the wood, and even the stones, dust, and water. Then, Elijah captured the prophets of Baal and killed all four hundred and fifty of them by the brook at the foot of the mountain.

Then he ascended to the summit of Mount Carmel, bent down to the ground in prayer, and hid his face between his knees. He said to his servant, "Go and look toward the sea!" The servant

---

[24] I. Hołowiński, *Pielgrzymka do Ziemi Świętej* [A pilgrimage to the Holy Land], Petersburg, 1855, p. 258.

returned, saying, "I see nothing." He walked seven times to see, looking seven times. The seventh time, he cried out, "Behold, a cloud as small as a man's hand is rising from the sea!" Soon, the clouds covered the entire sky, a strong wind arose, and a torrentuous rain fell, bringing life and joy.[25]

Today, whoever listens to the legend of the sacred mountain is primarily interested in the mention of the ecstatic cults of Baal and the bloody conflicts between the followers of various gods, but the motif of miraculously bringing rain is common in the legends of many peoples. As for the rebels led by Antigonus, they understood that ancient tale differently from us. They probably imagined that, just as Elijah had ruthlessly crushed the foreign cults on Mount Carmel, they would now destroy and crush the impure regime in Jerusalem. Just as Mount Carmel was the site of a miracle back then, it would now bring a life-giving breath of true liberation.

A vast coastal plain stretches south of the mountain. It was called Sharon. There, by an oak grove, the supporters of Antigonus engaged in their first successful skirmish against the followers of Hyrcanus and the *tetrarchs*, Herod and Phasael. Inspired by this victory, they marched on Jerusalem. They behaved boldly because from the north, Parthian troops were advancing behind them.

The Pentecost of 40 BC

Fighting broke out in Jerusalem, too. A fierce battle between the armed supporters of Anitgonus and the supporters of the Idumeans took place in the main square of Jerusalem. Herod's men emerged victorious, trapping their opponents in the Temple. However, some of the inhabitants of Jerusalem came to the aid of the besieged, attacking Herod's guards and setting their stations on fire. Dozens of Herod's men perished in a burning house. Herod avenged the death of his men, but the Temple and a part of the city remained in the hands

---

[25] A paraphrase of the 18th chapter of the First *Book of Kings*

of his opponents. The fighting continued on and off, and neither side was able to gain the upper hand.

The sons of Antipater now proved that they did not rule by the will of the Romans alone. There were no more Romans in the East, and no one knew whether they would ever return. The Parthian army was drawing near. Almost all neighboring lands had gone to their side, and the claimant, Antigonus, was in league with the invaders. Yet, for all this, Phasael and Herod did not consider giving up. They faced their enemies, sword in hand, and still commanded numerous supporters. And those supporters were not acting out of hate or fear of the Parthians. For though the invaders from across the Euphrates were not exactly welcomed in Judea—no one likes a foreign army in their home—they were driving away the hated Romans, and this was a strong argument in their favor.

Besides, the Parthians were not an unknown quantity to the Jews. Populous and prosperous Jewish communities thrived in Mesopotamia under Parthian rule. Those Jews were in close and constant contact with the Palestinian homeland, and this allowed the Jews of Judea to know what to expect from the new rulers. And the prospect wasn't terrible, especially since the Parthians were coming as allies of Antigonus, the rightful heir of Aristobulus.

Given all this, why did the Idumeans not capitulate? How could Herod and Phasael still count on support in Judea? In part, perhaps, they owed this to the sharp divisions within the Jewish society. The historical record for the events of 40 BC is sparse, and we have to rely on conjecture, but some general facts seem beyond doubt. Some sectors of the population of Judea feared that Antigonus—were he to seize power—would continue his father's policy of favoring the Sadducees and the great aristocracy. These people—among them surely the Pharisees—preferred to support Hyrcanus and the sons of Antipater.

Days and weeks of fighting came and went, and neither side in Jerusalem was able to gain the upper hand. Meanwhile, Antigonus deliberately postponed an attack on the city, awaiting the execution of a cunning plan.

Finally, the Feast of Pentecost came. It was called Pentecost ("Fiftieth") in Greek because it was celebrated fifty days after the Feast of Passover. It came in the month of Sivan, corresponding to our May and June. It was also called the Festival of Weeks (*Shavout*), or the Feast of Harvest, for it consisted of the offering in the Temple of the new harvest of wheat. (In Palestine, the wheat harvest concluded the period of grain harvests, which began in early spring during the Passover festivities with the gathering of barley).

As always, enormous crowds of pilgrims from all over the country came to Jerusalem. People camped around the temple, in the streets, courtyards, and suburbs. Many brought weapons with them. And now a great number of Antigonus' supporters arrived among them hoping to enter the city and take it by surprise. Hyrcanus and the *tetrarchs* held only the royal palace and some fortifications near the city walls.

But in the decisive moment, Herod, leading a small detachment, made a bold raid on the disorderly masses of Antigonus supporters encamped before the city. He slew many of Antigonus' men and drove them off in panic. Yet, both the Temple and a portion of the city still remained in enemy hands.

Such were the celebrations of the Feast of Pentecost in Jerusalem in the spring of 40 BC.

Negotiations and Treachery

Since his plot to take Jerusalem during the Feast of Pentecost failed, Antigonus now tried a different approach. He turned to Herod and Phasael with an appeal to stop the fratricidal bloodshed: why not let the new rulers of the East, the Parthians, mediate in the dispute? There already was a detachment of several hundred Parthian cavalry in Palestine—why not ask them? Phasael agreed to this proposal. Indeed, why not negotiate with the Parthians? The confrontation in Jerusalem showed that he and Herod were not weaker than Antigonus. Given the balance of power, the civil war could drag on for a long time, and since the Idumeans could not rely on speedy Roman assistance, it was perhaps wiser to try to settle with the new overlord. Perhaps some compromise solution was possible?

Thus reasoned Phasael. Soon, with the consent of both factions, a Parthian detachment was let into Jerusalem. Its commander held amicable talks with Phasael. He suggested that a compromise was possible indeed, but the matter required the decision of a higher authority—the satrap, Barsapharnes, who was already in Galilee. Despite Herod's reservations, Phasael decided to go to the headquarters of the Parthian leader, and Hyrcanus accompanied him. Some Parthians went with them, while the rest remained in Jerusalem as guards and hostages.

Barsapharnes warmly welcomed his distinguished guests and lavished them with gifts but asked them to proceed to the Phoenician coast to the headquarters of Prince Pacorus, where they could conclude the final treaty. Hyrcanus and Phasael set out that way.

They stopped at the small coastal town of Ekdippa,[26] halfway between Mount Carmel and Tyre, which the Parthians still besieged. Here, they understood the situation.

Well-informed individuals told Hyrcanus and Phasael that Antigonus had obtained Parthian support by promising to pay the tribute of a thousand talents of gold and to provide five hundred women from the leading Jewish families (naturally, wives and daughters of his enemies). Both dignitaries also noticed that their Parthian retinue never let them out of sight. Why hadn't they been imprisoned until now? The Parthians had wanted to draw them as far away from Jerusalem as possible to conceal their impending arrest from Herod.

Phasael's influential friends in the region strongly advised him to flee. They offered to give the prince good horses or a fast boat. However, he refused. He believed that in the moment of greatest danger, his place was with Hyrcanus. Instead, he tried a different tack.

He and Hyrcanus turned back and presented themselves before the satrap again. In a frank conversation, Phasael revealed

---

everything he had learned. He promised to give much more money
than Antigonus had promised if the Parthians would only allow him
a free hand in Judea. However, Barsapharnes denied everything. He
swore that the reports of impending treachery were false and baseless
and spread by enemies of peace. After this conversation, Barsapharnes
left the hall.

And Hyrcanus and Phasael were put in chains.

JUDEA LOST

Masada

And now, at night, in secrecy, hundreds of people left the royal palace in Jerusalem. Women and children traveled in carts and on pack animals. Armed men on horseback surrounded them. The unit moved quickly and quietly along the road leading south, through Bethlehem and Hebron, towards Idumea.

Herod and his closest associates were fleeing Jerusalem.

It was high time. Just the day before, Herod learned that a messenger carrying letters from Phasael had been detained by the Parthians. He immediately intervened with the Parthian commander. The latter expressed great surprise. He said:

"I am convinced that nothing like this could have happened. The messenger undoubtedly carries a report from Phasael and Hyrcanus on the course of the negotiations. It will be best if you go out to meet him and receive this message yourself."

These words might well have convinced the prince, but as he tried to decide the matter, Aleksandra, Hyrcanus's daughter and Mariamne's mother, intervened. Her intended son-in-law highly valued her wise advice. The princess, driven by fear for her father's safety, did not trust the Parthians. She implored Herod not to believe the treacherous suggestion: death and betrayal lurked everywhere, and Herod should not allow himself to be lured away from his men under any circumstances.

And then a report reached Herod through a secret channel that resolved all doubts: the Parthians had imprisoned Hyrcanus and Phasael; they were colluding with Antigonus; and now they were trying to lure Herod into an ambush.

There was no time to waste. Herod immediately prepared to escape. He had to save the women intended as booty for the Parthians: he took his mother Kypros, sister Salome, Princess Alexandra, and her daughter Mariamne; and his youngest brother Pheroras. There were also other women—wives and daughters of friends.

The women wept. They were leaving their homeland and heading into the unknown. Even if the escape succeeded, what would the coming months bring? How long would their exile last? Herod comforted them and encouraged them to remain calm and steadfast. There was no turning back. And if they managed to reach the protective walls of the fortress of Masada, they would be safe—at least for some time.

But, in the vicinity of Bethlehem, a mishap showed that Herod himself did not have tremendous confidence in the success of his plan. His mother's wagon overturned. At first, it seemed that something terrible had happened to the old woman, and Herod was deeply attached to her. He would never abandon her. Could they continue their trek without risking Kypros's life? What to do, since the Parthian cavalry was undoubtedly on their heels? In a moment of despair, Herod drew his sword: it was better to die by his own hand than fall into the hands of the enemy. His friends wrestled the sword from him. Only after his mother came to and the procession was able to resume its march did the prince calm down.

Soon, they faced a detachment of Jewish supporters of Antigonus, and a fierce battle ensued. Although the numbers involved were small, the fight was bloody and perhaps the most dramatic clash Herod had ever won. In later years, he often remembered that victory.

The journey to Masada, leading through the desert, took only a day. The formidable walls of the fortress soon rose ahead of them on a vast rocky platform, dropping almost vertically on all sides. A magnificent view of the surrounding wilderness and the blue expanse of the Dead Sea stretched from it; beyond the sea, to the east, the Moabite mountain range closed the horizon. The naturally defensive fortress was almost impregnable. Vast stocks of food had been hoarded there, and rainwater collected during winter rains into huge cisterns carved into the rock.

But Herod stayed only for a short time. He soon was on the road again with a handpicked retinue.

Nabatean Friends

The prince was in a great hurry to reach Petra, the capital of the Nabateans. He hoped to obtain from the ruler of Petra the money he needed to ransom Phasael. Antipater had lent significant sums to the royal court in Petra in the past. Herod intended to collect those old debts and borrow more to raise three hundred talents. It was a vast sum, yes, but Herod was prepared to pay even more if it meant saving his brother. As a precaution, he brought along his seven-year-old son, Phasael, to leave as a hostage in Petra if the Nabateans demanded a security.

The border between Idumea, Egypt, and the Nabatean territory ran through uninhabited areas of the Negev Desert. In an abandoned temple, the prince left part of his team and set off for Petra with an even smaller group. They did not get far. Envoys from the king of the rock-cut city intercepted them, delivering bad news: Herod and his party must immediately leave the Nabatean kingdom. The Nabateans did not wish to become involved in any action that could lead to a conflict with the Parthians.

This was only part of the truth. The matter wasn't just about the Parthians but also—about the money. The rulers of Petra guessed that Herod planned to ask for it. But what merchant extends a loan to a loser?

And thus, even those who had been friends of Antipater's family for a generation now abandoned him. Herod did not hide his outrage. In sharp words, he condemned the conduct of the rulers of Petra to the envoys. But he had no choice except to turn back.

He gathered his men and, by the following night, was already on the Mediterranean Sea in a small town two days' journey from the great Egyptian fortress of Pelusium. It was only here that he learned about Phasael's fate.

The Parthians had handed him over to Antigonus. Knowing he was lost, Phasael decided to commit suicide. His hands were bound in chains, so he had only one way out—he smashed his head against a wall. Some later claimed that the damage was not fatal, but a doctor sent by Antigonus—supposedly to save the prisoner's life—administered poison to him. Before the prince breathed his last, a woman servant managed to whisper to him that Herod had safely escaped. Antipater's eldest son died in peace: his avenger lived.

Hyrcanus's fate showed that the tortures that had awaited Phasael would have been terrible, indeed. Hyrcanus was an old man, the High Priest, and Antigonus' uncle. Nevertheless, the new ruler of Jerusalem ordered his ears to be cut off—to prevent him from holding the office of High Priest ever again. (According to the Law, an invalid was not worthy of serving in the Temple). The rumor went about that Antigonus removed the ears himself—some said, by biting them off. Later, the Parthians took Hyrcanus to Mesopotamia, where the local Jews revered him greatly.

The Parthians were now the true masters of Judea. Immediately after Herod's escape, they looted all the houses of his associates in Jerusalem. They did not find any valuables, though, because the Idumeans had either hidden or taken everything away. All the more eagerly, the Parthian cavalry began to plunder the entire country, especially Idumea, the province faithful to Herod.

In Egypt

Just as Herod reached Pelusium, new envoys from the king of the Nabateans caught up with him. They begged forgiveness for the previous "misunderstanding" (as they put it) and warmly invited the prince back to Petra.

The prince refused. Now that he knew about his brother's death, there was no reason to go to Petra anymore. On the contrary, it could only be dangerous, for if the ruler of Petra had also learned about Phasael's fate, then why the sudden change in attitude towards Herod? Could this be a plan to seize Herod and hand him over to Antigonus and the Parthians? That would be a nifty way to liquidate the debts he owed to the Antipatrids: to liquidate the creditor.

Herod had already formed a different plan. To implement it, however, he had to get to Alexandria. This proved a challenge. Captains in the port of Pelusium did not want to take the exiled prince on board. They acted prudently: why should they get involved in Palestinian politics? Herod then turned to the commander of the fortress for help. He showed more understanding for a man whose father had captured Pelusium and saved his present queen, Cleopatra. He escorted Herod to the capital of Egypt with all honors.

And now, Herod and Cleopatra met face-to-face for the first time. It was a meeting of two of the most prominent personalities in the Middle East of the day. Both had tied their destinies to Antony, and while this did not prevent future conflicts, their interests were aligned to some extent at the moment. The Parthian invasion of Syria and Palestine created a dangerous situation for Egypt. Who could guarantee that the rich lands on the Nile would not tempt the Parthians? Anticipating just such a risk, Cleopatra wanted to retain Herod in her service. She spared no effort to win over the Jewish prince, about whose military prowess she had heard so much.

But Herod proved that he could resist a woman whom neither Caesar nor Antony had been able to refuse. Although it was already autumn—a dangerous time for navigation, and disquieting news of the conflict between Antony and Octavian came from the west—he decided to embark for Italy immediately.

On the Capitol

To those who had seen Alexandria and Antioch, contemporary Rome had to come as a disappointment. Although large and scenically situated on several hills overlooking the Tiber, the city had been built chaotically. Its temples and palaces could not compare to the architectural wonders of the capitals of the East. Even the city center— the Roman Forum—was little more than a disorderly collection of buildings from different eras thrown together haphazardly along the Via Sacra—a street leading from the Palatine to the Capitol. The

Temple of Jupiter, the Best and the Greatest, stood on the latter hill, but it seemed too small and too modest to be the main sanctuary of a city that ruled the world.

Twenty years earlier, in that very same temple, Pompey had thanked Jupiter for his victories over the Eastern peoples, including the Jews. And the defeated king, Aristobulus, stood at his side in chains.

But now, and at the end of 40 BC, the King of the Jews offered a sacrifice at the same altar for the prosperity of the Roman people and of the people of Judea. Both *triumvirs*, Octavian and Antony, stood by his side, showing their respect to the crowned head of an allied state. And the King of the Jews—was Herod.

Yes. Herod.

He had attained this dignity contrary to all expectations.

Only a few weeks earlier, he had brushed past death's door. When he sailed from Alexandria to Italy, a storm surprised him off the coast of Asia Minor. The entire cargo, including his personal baggage, had to be thrown overboard to save the ship. Thanks to such desperate measures, Herod managed to reach the island of Rhodes, but he was now penniless. How to find passage for further travel?

As happened again and again, luck favored Herod. He met old Greek friends. They were wealthy and influential people, and they provided him with all necessary help. The prince was not only able to hire and equip a large *trireme*[27] but also to offer a significant sum of money towards the reconstruction of the city of Rhodes, which had been sacked three years earlier by his (then) friend and ally, Cassius.

When Herod landed at the southeastern tip of Italy in Brundisium, he learned, to his great joy, that the Roman political crisis had passed. That crisis, you will remember, had been occasioned by the

---

[27] A *trireme* was a kind of galley, with with three banks of oars. *Triremes* were usually warships. Hiring a *trireme* at a moment when he was penniless, shows Herod's determination not to skimp on costs but pay up for appearances during his Roman "Hail Mary Pass."

outbreak of the civil war between Octavian and Antony's brother, Lucius. But by the time Antony arrived in Italy, Lucius, besieged for a long time in Perusia, had already surrendered.[28]

The *triumvirs* stood facing each other for some time near Brundisium; minor skirmishes occurred between their troops for a while, but their friends managed to mediate an agreement, the conclusion of which lay in the interest of both sides. Antony had to hurry back to the East and drive out the Parthians from his part of the empire, while Octavian awaited a showdown with Sextus Pompeius, the son of Pompey, who had taken control of Sicily and built a pirate state. He blockaded Italy and threatened Rome with food shortages.

The agreement concluded in Brundisium in the late autumn of 40 BC divided the spheres of influence of the two *triumvirs*. Antony received the eastern provinces, while Octavian got the western ones. The border ran through what is now Albania. They recognized Italy as a territory subject to both. They left Africa for the also-ran *triumvir*, Lepidus.

And now, Herod found both Antony and Octavian in Rome. They were dealing with administrative matters and preparing for their wars. The Idumean immediately appealed to them both. First, he turned to Antony, who had ruled in the East and who knew him. Later, he contacted Octavian; it was their first meeting.

Caesar's adopted son was twenty-three years old. He was slim and medium height, which made him look even younger. The calm and composed and diminutive figure of this young man of delicate health contrasted sharply with the robust strength of the temperamental Antony, who, built like an athlete, liked to pose as Hercules. It did not take too much insight to foresee that the conflict between the two would renew sooner or later. However, for now, the two acted in harmony, including the matter of Herod.

---

[28] Bocheński reminds us that on that occasion Octavian sacrificed 300 defenders of Perusia on the altar of his adoptive father, Divus Julius. See *Naso the Poet, p. 134:* "In Perusia, I was right when I announced that I was sacrificing these three hundred to god, my father Julius, and ordered them to be killed on his altar. It was the right thing to do, it was not a mistake, nothing possessed me then."

After hearing his account of the events in Palestine, the *triumvirs* decided to provide him with all possible assistance without delay. The decision was as obvious as daylight. Faced with the Parthian invasion, Rome could not leave Palestine in the hands of Parthian allies, and Herod had proven both his loyalty to Rome and his political and military talents.

However, here, a formal issue arose. Antigonus claimed for himself the title of the king of Judea. He claimed it as the heir of a dynasty that had ruled Judea for a hundred years. To oppose him, Herod had to match him in dignity and somehow fight not in the name of Rome but in the name of the rightful king of the Jews. And since Hyrcanus was held in Parthian captivity, there was no way of putting him forward as king.

Herod proposed proclaiming Aristobulus king, the younger brother of his fiancée Mariamne. This Aristobulus was the grandson of both Hyrcanus and Aristobulus. In his veins, he united the blood of both branches of the Hasmonean dynasty. However, the *triumvirs* had a different idea. They believed that they should dispense with the fiction of a child-king, which opened a whole new can of worms. Just as they did themselves, they thought that Herod should conduct this war *in his own name*.

For the sake of formality, they presented the matter to the Senate. One of the speakers was our old friend, Valerius Messalla, the same man who had advocated for Antipater's sons in Daphne. The Senate passed unanimously a resolution recognizing Herod as the *King of the Jews*.[29]

Immediately following the Senate session, Herod and the *triumvirs*, preceded by consuls and high officials, went in a solemn procession through the Roman Forum to the Capitol to offer a sacrifice to Jupiter and to place in his temple as a perpetual memorial, the text of the Senate's resolution.

On the same day, Antony entertained the new king with a

---

[29] Josephus, *The Jewish War*, 1.14.4

feast: the king without a kingdom. Shortly afterward, Herod left Italy. He had spent a mere seven days in the capital on the Tiber.

THREE YEARS OF WAR

39 BC: Preparations

And thus, Judea now had two kings: Herod by the grace of the Romans and Antigonus by the grace of the Parthians. The latter took the dynastic Hebrew name Mattathias, to which he was entitled since his ancestor, the leader of the revolt against the Seleucids and the father of Judas Maccabeus, had borne it over a century ago. However, the new Mattathias was in no way equal to the old Mattathias, either in energy or in ability.

We know little about the internal policies of Antigonus II Mattathias, but it is clear that he was unable to resolve the long-standing social, ethnic, and religious disputes that had shaken the Hasmonean state. Following his father's policies, he relied primarily on the Sadducees and the great aristocracy, which must have alienated a significant portion of the population and the Pharisees. As an enemy of the Romans, he had the population of Judea on his side, but the Samaritans were hostile to him, as were the Idumeans and the Galileans, who had old ties to the Antipatrids. And the last two regions had been the hardest hit by the Parthian occupation. The fact that Mattathias imposed heavy taxes further fueled the hostile feelings towards him. But he had little choice: he had to pay the Parthians the promised thousand talents. He also needed money to bribe the Romans. And above all, he needed funds to expand his army to defend himself against Herod.

Herod landed on the Phoenician coast in the city of Ptolemais at the beginning of 39 BC. He could not take action immediately, for he had no troops. What was worse, Herod had no money either. After all, he had had to borrow money in Rhodes just to sail to Rome! The *triumvirs* had not given him a penny, as they, too, were in financial straits. So, where could he find the means to recruit and maintain an army?

He probably obtained it from the wealthiest man in Syria,

Saramallas. Saramallas was a Jew long bound by friendship and business to the house of Antipater. It was Saramallas who had warned Phasael in Ekdippa a few months earlier that Antigonus and the Parthians had reached a secret deal and who tried to facilitate his escape. In the later years, the Syrian magnate was to play a significant role at Herod's court.

Thanks to the loan, Herod was able to assemble a group of mercenaries. They were mainly Greeks and Syrians, but Jewish volunteers soon began to flock to him because many Jews had already come to know Herod's military and political talents and believed in his star. Moreover, the house of Antipater still had many supporters, and they all had reason to fear Antigonus. The masses of the Judean population remained indifferent, aligning with neither Herod nor Antigonus; they waited to see who would prevail to join the stronger side.

Herod had Antony's official support, but this meant little in practice. Antony had married Octavia, Octavian's sister, and went to Greece. There, he extorted the cities and partied in Athens. He sent his deputy, Ventidius, a capable general, to fight in the East. Ventidius managed to drive the Parthians out of Syria and Palestine; for some time, his army stood near Jerusalem, ostensibly on their way to aid Joseph, Herod's brother, who had endured many months of siege at Masada. However, the whole adventure ended with Ventidius taking a large bribe from Antigonus and abandoning Judea. He decided that he would not interfere in the internal Jewish affairs. Since Antony's instructions had bound him to support Herod, he left his subordinate, Silo, in his place. Supposedly, Silo's assignment was to assist Herod in capturing Jerusalem, but he showed little eagerness to fight. Not surprisingly, since he, too, took money from Antigonus.

Masada and Jerusalem

And so, Herod was on his own.

Nevertheless, in the autumn of 39 BC, he began offensive

operations. He marched through Galilee, and most of its towns immediately went over to his side. He captured the coastal and wealthy city of Joppa. He reached Idumea and relieved Masada. The garrison of the fortress had victoriously repelled all enemy attacks during all the months of Herod's absence. The worst days came when the water in the cisterns ran out. Joseph was preparing for a desperate sally to break out of the encirclement when, at the last moment, heavy rain fell, saving the garrison and the women and children in Masada from certain death.

Idumeans flocked to Herod, swelling his ranks. Now, he could finally begin the siege of Jerusalem. He set up his camp near Silo's, on the hills west of the city, and sent heralds to walk around the city walls shouting:

"Your king has come to save the city! He forgives everyone, even his enemies!"

Some of the city's inhabitants were receptive to the summons, and when Antigonus forbade people from going onto the walls to hear it, Herod ordered his men to start the attack. A hail of arrows and missiles rained down on his men from the walls.

Meanwhile, Antigonus conducted secret negotiations with Silo, arguing through his messengers:

"I understand that Romans do not want to recognize me as the king of Judea because I seized the throne with the help of the Parthians. But why should the diadem be given to Herod? How can Romans enthrone a commoner and a half-Jew? There are other Hasmoneans, besides me, who have a better claim on power!"

Antigonus made this concession to sow discord between Herod and his allies.

As the talks progressed, so much money flowed into Silo's pockets that soon the Roman commander threatened to abandon Herod. He justified it with his soldiers' complaints about the shortage of supplies. The surroundings of Jerusalem, never terribly fertile, had suffered so much devastation over the years that food supplies were indeed scarce.

Herod immediately began organizing food supplies and

ordered his people to fetch grain, oil, wine, and cattle from further afield. Antigonus ordered his men to attack Herod's supply columns near Jericho. Learning of this, Herod quickly led five Romam cohorts and an equal number of his soldiers against them. He broke up Antigonosus's men and captured many hiding in the caves of the nearby mountains. Meanwhile, the Romans marched on to Jericho and... sacked it.

And then winter came, and the siege of Jerusalem had to be suspended. Herod prepared winter quarters for Silo's men in the loyal districts of Idumea, Samaria, and Galilee. But by now, Silo had adopted a very ambiguous stance. He agreed to Antigonus's proposal for some Roman cohorts to winter in the city of Lydda,[30] controlled by the Hasmonean. Indeed, the city could serve well as winter quarters since it was one of the richest in Judea: it lay on the road from Jerusalem to Joppa, at the entrance to the fertile coastal plain. The problem for Herod, however, was that Lydda's inhabitants were faithful supporters of Antigonus. In this way, all of Judea was led to believe that the Romans were not wholeheartedly supporting Herod.

In Galilee

It took only an hour and a half to travel from Nazareth to Sepphoris. Sephhoris was the best-fortified city in all of Galilee. It sat atop a high mountain, offering a magnificent view. From its battlements, a dark line of the Mediterranean Sea stretched out to the west; it was only a three-hour journey to the foot of Mount Carmel. Heading east, one could reach the shores of the Sea of Galilee in half a day. Cana of Galilee, located north of Sepphoris, could be reached in four hours.

In short, the fortress lay at the heart of Galilee. Whoever controlled Sepphoris held sway over the most important routes in the region and could command many of its settlements.

And Herod captured Sepphoris in the winter by surprise

---

[30] Lod

during a snowstorm. He approached the mountain unexpectedly. Terrified by the sudden appearance of the enemy, Antigonus' soldiers fled, leaving ample supplies behind.

Despite this success, Herod's situation in the winter of 39/38 was dire. The siege of Jerusalem had failed. Silo had proved unreliable. News spread of the Parthians preparing a new invasion, encouraging Herod's opponents to redouble their resistance. And the population of Palestine watched the unfolding events and adjusted their attitudes accordingly. A few months ago, when Herod began his march from Ptolemais to the south, he had found many supporters. Now, having achieved little besides the relief of Masada and the capture of Sepphoris, he had to reckon with the people abandoning his cause. Hostile sentiments towards Herod became more widespread because he had to collect high taxes to feed his troops *and* Silo's legions. The mechanism that had worked against Antigonus was now working against Herod.

Even Herod's homeland, Idumea, was uncertain. Herod sent his brother Joseph to deal with it while he himself remained in Galilee. There were still Antigonus garrisons in various places, and signs of hostility among the population were growing.

Nine years had passed since Herod's annihilation of the band of Hiskias. During those years, full of turmoil and wars as they were, the Zealots regained strength in Galilee. They did not support Antigonus. They despised the entire Hasmonean line, claiming that it had usurped the royal dignity, which belonged only to the line of David. And they refused to accept a king who had been installed by the Parthians. But the Zealots saw Herod as their main enemy: he was a descendant of Israel's ancient foes, the Edomites, and he had committed blasphemy by offering a sacrifice to a foreign deity on the Capitol, and he was an appointee of the hateful Romans.

The Zealots now gathered in the hilly region around Arbela, a town located a few miles west of the Sea of Galilee. Numerous caves in the rocky slopes of the surrounding hills served as excellent shelters for their fighters. Immediately after the capture of Sepphoris, Herod sent part of his forces to Arbela. They were to drive away the "bandits," as he always called them. The initial action did not go well, so forty days later, he himself arrived in Arbela with his entire army. A battle ensued. The Zealots fought so fiercely that the left wing of the royal forces found themselves in danger. Herod commanded the right wing and won the day. Masses of the poorly armed and poorly trained Zealots fled. The king's soldiers pursued them all the way to the Jordan. Some managed to escape the massacre by fleeing across the river. Others hid in caves.

38 BC: Galilee Again

Herod's soldiers went into winter quarters, but the king could not afford to rest. Suddenly, Antigonus stopped supplying Silo's cohorts stationed in Lydda, and the burden of organizing their provisions fell on Herod. He managed it with the help of his youngest brother, Pheroras, who also took charge of rebuilding the great fortress of Alexandrion.

In the spring of 38 BC, the news came that the Parthians had again crossed the Euphrates. In response, Ventidius recalled Silo from Judea. Herod bid farewell to the corrupt and ineffective commander without much regret. However, without Roman troops, he could not hope to resume the siege of Jerusalem. He decided to turn his attention to the Galilean rebels still hiding in caves.

The caves were almost inaccessible, with entrances set high in steep cliffs. It was only possible to reach them by climbing single-file, and even then, one had to hold on tightly to the rock with his hands and feet. How could one even think of fighting when every move risked a fall into the abyss?

Herod ordered his soldiers to occupy the tops of the cliffs and lower large wooden crates on iron chains from the edge of the precipice. Soldiers lowered in these crates expelled the "bandits" from their hideouts using hooks, spears, and bitumen fire.

Many rebels, terrified by the king's resourcefulness and determination, surrendered. However, others preferred death to captivity. In one of the caves hid an older man with his whole family—his wife and seven children. The family wanted to surrender. The man seemingly agreed but stood at the cave's exit and systematically killed those who came out, throwing their bodies over the precipice. Herod, who saw it from the opposite mountain, shouted to him that he spared his life. But the older man cursed and insulted him and then threw himself into the abyss.

If the king assumed that he had completely wiped out the "bandits," he was soon disabused. As soon as he left Galilee, small groups of rebels seemed to spring up everywhere. They attacked unexpectedly and quickly withdrew to inaccessible places. They assassinated one of his governors. They were all the more difficult to capture because they received the support of the local population. Although the king was already in Samaria, preparing to fight Antigonus, he immediately turned back. He defeated the opponents in several skirmishes, destroyed their strongholds, and imposed fines on those cities of Galilee that did not take the appropriate steps to deprive the Zealots of support.

Macheras

At the beginning of June, the Parthian army suffered a devastating defeat near Gindaros in Syria. Their commander, Pacoras, the heir to the throne, was killed. The victorious Ventidius besieged the wealthy city of Samosata near the Euphrates in northern Syria. Now, he was free to come to Herod's aid again. He sent two legions and a thousand cavalry to Palestine under the command of Macheras.

It soon became apparent that Macheras was a worthy successor to Silo. Against Herod's advice, he started talks with Antigonus as soon as he approached Jerusalem. He probably thought that the mere appearance of the Roman army would be enough for the terrified inhabitants of the capital to open the city gates. Alas, a hail of stones and arrows greeted him. Enraged, the commander withdrew to the town of Emmaus, killing all Jews he encountered along the way, not asking whose supporters they were. Outraged by this thoughtless cruelty, Herod confronted him sharply. The consequences of this altercation could have been dire: it threatened to pit Herod against the Romans *and* Antigonus at once.

But it did not come to that. Antony finally arrived in Syria. He showed up at Samosata and took command of the siege. One of his first actions was to depose Ventidius. Ventidius had become too popular among the legionaries, so he was sent back to Italy under the honorable pretext of celebrating a triumph in Rome.

Herod decided to go to Samosata. He wanted to report to Antony on the massacre in Emmaus and all the less glorious aspects of Roman "assistance" in Palestine. The departure of Ventidius—whose deputies Silo and Marcheras were—would work in the king's favor.

He was on his way to Samosata when Macheras, terrified, caught up with Herod. He managed to appease him, but the king did not change his mind about meeting Antony. During his absence, he appointed his brother Joseph, famous for his defense of Masada, as the commander of his troops in Judea.

Joseph

The dream was so dreadful that Herod jumped out of bed, even though it was still dark. He had dreamt that Joseph was dying.

During his entire several-week journey, the king had worried whether Joseph followed his instructions not to engage in fighting before Herod's return from Syria.

Herod was now in Daphne, near Antioch, on his way back to Palestine. He was pleased with the results of his meeting with Antony. It had strengthened their friendship. On the way to Samosata, Herod had routed a large contingent of Syrians fighting against the Romans. Later, in battles right in front of the fortress, the Jewish king once again distinguished himself with valor. Seeing all this, Antony proved very gracious. Immediately after the capitulation of Samosata, he ordered Sosius, the new governor of Syria, to provide all possible assistance to

Herod. Sosius's legions were even now marching towards Palestine.

As Herod woke from his nightmare in Daphne, his attendants brought messengers from Judea into the king's chamber. The men's faces were grim. Before they even started speaking, Herod guessed the news.

Joseph had died in battle near Jericho. He had gone there with five Roman cohorts to collect grain. The enemy surprised them in rugged terrain along the way. The legionaries were fresh recruits from a recent levy and fell like flies. Joseph jumped into the thick of battle and met his end. Antigonus had his head cut off; Pheroras, the youngest brother, paid 50 talents to ransom it.

There was no time for mourning and sorrow, and the king left Daphne immediately. With forced marches, he reached the northern slopes of Mount Lebanon, where he enlisted eight hundred hill tribesmen and joined forces with the Roman vanguard, advancing ahead of Sosius's main force.

From Lebanon, Herod continued southward along the Phoenician coast. He passed by Sidon and Tyre. He ascended the pass known as the "Steps of Tyre." There, the high mountains reach almost to the sea. The road winds up steep slopes. Overhead, white limestone cliffs tower to the sky, adorned with meager shrubs, while below, foaming waves crash against the coastal boulders.

After negotiating the pass, the king entered a vast valley, enclosed on the south by the long ridge of Mount Carmel, on the east by the hills of Galilee, and on the west by the blue expanse of the sea. Streams flowing from the Galilean mountains watered this plain abundantly. As far as the eye could see, stretched fertile fields, gardens, and pastures. The main city of this wealthy region was Ptolemais, famous in later ages under the name of Acre.

Only here did Herod turn eastward and enter the heart of Galilee.

Galilee, for the Third Time

Following the death of Joseph, Galilee had risen. The current uprising had a different character from previous troubles. This time, it did not consist of small bands of Zealots but of vast masses of disaffected peasants. The people rose against their landlords and the royal officials. They dragged them from their homes and drowned them in the lake. Their anger was entirely understandable. Levies and taxes rained upon the people incessantly. Collectors and customs officials squeezed out their last penny and their last speck of grain on behalf of Herod to cover the costs of his army and to satisfy the ever-hungry appetites of his Roman masters. The wealthy did their level best to shift the heaviest burdens onto the shoulders of the poor. And now, in summer, the peasants were particularly bitter, seeing how the fruit of their labor passed into other hands, into the royal and lordly granaries.

The rebels faced Herod in the open field. They were defeated and escaped to a fortress. A sudden storm forced Herod to call off his first attack on its walls. Meanwhile, the second legion of Sosius's army arrived. When the king led the troops to the walls of the fortress on the following day, it turned out that there was not a soul there: the defenders, terrified by the enemy's superior numbers, scattered at night. The uprising was over.

Straight from Galilee, Herod hurried south. He soon arrived near Jericho, which had seen the defeat and death of his brother just a few weeks earlier. Antigonus' forces occupied the mountains west of the city to block the main road to Jerusalem.

On the evening before the ensuing battle, Herod gave a feast. Afterward, after the guests dispersed, the roof of the building collapsed. No one suffered the slightest harm. The event significantly lifted the spirits of the king and his men. Many believed that this miraculous escape was a sign of special providential grace.

There were only six thousand Antigonus's men near Jericho. They held superior ground and refused battle in the open field. They remained dug in in their crags, and as Herod's men advanced, they peppered them with stones and arrows. The king narrowly escaped death once again. He was wounded in his side by a javelin as he circled his ranks on horseback, urging his men on.

Isana

Sosius's main corps advanced slowly. They were still on their way, and there was no question of immediately besieging Jerusalem. Therefore, Herod set about capturing small towns in Judea. Five of them went up in smoke, and two thousand of their inhabitants perished. Antigonus, wanting to divert Herod from Judea, sent troops led by a man named Pappus to Samaria. Macheras defended the region but was not very effective. Herod moved north. Now, people flocked to him again as he seemed the stronger party.

Perhaps to prevent a further swelling of Herod's forces, Pappus decided to give battle. The meeting occurred near Isana,[31] a village located on the main road from Jerusalem to Samaria. The fierce battle ended in Pappus' defeat. His fleeing soldiers fled to Isana and defended themselves in its houses. The Romans and Herod's men cleared the houses one by one. They collapsed each roof onto the men hiding inside. Those who wanted to save themselves rushed out straight into the waiting swords of the legionaries. To avenge Joseph's memory, the king ordered that no prisoners be taken. Only a violent storm put an end to the massacre.

Perhaps only this tempest preserved Antigonus' rule for another year because Isana lies only half a day's journey from Jerusalem, and Herod's men could well have reached the capital on the heels of the runways and perhaps stormed the gates, taking advantage of the confusion.

Still, luck did not leave Herod. After a day of bloody toil, covered in dust and heated by the excitement of victory, he decided to

---

[31] 'Ein Siniya, 8km east of Ramallah.

take a bath in one of the few surviving buildings of Isana. He had only one boy attendant with him. Everyone, including his bodyguards, could barely stand with exhaustion and had already begun to disperse with the king's permission. As Herod lay in his bath, completely naked, suddenly, several armed men burst in from the next chamber. They were Pappus's men who had survived the slaughter and hidden in the house. They could have murdered the king but proved even more frightened than he was. They ran through the bathroom and out into the garden and fled. Having escaped death by a hair, Herod chose not to pursue them.

37 BC: The Wedding

In the early spring, in Samaria, Herod married his fiancée Mariamne, the granddaughter of Hyrcanus and Aristobulus.

How were weddings conducted in Judea at that time? It was not a religious ceremony. The bride was simply escorted from her parent's house to her husband's house. Both the bride and groom were beautifully dressed and adorned with wreaths of flowers. The girl was carried in a sedan chair decorated with myrtle branches. The groom's best man, one of his closest friends, led the wedding procession; he held a staff wrapped in myrtle as a sign of his office. Everyone eagerly rushed to see the procession and join in the general joy. Often, they lit torches because the processions typically set off at dusk. Thick incense smoke, saturated with the scent of myrrh, rose from censers. There was pipe and lute music.

The people raised cheerful cries, exchanged jokes and taunts, sang songs, and danced. To ensure the young couple's well-being, they poured wine and oil in front of them and scattered nuts and grain. A feast awaited them in the house of the groom. The groom took the seat of honor. Invited guests arrived with gifts, sometimes precious ones. The feasting went on for seven days.

Through this marriage, Herod became a relative of the Hasmonean dynasty, which was not without its significance in the struggle for the throne of Judea. Straight from the wedding ceremony, the king hastened to Jerusalem, where he had previously stationed his troops, and began the siege work on the northern side of the temple, the same side that Pompey had stormed twenty-six years ago.

Jerusalem Captured

The king now had over thirty thousand men. Soon, Sosius arrived, leading the remaining legions. Despite such significant forces, the siege lasted a long time, nearly five months, from spring to autumn. The besiegers launched daily attacks on the walls; they constructed tall siege towers and dug tunnels under the fortifications. And they used ingenious machines to hurl projectiles at the city. Nevertheless, the besieged defended themselves with desperate courage: they knew there would be no mercy once the city fell.

Antigonus's supporters did everything they could to sustain the spirit of resistance among the population. New, heartening prophecies spread among the crowds gathered in the city. Every day, they anticipated a miracle, believing that the hand of the Lord would annihilate the enemies of the Temple. The crowds in the streets of the capital and in the courtyards of the sanctuary lived in the intoxication of these mystical prophecies, which heralded the imminent manifestation of some great event.

The voice of reason was heard from only one-quarter of the condemned city. Several legal scholars dared to call for the surrender of Jerusalem. Among them were Shemaiah and Abtalion. It was the same Shemaiah who, ten years earlier, demanded that the Sanhedrin punish Herod in the matter of Hiskias. But Shemaiah had never been a friend of the Sadducees or the great aristocracy, the primary supporters of Antigonus' rule. Moreover, he knew well the consequences of a prolonged siege: the enraged victors would massacre everyone.

But the young fighters believed in their arms more than in the prophecies or in the sober advice of scholars. They made constant sallies against the enemy to hinder the progress of siege works. They set war machines on fire and dug counter-mines against the mines. Others conducted sorties further afield to interrupt the enemy's lines of supply. But all these efforts proved futile. Judea was already completely devastated, and Herod, with his usual energy, organized regular food supplies from very distant parts of the country.

After forty days of siege, the first defensive wall of the Temple fell, and after another fifteen—it was already the beginning of October—the second. The attackers now occupied the first courtyard of the temple and the districts between the Tyropoeon and Kidron valleys. Despite the hopelessness of their situation, Antigonus's men continued to defend themselves in the inner sanctum of the temple and in the western districts.

No one thought of salvation anymore: everything was lost. Nevertheless, the priests never neglected the offering of sacrifices. Herod made a pretty gesture to show how devout he was; he agreed to a short break in the fighting so the priests could bring in sacrificial animals. Immediately afterward, the final assault began. It soon turned into a massacre. The conquerors killed everyone—the elderly, women, children. They killed them in houses, streets, and at the altar.

The massacre horrified Herod, and he tried to stop it, but no one listened. A blood frenzy gripped both Romans and Herodians. At the same time, a crowd of legionaries pressed into the temple, eager to see with their own eyes what treasures were held in the sanctuary so jealously guarded by the Jews. Herod remembered from his boyhood what horrible impact Pompey's entry into the Holy of Holies had had on all the Jews of the world. He was frantic to prevent a repetition of the crime for which the people would blame him. He begged and threatened, ready to draw his sword and fight. Desperately, he called out to Sosius:

"Shall I be a king of a desert? I would not want to be the master of the whole world at the price of such a slaughter!"

But Sosius replied with complete calm:

"My men have suffered. They will be avenged."

It ended with Herod compensating the Romans for their

sufferings and redeeming the lives of the inhabitants of Jerusalem by paying their ransom from his own treasury. Soon, the legionaries departed, laden with gold, satiated with murder and blood and treasure. They took Antigonus with them, bound in chains, the last Hasmonean to sit on the throne of Judea.

When Jerusalem fell, and blood flowed everywhere, Antigonus had come out of the palace and fallen at Sosius's feet, begging for mercy. The Roman commander burst out laughing. He roared at the top of his voice:

"This is not Antigonus. This is Antigone!"

Shortly thereafter, in Antioch, Antigonus was beheaded on the orders of Antony.

Part Two
HEROD THE KING

HEROD AND CLEOPATRA

The Heiress to the Pharaohs

"Palestine must be Egyptian. The pharaohs ruled it a thousand years ago. Less than two centuries ago, it belonged to the Ptolemies. It holds immense significance for Egypt, guarding the eastern approaches to the Nile Delta. It is just and necessary for it to be restored to the heir of the Pharaohs, the scion of the Ptolemaic dynasty, the rightful ruler of the monarchy of the Nile—Cleopatra."

Antony spent the winter of 37/36 BC in Antioch. There, after a four-year hiatus, he met Cleopatra again, and there she presented her demands. She felt she had a moral right to make demands. Antony had betrayed their love. He married Octavia. Then, for several years, Antony stayed away in distant lands. If he truly desired the return of the old, sweet times, he should wipe away the tears of the wronged woman—and wipe them with a proper royal gift.

He should do this all the more because Cleopatra was the mother of his children. She brought the three-year-old twins, a daughter and a son, to Antioch. Antony acknowledged them as his own by taking them into his arms before witnesses, as the ancient Roman custom demanded. They received beautiful names: Alexander Helios and Cleopatra Selene.

Although the arguments of the Queen of Egypt were not without merit, in truth, Octavia was the more wronged woman. Just the previous winter, in 38/37 BC, after the capture of Samosata, Antony had gone to her in Athens. The couple spent several pleasant months together, rejoicing in their two-year-old daughter. Then, in the spring of 37 BC, they sailed together to Italy, where Octavia contributed significantly to the reconciliation between her husband and her brother, Octavian. As a reward for all this, Antony sent her back to Rome from the island of Korkyra in the autumn of 37 BC and hurried east to Syria, straight into the arms of Cleopatra.

Their reunion was tender and sweet, but the triumphant queen/lover did not forget for a moment that she was a queen first and that it was her duty to look after her state and expand its borders.

And thus, a serious threat now hung over Judea: the threat that it might fall into Egyptian hands. What would this mean for the population of this land, so ravaged by years of war? Above all, it would mean ruthless exploitation by the efficient and unforgiving fiscal system perfected over the millennia on the Nile. Again, it would mean exploitation for the benefit of a foreign court, for the ambitious political goals of a ruler ready to sacrifice everything for her own glory and power.

Life in Egypt under the rule of Cleopatra was not idyllic. Arrests, confiscations of property, forced labor—often with the whole family—in the mines in the Nubian desert awaited anyone who failed to satisfy the demands of the state treasury or fell under the suspicion of not appreciating fully the blessings of the queen's government. Secret denunciations thrived. Cleopatra did not invent the system, but she used it extensively.

The threat to seize Judea was all the more real since Cleopatra received from Antony the entire coastal strip of Palestine and Phoenicia—except for the cities of Tyre and Sidon. She also gained control of the principality of Chalcis and its neighboring lands, thus effectively taking control of almost all of central Syria. (The ruler of Chalcis, Lysanias, had been sentenced to death by Antony for allying with the Parthians). Even some Nabatean territory by the Dead Sea was handed over to Cleopatra. For though the rulers of Petra were officially independent from Rome, it was obvious that they would not dare to defy the will of the masters of the universe.

Herod's kingdom, which he had won at such a high cost, was now surrounded on all sides by the possessions of Cleopatra, and it was only to be expected that the queen would now demand Judea. However, Antony steadfastly refused her. He did it because Herod owed the title of king to him and also because he knew his loyalty and energy.

But to appease Cleopatra, Antony took away from Herod and granted to the queen the wealthiest city of Judea: Jericho. Thus, Herod lost this beautiful oasis of palm groves and balsam plantations. He consoled himself with the thought that he retained the rest of his lands.

Had Antigonus, a Parthian puppet, still sat on Jerusalem's throne, Antony would certainly not have hesitated to give the entire kingdom to Cleopatra. Thus, if Judea now survived as a separate state, it was entirely due to Herod. Although the establishment of his rule had come at the cost of death and slavery of thousands and wholesale devastation of the land, it brought at least this one benefit to the unfortunate country: it would not be bled to death by Egypt.

The Beginnings of Herod's Rule

Given Cleopatra's designs, the external position of Herod's kingdom was precarious. Internal affairs were none too stable, either. Years of war had ravaged the country, yet the king urgently needed money. He had to maintain friendly relations with Antony and his entourage, and this required a constant stream of costly gifts to all the prominent Romans in the East. It was also clear that Herod had to help finance Antony's planned expedition against the Parthians.

One of the first moves of the new ruler of Jerusalem was to sentence to death forty-five of the most prominent aristocrats and Sadducees, supporters of Antigonus. He confiscated all their property. Guards at the gates carefully searched even coffins leaving Jerusalem to make sure that the families of the murdered were not smuggling out valuables. In this way, Herod cast terror on all the magnates, removed his most bitter enemies, and restocked his treasury all at once.

Next, he levied special contributions on the wealthy. He taxed even jewelry and weapons.

Then, he removed all the supporters of the last Hasmonean from office, appointing his own men in their place. Thus, gradually, a new faction—the Herodians—emerged. It consisted of people whose livelihood and position depended entirely on the new king, for they were neither independently wealthy nor well-born. Of course, as a group, they were too weak and too few to constitute a reliable social foundation for the new government. Therefore, Herod diligently courted the powerful faction of the Pharisees. He showed particular respect to Shemaiah and Abtalion.

Naturally, the Pharisees hated having an Idumean usurper on the throne of Judea even more than they had hated the Hasmoneans. Nevertheless, the king gained at least this much: some of the Pharisee leaders advanced the position that it was right and proper to submit to the rule of Herod, for it was a punishment from God for the godless sins of the Jews.

In the secrecy of their hearts, the Pharisees probably thought even more profound thoughts to explain to themselves the meaning of the tragic events: God must have placed Herod on the throne of Judea to fulfill some divine plan. The king fulfilled it when he removed the wicked Hasmoneans. He fulfilled it further when he sentenced to death the leaders of the Sadducee faction. Of course, this half-Jew, blasphemer, and murderer would not endure long on the throne in the Holy City. He was only God's rod and broom; he cast out of Judea one set of abominations and would soon be cast away himself. Sooner or later, the people would overthrow him, and perhaps even those who had raised him—the Romans. Who will then remain in Palestine to assume power according to the Law and to bring the kingdom of the Messiah closer?

Why, the Pharisees.

But Herod did have genuine supporters, too. They came from those groups of the population of Palestine that had hitherto been treated with contempt or even hostility by the Judean elites. They were Idumeans, Samaritans, Greeks, and even some Galileans, especially those from southern Galilee.

The Royal Visit

Meanwhile, the spring of 36 BC came, and Antony marched against the Parthians. Cleopatra escorted the great army—the largest the Romans had ever raised in the East—up to the banks of the Euphrates. Then, she returned to Egypt through Damascus, Apamea, and Jerusalem. Here, she stopped for a while.

Herod put on great celebrations to receive his distinguished guest. He showered the queen with gifts and tried to gain her favor in every way. But, for all his efforts, another humiliation awaited him. Cleopatra never lost sight of her goals. To "reward" the king for his friendly welcome, she graciously leased "Egyptian" Jericho to him. The rent—200 talents a year—was confiscatory, but Cleopatra went even further in her "favor." She ordered the Nabatean King Malchus to pay the same amount for leasing back his former properties by the Dead Sea—another 200 talents. The queen now granted Herod the great "privilege" of collecting this payment from Malchus and forwarding it to Alexandria. This meant, in effect, that the King of Judea had to guarantee the debts of the Nabatean king. In this way, the queen planted more seeds of discord between the two kingdoms.

They were soon to bear fruit.

When, many years later, Herod wrote his memoirs, he did not fail to immortalize the figure of the queen and his impressions of her stay in Jerusalem. He did so in more or less the following words:

"Cleopatra often met with me. She sought *specific contacts*, which did not surprise me, for she was a woman completely devoid of shame and given entirely to debauchery. She now pretended to be in love with me. However, I was on my guard, understanding that in this case, only two eventualities were possible: either she was indeed debauched and, in that case, worthy only of contempt, or she was setting a trap for me.

"Therefore, I remained indifferent to her attentions. I did ask my friends in great secrecy whether it would be prudent to eliminate the Egyptian queen. By doing so, I would have done a great favor to her numerous enemies in Rome and perhaps even Antony himself. However, my friends dissuaded me from this plan, pointing out that it could bring great disaster upon me, my entire family, and the country, for Antony, infatuated with Cleopatra, might choose to seek revenge."[32]

Thus, Herod avenged himself for the humiliations and misfortunes inflicted upon him by the queen of Egypt. Of course, this report was probably a lie: Herod genuinely hated Cleopatra, but the idea to kill her—her, who was by then the common-law wife of Antony, the Roman ruler of the East—certainly did not arise in his mind. But he could not deny himself the pleasure of erecting a monument to his courage and foresight. He wrote these words long after Cleopatra had died, and Rome had officially condemned her memory.

When Cleopatra departed from Palestine, Herod respectfully accompanied her to the gates of Egypt at the Pelusium fortress. They parted with the pretense of complete harmony and warm friendship.

Not a year passed, and everyone learned what that friendship looked like.

---

[32] A reconstruction on the basis of Josephus, *Antiquities*, 14,4,2

HEROD AND ARISTOBULUS

The Portrait

Antony's great expedition ended in defeat. Snow and frost claimed thousands of casualties during his winter retreat through the mountains of Armenia. He had failed to capture his objective, the capital of Parthian allies, the Medes. Demoralized, starved, and ragged remains of his colossal army barely reached the borders of the Empire. Antony himself outpaced his legions. He swiftly arrived in Syria; there, in one of the coastal towns, he awaited the arrival of Cleopatra. Trying to forget about the defeat, he sought solace in wine. At last, the queen arrived; her ships carried supplies for the army. Then, the two sailed for Alexandria.

At the same time—at the beginning of 36 BC—an elegant Roman aristocrat, Quintus Dellius, visited Jerusalem. He was a man of great intelligence but devoid of any scruples. He gladly hired out his talents to victors and abandoned his former friends the moment fate became less kind to them. He had first associated with Dolabella, then transferred his loyalties to Cassius, then to Antony. He now belonged to the circle of Antony's closest friends.

He had taken part in the ill-fated Parthian campaign, and, as he was full of literary ambitions, he documented it in a unique work which he published some years later.[33] Following his commander, he was now on his way to Egypt. However, he did not rush and did not miss the opportunity to recuperate after the hardships of war at the court of the Jewish king.

Here, Dellius got to know Herod's family. He was dazzled by the beautiful young Mariamne. The Roman was equally pleased by her handsome brother, the sixteen-year-old Aristobulus. A polite and charming man, Dellius praised this beautiful pair to their mother,

---

[33] *Bellum Parthicum*, now lost, was presumably Plutarch's source for his life of Antony.

Alexandra. He hinted that Antony, a sincere admirer of all things beautiful, would be delighted to see the portraits of the siblings. Indeed, he would not hesitate to bestow his favor upon such charming beings.

The request was not just a mere courtesy. Dellius specialized in drawing the *triumvir's* attention to beautiful women and boys. Dellius had even arranged the meeting between Antony and Cleopatra in Tarsus four years earlier. It was said—both then and later—that much warmer and closer relations existed between Dellius and the queen than Antony suspected or wished. Decades later, with no small delight, love letters of the two were circulated in Rome—whether factual or fabricated, no one knew. Though involved with Cleopatra, Antony still took interest in other beautiful beings. Of course, he had to do so discreetly, considering the queen. But in such matters, Dellius was invaluable.

This was the background of Dellius's tactful suggestion to send the portraits of the siblings to Alexandria.

Now, portraiture was against the Jewish Law:

> Thou shalt not make unto thee any graven image, or any likeness of any thing that is in heaven above, or that is in the earth beneath, or that is in the water under the earth. [34]

However, the mother had good reasons to seize on Dellius's idea. She quickly calmed her conscience: after all, it would not be she who made the likeness, and it would not even be made for a Jew. Thus, just a few weeks later, in the palace of Alexandria, Antony admired the portraits of Mariamne and Aristobulus sent to him in secret. What the artist's brush had not captured was rounded out by Dellius's praise and compliments.

Of course, Antony could not ask the King of Judea to send him his wife. Setting aside the question of Herod's objections—his love for Mariamne was well known—Antony knew that Cleopatra

---

[34] *Exodus*, 20:4

would not tolerate any other woman at Antony's side. However—and Dellius had thought of this from the beginning—young Aristobulus *could* be invited to the capital of Egypt.

An appropriate letter was sent to Jerusalem. The response came soon. Herod pointed out that sending the youth out of the country could have undesirable consequences; it would undoubtedly raise hopes among some Jews that the Romans intended to give Judea to this last descendant of the Hasmonean line.

Antony considered the matter closed. If only he could have guessed what chain of events this half-joking invitation would initiate.

High Priest Aristobulus

There had been tensions in Jerusalem for months, even before Dellius visited the Jerusalem court. A fierce dispute raged over who should hold the office of High Priest, and the young Aristobulus played a significant role in it.

Herod could not serve as High Priest because he did not come from a priestly lineage. Thanks to Herod's efforts, Hyrcanus had recently returned from Parthian captivity in Babylon. He had enjoyed total freedom there, and the Babylonian Jews, proud to host a descendant of the Maccabees, spared him no honors or gifts. In Jerusalem, Herod honored Hyrcanus but could not reinstate him to the office of High Priest because of the severed ears. Ultimately, the king decided to entrust the high priesthood to a priest named Hananel—a totally unknown quantity in Judea. Hananel came from an ancient Jewish family that had been settled in Babylon for centuries and had long maintained friendly relations with the Antipatrids.

The priestly aristocracy of Judea, who considered this office their own, were outraged by this decision. Many believed that by this appointment, Herod sought to demote the importance of the highest religious office. Clearly, the king was not fond of the consistently hostile Judean priestly families, nor did he see any reason to uphold an independent and unfriendly ecclesiastical authority in his state.

However, the public opinion in Judea received Hananel's appointment with as much hostility as the Jews in Babylon received it with joy. After Palestine and Egypt, Babylon was the world's most significant center of Judaism. Hananel's appointment to the high priesthood demonstrated that it was a universal office, an office for all the Jews in the world. It also served to convey that Herod saw himself as the king of all Jews, whether in Palestine or abroad.

However, more than the Judean priests, the choice of Hananel as high priest offended Alexandra, the mother of Mariamne and Aristobulus. She was deeply convinced that this office should belong to her son. His young age was no obstacle, as the Law was silent on this matter. Since all her pleas to Herod were in vain, she sought support from Cleopatra and Antony. Even before Dellius's arrival, she had sent a letter to the Egyptian queen, which some lute players secretly delivered. Later, at Dellius's urging, she tried to secure Antony's support by sending him the boy's portrait.

The invitation of Aristobulus to Alexandria convinced Herod that the matter of high priesthood had taken a dangerous turn, and he had to make a concession. Of course, he never doubted who the true instigator of Antony's sudden interest in Mariamne's brother was.

Herod invited Alexandra to a meeting of the royal council, where he presented the situation. Thanks to his well-developed system of espionage and informants—both in Jerusalem and at the Egyptian court—he had much evidence in his hands. He accused Alexandra of secret plots, planning to overthrow him and hoping to elevate Aristobulus to the crown. That could mean pushing the country, which had already suffered so much, into the abyss of a new civil war. For all that, Herod would act justly and with forbearance. Since Alexandra cared so much about granting the high priesthood to her son, he would take the office away from Hananel—though it was contrary to the Law because the office was for life—and give it to Mariamne's brother.

Touched by this kindness, Alexandra made her apologies and offered her thanks with tears in her eyes. Both sides shook hands, and harmony and love returned to the family.

The Feast of Tabernacles

A year passed, and the autumn of 35 BC arrived, bringing the joyful Feast of Tabernacles. The people built huts of branches of olive, pine, myrtle, and palm on the flat roofs of their houses, in courtyards, streets, and squares. Whole families moved into these booths for eight days. The priests said this was done in memory of the tents in which their ancestors lived during the long years of wandering through the desert on their way to the Promised Land. In fact, it was a joyous festival celebrating the abundance of the land. The people made bouquets from the fruits of the most beautiful trees and branches of willows growing by the streams. Holding them in their hands, they circled the temple altar and repeated the words of a psalm:

Preserve us, O God: for in thee we put our trust. [35]

This year, the celebrants looked with special joy at the high priest, at his beautiful, slender, youthful figure. Clad in magnificent robes, he conducted the rites and offered sacrifices with gravity and pomp. Everyone recalled that he was the grandson of King Aristobulus, an enemy of the Romans and the only surviving legitimate heir of the Maccabees. Everyone showed him devotion, loyalty, and love.

Herod took part in the processions along with others, rejoicing and singing joyful psalms at the altar.

Immediately after the festival, he left with his family for Jericho. He liked this charming oasis of greenery, abundantly irrigated by the waters of many streams.

They were guests in the house of Princess Alexandra. There was love and harmony between her and Herod, though a certain untoward event had recently taken place.

The distrustful and cautious king had ordered his men to watch Alexandra closely. She felt like a prisoner in her own

---

[35] *Psalms* 16:1

apartmments. She contacted Cleopatra and, at the queen's suggestion, decided to flee to Egypt. And thus, one night, her servants carried two coffins out of the palace. One contained Alexandra, the other Aristobulus. However, Herod had received a timely warning. The coffins were opened in his presence. Once again, he showed admirable forbearance, forgiving the two for their attempt to escape.

And now, a great time was had by all in Jericho. The feast was splendid; the king joked and amused himself with his young brother-in-law, the High Priest. But Jericho is known for its heat. It is no wonder: it lies in the Jordan Valley, in a deep depression, close to the Dead Sea. So, in the afternoon, the revelers moved from the palace chambers to the side of the beautiful bathing pools formed by one of Jericho's many streams. They swam and frolicked in the water until late evening. It was already dark when suddenly a scream of terror rang out: Aristobul had drowned!

Many widely speculated that the king's trusted courtiers, taking advantage of the darkness and, under the pretext of rough horseplay, forcibly held the young High Priest underwater a tad too long. However, no one could prove this.

Mariamne and Joseph

In the spring of 34 BC, Herod left Jerusalem with a heavy heart and a sense of foreboding. He was setting out for Laodicea near Antioch in response to Antony's summons. Antony had stopped there on his way to the East in preparation for a campaign against Armenia—retribution against its king for treacherously abandoning the Romans during the disastrous Parthian War two years earlier.

It was clear that Antony's summons was somehow related to the death of Aristobulus. Princess Alexandra had informed Cleopatra of the events in Jericho, adding appropriate commentary. The Egyptian queen immediately seized upon this heinous crime to incite Antony. If she could overthrow Herod now, Palestine would be hers.

Herod was concerned for his wife, Mariamne, of whom he was

extremely jealous. Before his departure, he appointed his uncle, Joseph, as his plenipotentiary. Joseph, who was married to Herod's sister Salome, was thus also his brother-in-law. Herod asked him to keep an eye on Mariamne.

What exactly occurred at the royal palace after Herod's departure was known only to a few house servants. But it did not escape the eyes of the courtiers that Joseph visited the queen's chambers often and engaged in lengthy confidential conversations with her and her mother, Princess Alexandra. Of course, he had every right to do so—as a family member and the king's deputy.

Then, one day, the rumor spread that Antony had tortured and executed Herod. The city immediately erupted in turmoil, and Alexandra put in motion another of her grand plans. She went to Joseph and demanded that he move to the Roman military camp near Jerusalem.

But before Joseph could make up his mind, a letter from Herod arrived, informing him that the business in Laodicea had been resolved favorably: Antony dismissed all accusations against the king. And in any case, changes in Palestine could only be contemplated after the Armenian campaign. As usual, Herod's lavish gifts probably played a significant role. So, Cleopatra suffered a setback, and Herod returned to his capital in triumph.

However, a painful surprise awaited him here. Various persons in the palace felt it their duty to inform the king of what had transpired during his absence. These individuals included Herod's mother, Kypros, and his sister, Salome. A fierce struggle had raged for years between the two on the one hand and Mariamne and Alexandra on the other. The proud Hasmonean women openly showed their disdain for the Edomites, pointing out their low, half-Jewish origins. Now, they added sexual jealousy to the mix. Even more suspicious by nature than her brother, Salome was convinced that her husband, Joseph, had discussed with Mariamne matters that went well beyond politics. Why else would he even have considered moving to the Roman camp? Perhaps Joseph intended to marry Mariamne and seize power in Judea for himself?

Faced with the charges, Mariamne refused to deny them or make excuses. She went on the offensive instead. If Herod truly loved her—as he claimed—why had he given to Joseph the secret order to kill Mariamne if he didn't return from Laodicea alive?

The queen did not realize that by repeating those words to Herod, she passed a death sentence on Joseph. Herod flew into a rage. In his eyes, the revelation of his secret order was clear evidence that Mariamne and Joseph had been plotting together. Joseph had tried to turn her against him, win her favor, and pave his own way to the throne!

Joseph was killed.

Herod loved Mariamne too passionately to do her any harm, but now his suspicions and jealousy only intensified.

And thus, gradually, Herod's court became the stage for a -procession of gloomy tragedies. Their chief cause lay in the king's constant fear. He had only recently acquired power and did not yet feel secure on the throne. He feared that Cleopatra might wrest his hard-won kingdom away from him by using members of his own family for that purpose.

Meanwhile, the year 33 BC arrived, heralding a great war that would change the face of the Mediterranean completely.

HEROD AND THE WAR OF THE GIANTS

Sibyl

The reign of an immortal king will descend upon the Earth when Rome conquers Egypt. Then, a divine lord will arise and rule the world for all eternity. This will happen when the might of relentless Latins is threatened, and the Three inflict a terrible fate upon Rome. In those days, Beliazar will come. He will raise mountains, halt the sea's waves, the bright moon, and the blazing sun. He will resurrect the dead and perform many miracles. However, there will be no perfection in him, only deception. He will mislead many, both the Hebrews and those ignorant of the Law. And behold, the terror of mighty God draws near as sheets of fire descend upon the earth! Beliazar and all those who have placed their hopes in him perish. This will all occur when the world is ruled by a woman, and everyone obeys a widow. And when these events unfold, the day of God's judgment will come.[36]

This prophecy had circulated in Judea and among Jews of the Near East for several years prior to 31 BC. It was written in verse, in Greek, and attributed to Sibyl,[37] an ancient Greek oracle. In reality, these intentionally vague and confused visions expressed the hopes and fears that preoccupied the Jewish society during the anxious days preceding the outbreak of the new civil war in Rome.

Everyone realized that a war between Octavian and Antony

---

[36] *Oracula Sybillina*, 5:36-90

[37] The sibyls were prophetesses or oracles in Ancient Greece and prophesied at holy sites. A sibyl at Delphi has been dated to as early as the eleventh century BC by Pausanias. At first, there appears to have been only a single sibyl. By the fourth century BC, there appear to have been at least three more, Phrygian, Erythraean, and Hellespontine. By the first century BC, there were at least ten sibyls, located in Greece, Italy, the Levant, and Asia Minor. Renaissance church decorations in Europe often represent the Sybils alongside the Jewish prophets as prophesying the coming of Christ.

was inevitable. The fundamental reason for the conflict was that there was not enough room in the world for two such extraordinary giants. But the two sides also presented other complaints. Octavian, the ruler of Italy and the West, accused his fellow *triumvir* of betraying Rome's interests, pursuing a policy dictated by Cleopatra, and transferring Imperial possessions to the Egyptian queen and her cronies. In turn, Antony accused Octavian of ousting Lepidus from power, illegally seizing Sicily and Africa, and preventing Antony from recruiting for his legions in Italy.

The war was going to be terrible; no one had any illusions about that. Hence, the prophecy of Sybil painted a dark picture of "Beliazar's days," combined with a warning not to believe in false Messiahs even in the most trying times. Antony's military prowess and Cleopatra's vast wealth suggested they might emerge victorious. Antony's love for Cleopatra subjected him to her will, which could lead to the fall of the Roman Empire and the rule of a woman.

Contemporary readers knew why Sybil referred to Cleopatra as a widow: she had poisoned her most recent husband and brother. But never mind, the triumph of Beliazar would be short-lived, and Cleopatra's rule would end quickly. For soon upon their heels, the long-awaited, true Messiah would come. The time was at hand! In their apprehensive anticipation, Herod's subjects consoled themselves. They saw Herod as one of Beliazar's temporary puppets.

Herod himself lived in tormented uncertainty: how to navigate his affairs in the face of the impending storm and preserve his throne and his country? If Octavian were to triumph, he would severely punish his enemy's allies. But if Antony prevailed, nothing would shield Judea from the greed of his heart's beloved and now officially wedded wife, Cleopatra.

The Nabatean War

In the spring of 32 BC, Herod led his troops to southern Syria. He was on his way to join Antony's forces, which were concentrating in Asia

Minor and Greece in preparation for an invasion of Italy.

On the way, Herod received an order from Antony's headquarters: his help would not be needed; he was to turn back immediately and set out against the Nabateans, whose behavior was causing concern.

Herod took on this task willingly, as he had his own scores to settle with the King of Petra. For years, the Nabateans had refused to pay the lease that Herod had guaranteed to the Queen of Egypt—and as a result, he had had to pay it himself. But the sudden outbreak of the Nabatean affair had a different cause. Cleopatra wanted to keep Herod as far away from Antony as possible. She wanted to ensure that the King of Judea would have no part in Antony's victory over Octavian—a victory of which she felt confident. By sidelining Herod now, she calculated, she prepared the ground for a quick seizure of his kingdom when the new world order was settled after the victory. Meanwhile, the Jews and the Nabateans should bleed each other for the benefit of a third party.

Herod understood the queen's reasoning but had no choice: he had to go to war against the Nabateans. The future would show how great a favor Cleopatra had done him by sending him to that war.

The Judeo-Nabatean war took place in the lands east of the Jordan, in the supposedly "free" territories of the Greek cities of the Decapolis. Cavalry played the primary role on both sides. The first serious clash occurred near the city of Dion, and Herod emerged victorious. Later, the Nabateans gathered their forces near the town of Canatha, in the wild, rocky land of Auranitis, at the foot of a massif of extinct volcanoes now called Jabal-al-Druze.

The victory at Dion made Herod and his men overconfident. When they arrived at Canatha, they did not even bother to fortify their camp. Later, Herod maintained that this happened against his explicit orders. He also said that he led his men straight into battle because— enthused—they pressed him to attack: they thought they would repeat the success of Dion. In the first charge, the Judean cavalry pushed back the masses of Nabatean warriors; victory seemed at hand, indeed.

And then, suddenly, panic broke out in the rear of Herod's

ranks. There, a new enemy struck, seemingly emerging from nowhere. It turned out to be the local population acting on the orders of Athenion, the Egyptian deputy of Cleopatra in those parts of Syria Antony had given her. Herod had considered him an ally and assumed that he had mustered his levies to reinforce their joint effort. Meanwhile, Athenion's objective was different: to ensure that the Jews did not wholly rout the Nabateans. Of course, in doing this, he acted on Cleopatra's secret instructions. He risked nothing, as he could always claim in the end that the inhabitants of Auranitis carried out the attack without his knowledge.

Thousands of Jews fell in that battle. Now, the Nabateans moved forward, hunting down the units of Jewish cavalry scattered among the ravines, crevices, heaps of boulders, and lava. The defeated had nowhere to retreat to. Their camp—never fortified and defended by only a handful of survivors—was taken by the enemy on the first assault. Herod saved himself by a swift escape. Later, in his autobiography, he claimed that he rode off at full gallop only to summon reinforcements.

Thus, the great battle of Canatha ended in a shameful defeat for Herod.

From then on, the war took on a different character. The king prudently avoided major battles, stuck to mountainous terrain, and devastated the land of the Nabateans with guerilla raids. Thus, he tried to erase the ignominious memory of Canatha among the people and the army.

First a Disaster, then a Triumph

In the spring of 31 BC, Judea experienced a terrible disaster—an earthquake. It probably happened at night because about thirty thousand people and tens of thousands of head of cattle lost their lives under the rubble of collapsing buildings. The cataclysm did not directly affect the army in the field, but it shrouded the entire country in mourning. Like most people, Herod's soldiers considered this tragedy a sign of the wrath of the Lord: their king had angered God!

The Nabateans welcomed the news of the disaster with joy. They considered it a just vengeance sent from heaven to punish their hated enemy, and hordes of Nabatean looters set out to plunder the ruined land. Herod, through messengers, begged for mercy and proposed a truce because, in the face of such a monstrous catastrophe, every man and every nation was powerless, and therefore, all feuds should cease. The only response from the Nabateans was to murder the Jewish envoys.

If Herod ever proved to be a provident master of Judea, it was then. The king's fervor inspired everyone capable of bearing arms to fight. The Jewish army crossed the Jordan to block the invaders. The two armies met near the city of Philadelphia in the Decapolis.[38] The place had a special significance for the Jews and inspired them with extraordinary courage.

Philadelphia stood on the summit and slopes of a mountain above the Jabbok River.[39] The city's name was Greek, and many Hellenes had lived here for two centuries. However, everyone knew that the city of Rabbat Ammon had once stood here, the capital of Israel's ancient enemies, the Ammonites. Ten centuries ago, the Jewish commander Joab and King David himself captured Rabbat Ammon. The *Book of Samuel* told the story:

> And he took their king's crown from off his head, the weight whereof was a talent of gold with the precious stones: and it was set on David's head. And he brought forth the spoil of the city in great abundance.
> And he brought forth the people that were therein, and put them under saws, and under harrows of iron, and under axes of iron, and made them pass through the brick-kiln: and thus did he unto all the cities of the children of Ammon. Thus, David and all the people returned unto Jerusalem.[40]

---

[38] Today's Amman, capital of Jordan

[39] Zarqa River in Jordan today

[40] *2 Samuel,* 12:30-31

Why shouldn't the Jews return victorious from Rabbat Ammon again? And so it happened. Herod's forces defeated the Nabateans near Philadelphia. They killed five thousand of the enemy. Some who tried to defend themselves in the fortified camp had to surrender after a few days due to lack of water. The Jews captured four thousand and cut down another seven thousand who tried to break free.

And thus, they avenged Canatha. The people of Jerusalem joyfully welcomed their victorious king.

Shortly after this triumph, a shocking piece of news reached the court: on September 3, Octavian defeated Antony in a battle at Actium. Antony and Cleopatra fled to Alexandria. The victorious Octavian was heading east to establish a new order—to punish his enemies and empower his friends.

Would the defeat of Antony drag Herod into the abyss? This was the question everyone in Judea was asking, especially the king himself. Fortunately, Octavian was not in a hurry. There was time to prepare and find a way to save themselves.

Antony's Faithful Gladiators

Many months earlier, Antony had gathered several thousand gladiators in the city of Cyzicus on the shores of Propontis at the entrance to the Black Sea. There, they trained for the battles they were expected to fight to the death in the circuses of Rome to celebrate their master's expected victory over Octavian.

When they learned of Antony's defeat, they immediately marched south to offer him their assistance. They marched through Asia Minor, cutting their way through the lands of hostile princes and cities. Meanwhile, all the rulers of the East, who owed their rule to Antony, were abandoning him. His governors betrayed him. Cities and provinces revolted against him. To the best of their ability, everyone sought Octavian's favor, hoping to expunge through haste and zeal the stain of their previous service to his enemy.

Only the gladiators—the most scorned of men—stayed faithful to Antony. Armed only with swords, they pressed on, reaching as far as Syria.

The governor of Syria was Quintus Didius, hitherto Antony's most devoted ally. Upon hearing of the defeat at Actium, Didius immediately switched his allegiance to Octavian, and now he did everything he could to halt the gladiators' march and prevent them from reaching Egypt, where Antony desperately gathered the remnants of his troops. However, the gladiators quickly broke up the forces Didius sent against them and continued their march south. Egyptian garrisons guarded those Syrian territories that Antony had granted to Cleopatra, and they were already in view.

Suddenly—and very timely—Didius received assistance from an unexpected quarter. New forces arrived—they were small but just large enough to cut off the gladiators' further progress south. The faithful slaves did not give up. They sent messengers to Antony, asking for relief or orders what to do next. Weeks passed, and no response came. The gladiators concluded that Antony had perished.

In reality, Antony was still alive and well in Alexandria, and the gladiator's messengers had reached him. But the Lord of the East had already lost all hope and all will to fight. He alternated between revelry and despair. He did not grace his most faithful men with a single word.

After a long, fruitless wait, the gladiators made arrangements with the representatives of Octavian. They surrendered because they knew he would never employ them for combat in the arena. Octavian's men assigned Daphne, near Antioch, as temporary quarters for the gladiators and promised to enlist them eventually in the Roman legions as full-fledged soldiers. The gladiators received this news joyfully, as it meant gaining freedom, Roman citizenship, and land after completing their service. In small groups or even individually, they dispersed to their assigned units scattered throughout various regions of the great Empire. Strangely, none ever reached his designated unit. They all mysteriously disappeared without a trace along the way. [41]

But all that was still in the future. For now, let us go back a bit. Here is a question: Who prevented the gladiators from breaking through Syria? Who assisted the governor of the province?

Quintus Didius himself provided the answers to these questions. In a letter to Octavian, he praised the person as a loyal ally who promptly sent men to stop the "rebellious slaves."

The man was Herod, King of the Jews.

Death of Hyrcanus

In his memoirs, Herod wrote about those times like this:

"My friends considered my cause lost, and my enemies rejoiced. Now, the hateful Princess Alexandra, the cause of many intrigues and misfortunes, conceived of a new plan of action. Thinking that my downfall was imminent, she decided to escape from Jerusalem along with her uncle, Hyrcanus.

"She began to persuade him to turn to the king of the Nabateans with a request to grant the two of them asylum in his kingdom. She did this because she was sure that Octavian would depose me for having once been a friend of Antony. And then, who else but Hyrcanus could possibly rule over Judea?

"Hyrcanus was already an old man, well over seventy, and as he had always lacked energy and enterprise, he resisted her suggestions for a long time. But eventually, persistence and feminine guile prevailed. He wrote a letter to Petra, asking for a detachment of Nabatean cavalry to help with their escape. The man to whom Hyrcanus gave this letter—a fellow named Dositheos, showed it to me. This was all the more noteworthy because this man was a relative of that Joseph, who a few years earlier met his end on my orders as a

---

[41] Polish readers of this text would recall the story of 30,000 Polish army officers taken POW by Stalin in 1939 and strangely "disappeared without a trace." (They were in fact murdered by Russian security services).

traitor. Even earlier, another one of Dositheos' relatives had perished during the disturbances in Tyre when a group of Jewish emissaries sent before Antony demanded my deposition.[42]

"I now read Hyrcanus's letter and handed back it to Dositheos, telling him to deliver it to Petra. I was curious about what they would do in this matter. As I suspected, the king of the Nabateans immediately showed full readiness to come to Hyrcanus's aid.

"After intercepting the letter from Petra, I exposed Hyrcanus's machinations before the council. They sentenced him to death."[43]

If this version of events rings false in your ears, it does because it probably is. It does, however, illustrate the constant fear in which Herod lived: he constantly worried about losing his throne and perhaps even his life. And when in doubt, he did not hesitate. He wanted to fight, to defend himself, and to maintain his power at any cost. He reasoned that Octavian would only depose him if he had a plausible alternative. So, as a precaution, Herod got rid of the only such alternative: the last surviving Hasmonean male.

And so died Hyrcanus, the man to whom the clan of Antipater the Idumean had owed their political career.

A Meeting in Rhodes

"Ave Caesar! I became king thanks to Antony. That is true. I also admit that I served him zealously in every matter and in every situation. Had it not been for the war with the Nabateans, I would have fought against you at Actium at the head of my troops. Even so, I sent many men and tens of thousands of measures of grain to Antony to support his cause. Even after his defeat, I did not abandon my benefactor. Since I could no longer serve him with the strength of my arms, I became his best advisor. I tried to explain to Antony that there was only one hope of salvation in his catastrophic situation—to kill

---

[42] In other words, Desitheos was Herod's spy in the enemy camp.

[43] Based on Josephus, *Antiquities*, 15, 6, 2

Cleopatra. I told him that if he decided to get rid of the Queen of Egypt, I would provide him with money, fortresses, and troops and personally take part in the war against you. Unfortunately, his passion for Cleopatra was more potent than the voice of reason and friendship.

"I suffered a defeat along with Antony. Since fortune has abandoned him, I lay down my royal diadem at your feet. I place myself at your disposal, and all my hope of salvation lies only in your mercy and your righteousness. I hope that as you decide my fate, you will consider not whose friend I was but what kind of a friend I was."

Moved by these words, Octavian replied:

"And with these words, you are saved! Rule now with even more assurance than before. You deserve to rule because you defend your friends. Now, strive to be loyal to those whom fortune has favored more than it has your friends. I have great hope in the steadfastness of your character. It is a good thing that Antony listened to Cleopatra more than he listened to you because, through his error, we have gained a worthy friend. Indeed, you have already begun to serve us. Quintus Didius wrote to me in this letter that you had provided significant help in stopping the march of the gladiators.

"Therefore, I now confirm by a separate decree your royal dignity, and in the future, I will endeavor to shower you with such favors that you will never have occasion to mourn the loss of your former friend, Antony."[44]

Herod and Octavian supposedly delivered these moving speeches in the spring of 30 BC on the island of Rhodes. It was their first meeting in ten years—the first meeting since that day in Rome, when, on the Capitol, Herod had offered sacrifice to Jupiter in the presence of both *triumvirs*. How much the situation changed since then! Octavian was now the sole ruler of the world. Antony was still in the royal palace in Alexandria, but his days were numbered. Everyone had abandoned him. Even Cleopatra began secret negotiations with the victor. Herod, ten years ago, a king without a country, had won his kingdom and, sword in hand, removed all rivals.

---

[44] Josephus, *The Jewish War*, I, 385-392

Like Octavian was in Rome, he was now the last man standing in Palestine.

Herod quoted the speeches in Rhodes—both his and Octavian's—in his memoir, and his court historian did not fail to cite them. They demonstrated to posterity the nobility and beauty of the character of both interlocutors.

But they were probably never delivered in that form.

Herod did indeed receive confirmation of his royal office in Rhodes. However, beyond any doubt, this did not happen due to theatrical gestures and emotional speeches. Octavian was too astute a politician to be swayed by rhetoric. There were many practical reasons why the victor considered it expedient to keep Herod in power.

Above all, Octavian knew that Herod would serve him as faithfully and as loyally as he had served Antony, and before Antony, Cassius, and before Cassius, Caesar, and before Caesar, Pompey. Now, he would serve Octavian—and even more devotedly, as he had no choice, for henceforth, there would be only one ruler in Rome. It also worked in Herod's favor that he had not taken part in the Battle of Actium. And finally—and perhaps most importantly—Herod genuinely hated Cleopatra. Octavian was well-informed about this.

Octavian also realized that the situation in Palestine was complicated because of the constant conflicts among the various Jewish religious factions and the threat of a Nabatean invasion. Therefore, leaving political power in Judea in the hands of an energetic man who had always been loyal to Rome, who knew the local conditions, and who had at least part of the population behind him seemed like a far better solution than turning that land into a Roman province and trying to introduce the Roman administration, which could cause resistance, unrest, revolts, and likely was not worth the cost involved.

Jews' love of freedom and their unparalleled courage in defending it were well known to the Romans. Moreover, who could predict whether the Nabateans would not seek to take advantage of any unrest in Judea?

Octavian was not a petty or vindictive man. He confirmed in

their positions several other princes who had remained with Antony even longer than Herod. Furthermore, he decided that leaving or even expanding the system of small buffer states in the Middle East—states which, under the guise of independence, were, in fact, only subservient and feeble vassals of the mighty Empire—would remain Roman policy. Given these circumstances, such a solution seemed most advantageous, both politically and financially. Therefore, Herod would keep his kingdom.

Herod returned to Jerusalem joyful and triumphant, much to the chagrin of his numerous enemies. Among them were even people so obsessed with hatred for Herod that they were prepared to support his downfall, even at the price of incorporating Judea directly into the Empire. Others were critical that Herod had not fought and died in defense of Antony and Cleopatra, as honor would have demanded.

The king stayed only briefly in Jerusalem. After a few weeks, he left for the city of Ptolemais on the Phoenician coast to welcome Octavian, who was leading an army to Egypt by the coastal route. The Roman headquarters received Herod with appropriate honors. Then, Herod rode alongside Octavian in front of the advancing legions. Later, he entertained his officers with a splendid feast: they filled a hundred and fifty rooms. And when the Roman army moved further south towards the Egyptian border, Herod took on the responsibility for provisioning it.

On the first day of August, Octavian entered Alexandria. Antony, whose last men had deserted him, committed suicide by falling upon his sword. Cleopatra tried to negotiate with Octavian for a while longer. However, when she learned that she was to be taken to Rome to march in Octavian's triumph, she took her own life.

Herod had not taken part in the march on Alexandria but now hurried there to congratulate Octavian. His congratulations were sincere. The victor declared all of Antony's donations to Cleopatra and her children illegal. Then, the issue of Palestine arose. Octavian

Tyre from the Isthmus

decided that Jericho should return to Herod.

Furthermore, he also gave him a portion of the lands that Pompey had detached from Judea after his capture of the Temple: the coastal strip with the cities of Gaza, Antedon, Joppa, and the small town called Strato's Tower; all of Samaria; the cities of Gadara and Hippos to the east of the Sea of Galilee. And, as a personal gift—four hundred men who had previously constituted Cleopatra's bodyguard. It is not surprising, therefore, that when Octavian returned to Rome at the end of 30 BC, Herod, full of gratitude, accompanied him as far as Antioch.

HEROD AND MARIAMNE

Love and Politics

We read in the *Song of Songs*:

> Rise up, my love, my fair one, rise up and come away. For, lo, the winter is past, the rain is over and gone. The flowers appear on the earth; the time of the singing of birds is come, and the voice of the turtle dove is heard in our land. The fig tree putteth forth her green figs, and the vines with the tender grape give a good scent. Arise, my love, my fair one, and come away. O my dove, that art in the clefts of the rock, in the secret places of the stairs, let me see thy countenance, let me hear thy voice; for sweet is thy voice, and thy countenance is comely. [45]

Mariamne certainly knew this song, one of the most beautiful in the Old Testament. However, what kind of love did she have? Herod indeed loved her. However, their marriage, celebrated in the spring eight years ago in Samaria, had not been joyful. Straight from the wedding festivities, Herod hastened to the siege of Jerusalem. It was not a time for reveling in the spring bloom. To conquer the capital! To cut down Antigonus' men! That, and only that, was the topic of conversation at the royal court.

Antigonus was executed by the Romans that spring. Who was Antigonus to Mariamne? He was her uncle, the brother of her father.

Then, the tragic autumn of 36 BC saw the coming of their first child into the world. That autumn, Mariamne's young and only brother, Aristobulus, was treacherously drowned. He perished because Herod feared that Cleopatra might use him against him.

One crime led to another—the execution of Joseph, Herod's uncle, Mariamne's guardian. When Antony suffered defeat, what was

---

[45] Song of Solomon, 2:11-14

Herod's first move? He killed Hyrcanus under the pretext of a planned escape. He did it to remove the last of the Hasmoneans and to deny victorious Octavian any alternative ruler for Judea.

But Mariamne was Hyrcanus' granddaughter.

Herod knew human nature too well to imagine that these crimes did not affect Mariamne's attitude towards him. He had five children with her: three sons and two daughters united them. But four graves separated them, and he could never bridge that chasm. Herod's paranoia and suspicion grew with each new crime. Was Mariamne perhaps plotting revenge? The lust for power is the most hideous malady that can ever afflict a human heart. It kills everything, even the most humane feelings—even a man's love for the mother of his children.

The Death of Mariamne

And now they led Mariamne to her death. The royal council had sentenced her for attempting to poison her husband.

The queen walked calmly and with dignity, in a way befitting a woman of a great royal lineage that had ruled for generations. Suddenly, her mother, Alexandra, rushed out from her chambers. She threw herself at Mariamne, cursing and insulting her. She beat her and pulled her hair. She screamed at the top of her lungs, declaring that such a wicked daughter and wife deserved the just and righteous punishment that befell her. The crowd watched this repulsive scene with shock and disdain, but no one dared to step forward in defense of the tormented woman.

Mariamne remained composed. She did not respond to her mother as she publicly disowned her daughter and pushed her towards the grave, all in order to—save her own life.

Mariamne's fate entered the last stretch in the spring of 30 BC when Herod went to Rhodes to win over Octavian. The king, just as he had when he left for Antioch six years earlier, considered the possibility that this might be his last journey. If Octavian were to depose Herod, it would put his entire family in mortal danger. They would become victims of the hatred of their enemies, of which there was no shortage. Therefore, Herod appointed his younger—and only surviving—brother, Pheroras, as his deputy. He instructed him to move to the fortress of Masada with their mother, their sister Salome, and the children of Mariamne. Mariamne and her mother, Alexandra, were sent to another fortress in the north of the country: Alexandrion. In this way, Herod separated the four women who loathed each other and simultaneously deprived the children—the oldest of whom was only seven years old—of their mother's love.

The commander of Alexandrion, Soaimos, was a farsighted man. He realized that, regardless of how events unfolded, it was necessary to seek Mariamne's favor. If Octavian deposed Herod, she—the last Hasmonean—would become critically important. But if the king preserved his life and power, the goodwill of his wife and the mother of the heirs to the throne would be precious. To secure her favor, Soaimos, in great secrecy, revealed to Mariamne his master's secret order: that if anything untoward were to happen to Herod in Rhodes, both Mariamne and Alexandra should be put to death.

Soaimos did not know that Herod had given the same order to Joseph a few years earlier when he went to face his trial in Antioch, and therefore, he could not have anticipated how shocking this information would be for the queen. Certainly, the deaths of her brother, Aristobulus, and recently her grandfather, Hyrcanus, had come as great personal tragedies. However, ultimately, in both cases, she could at least delude herself into thinking that Herod was blameless. Perhaps Aristobulus had really drowned? Perhaps Hyrcanus did plan treason? Joseph might even have invented the story of Herod's order to murder Mariamne in order to convince her to help him seize power.

Now, however, there was no doubt. Herod's murderous and ruthless egoism revealed itself with terrifying clarity.

Upon Herod's return from Rhodes, his reunion with his wife did not go as Herod had expected, radiant with Octavian's favor as he was. Mariamne was sad and distant. The astonished king erupted in anger, pleaded, threatened, and—suspected. Meanwhile, Herod's mother and sister arrived in Jerusalem from Masada. Taking advantage of the situation, they again brought accusations against Mariamne. Herod raged. However, he did not have time to deal with family matters. First, he traveled to Ptolemais to wait on Octavian, then to Alexandria to congratulate him on his final victory over Antony and Cleopatra, and finally to Antioch to bid farewell to the ruler of the world.

The situation at the Jerusalem court remained unchanged. Mariamne did not hide her aversion towards her husband, and Herod became increasingly agitated and filled with wild suspicions. Salome encouraged them. Since the Joseph affair, the hatred between her and Mariamne had only intensified. The queen could not ignore the scornful glances cast at her, and she displayed her contempt for her husband's sister and mother all the more ostentatiously.

The intrigue that Salome invented was, in fact, quite crude. If not for chance, it would likely have come to nothing. Taking advantage of a moment when Herod, after one of their many quarrels, was particularly ill-disposed towards his wife, Salome sent a well-paid chamberlain to him. He testified that Mariamne had bribed him: he was supposed to give the king some bay leaves to rekindle their love; however, he, the chamberlain, suspected that the queen had deceived him and that the supposed bay leaves were really poison.

Despite everything, Herod was not inclined to believe this report. As a precaution, however, he ordered the most trusted servant of Mariamne to be tortured. Of course, the servant could not reveal anything about any bay leaves or poisons, as the entire story was fabricated from start to finish. However, as is often the case with tortured individuals, he blurted out everything he knew or suspected. He testified that the queen had been hostile to her husband since the day Soaimos revealed Herod's secret order to her.

And that was enough.

The king, full of morbid suspicions perpetually stoked by his sister, immediately began to shout that Mariamne must have had an affair with Soaimos if he had revealed that order to her. He, Herod, had been deceived by his wife and the officer he trusted the most. He had Soaimos executed on the spot. Shortly, the royal council convened. Herod himself accused Mariamne. In demanding his wife's death, he acted—from his point of view—not without justification. He understood perfectly well that matters between them had gone too far; Mariamne's hatred would only intensify; nothing would assuage her grief; and nothing would ever make him trust her again. The king feared that his wife would imbue their children with hatred for him. It was better for them never to see their mother again.

A Train of Crimes

> For love is strong as death; jealousy is cruel as the grave: the coals thereof are coals of fire, which hath a most vehement flame. Many waters cannot quench love, neither can the floods drown it: if a man would give all the substance of his house for love, it would utterly be condemned. [46]

Now came one of the most tragic periods in Herod's life. Mariamne's death nearly drove him mad. He sought forgetfulness in every possible way, oscillating between extremes. He feasted and reveled, only to weep bitter tears moments later, calling for Mariamne as if she were still alive.

> Behold, thou art fair, my love; behold, thou art fair; thou hast doves' eyes within thy locks: thy hair is as a flock of goats that appear from Mount Gilead. Thy teeth are like a flock of sheep that are even shorn, which came up from the washing; whereof every one bear twins, and none is barren among them. Thy lips are like a thread of scarlet, and thy speech is comely: thy temples are like a piece of a pomegranate within thy locks. O, thou art all fair, my love; there is no flaw in thee. [47]

---

[46] *Song of Solomon*, 8:6-7

[47] Ibid., 4:1-7

This is how beautiful Mariamne had been. Her body was already decaying.

A plague erupted in Judea. The people believed it was divine punishment for the king's unjust murder of an innocent woman. Herod shared this widespread conviction but could not admit it. He departed from Jerusalem to desolate, barren lands on a grand hunting expedition. Everyone at court knew the king was, in fact, tormenting himself with bitter regret. Soon, physically and mentally exhausted, he fell ill. Transported to Samaria, he lay in a fever, enduring excruciating headaches. He frequently slipped into unconsciousness. The physicians pronounced that no hope was left and said that Herod's days were numbered.

News of this reached Jerusalem. Alexandra, Mariamne's mother, attempted to sway the commanders of the two fortresses guarding the city and the Temple to her side. She argued that she was acting in the best interest of Herod's and Mariamne's sons—her grandsons. She wanted to secure their future in case of their father's death. However, the prudent commanders dispatched a messenger to Samaria. He found the king somewhat more lucid. When Herod learned of Alexandra's scheme, he flew into a rage. The messenger returned to Jerusalem with orders to execute the princess.

The death of Mariamne's mother marked the beginning of a grim procession of further deaths, even among the king's closest friends. One of the first victims was Costobarus, Salome's husband and thus Herod's brother-in-law. Hailing from Idumea, he governed that region and the city of Gaza on the king's behalf. He had learned the lessons of Antipater and Herod: if they had managed to overthrow the royal line and seize Jerusalem's throne, why should Herod's fellow Idumean, Costobarus, not be able to do the same? Some people had falsely accused Costobarus of conspiring with Cleopatra some years ago. However, this time, he was at the forefront of a wide-ranging conspiracy, planning to stage a coup while the king was ill.

Salome uncovered the plot. As Herod's sister, she would likely have been one of the first victims if her husband's plot had prevailed. Thus, she promptly informed her brother. Costobarus perished along with all his co-conspirators.

During the search of his estates, an exciting discovery came to light. In one of Costobarus's remote houses, several members of a collateral branch of the Hasmonean family lived in hiding. Costobarus had saved them back in 37 BC when the people of Jerusalem were massacring aristocrats and supporters of the Hasmoneans. Since then, they have lived quietly in hiding, and through them, Costobarus has established secret ties with Herod's most bitter enemies—the old nobility of Judea. Thus, in an ironic twist, fate had bound together recent mortal adversaries: the Idumean and Judean aristocracies.

HEROD THE BUILDER

Fortress Antonia

Construction was Herod's passion. In the early years of his reign, when the country lay in ruins, money was scarce, and war loomed on all fronts, the king could not devote himself to his beloved pursuit as much as he desired. He constructed only the indispensable fortresses.

He raised from the ruins the mighty Alexandrion, guarding the main road from Samaria to Judea. He also expanded and fortified the fortress of Masada, overlooking the Dead Sea, which had saved his family's lives many years ago. And he fortified the capital, Jerusalem.

A natural rocky steep promontory rose in the northwestern part of the Temple Mount. During the Hasmonean era, Jews had built a defensive tower on the site, called Baris. But Herod erected a genuinely awe-inspiring fortress in its place.

He ordered the rock on which the fortress walls were to rise to be faced from bottom to top with smooth stone slabs, which created the impression that the entire base, nearly twenty-five meters high, had been built by human hand. A parapet was built all around the top of the rock, and upon it, a grand quadrilateral structure, about twenty-five meters high. Four towers guarded its four corners. The tallest of them, the southeast, reached thirty meters and loomed directly over the temple courtyard. Whoever held the fortress controlled the heart of the religious life of the entire Jewish nation.

From the outside, the structure appeared to be an impregnable fortress, but its interior was a spacious and splendidly furnished palace. It lacked nothing that could enhance the life of its garrison in the event of a siege: there were even luxurious baths.

Herod named the fortress "Antonia" after his then-close friend and protector. This name stuck and remained—even after Antony's downfall and death.

Games

Shortly after Octavian's victory, when Herod's rule came to rest on a firmer foundation, and with the addition of new territories, his income also increased, the King of Judea began to erect magnificent public structures of the sort without which not even a second-rate Greek or Roman city could do at that time: theaters, sports stadiums, and hippodromes—this last being racecourses for chariots. Herod intended all these beautiful buildings to adorn Jerusalem to testify to its status as the capital of a ruler who loved Greek culture and, at the same time, to glorify his victories and might. Numerous inscriptions on the walls and entrances of the buildings attested to this, as well as the so-called "trophies"—fanciful arrangements of captured enemy weapons and armor.

These trophies caused grumbling among the inhabitants of Jerusalem, as they felt that these objects were just the sort of likenesses forbidden by the Law. Herod easily quelled this seed of unrest. When, at his invitation, the leaders of the Pharisees arrived at the amphitheater, he ordered the removal of all the armor from the trophies. The grumbling stopped when it became clear that the helmets and breastplates were not concealing statues but rested on ordinary pillars—which did not violate the Law.

Most severely, however, the Jews condemned the construction of the theater and the amphitheater. Every four years, in September, these structures were used to hold grand games in honor of Octavian's victory at Actium. And not just races, musical contests, and athletic competitions, but also bloody spectacles modeled after the wildest Roman shows—battles between predatory animals and men.

For the first time, these Actian Games—as Herod called them—were held in 27 BC. Ten conspirators decided to attempt to assassinate Herod on the occasion as he entered the theater. However, at the last moment, they were betrayed by an informant. They were arrested with concealed weapons. They boldly admitted they had hoped to kill the king and were put to death after terrible tortures.

They were likely connected with the oldest and perhaps most implacable enemy of Herod—the Zealots.

The man who betrayed the conspirators did not escape punishment. One day, someone recognized him on a Jerusalem street. The crowd immediately tore the informant to pieces, and his bloody remains were thrown to the dogs.

Samaria-Sebaste

According to the Bible, almost nine hundred years earlier, shortly after the death of King Solomon, the Jewish kingdom had split into two smaller states. The smaller of the two, known as Judah, had its capital in Jerusalem. The capital of the larger and wealthier northern state, Israel, was in Shiloh, then Shechem, then Tirzah. Some decades later, the seventh Israelite king, Omri, purchased a mountain for two talents of silver and built a city on it. He named it Somron after the mountain's former owner, Shemer. From this came its Greek name: Samaria.

The mountain was easily worth two talents of silver. It was high and broad, with gentle and fertile slopes, overlooking a vast fertile valley surrounding it on all sides. Fields and orchards adorned its slopes, the city sprawled on its extensive crest, and at the very summit stood a great fortress. Samaria served as the capital of the Kingdom of Israel and the residence and burial ground of its kings for over a century until 722 BC. That year, after a three-year siege, the ruler of mighty Assyria, Sargon II, captured it and destroyed it. Thirty thousand of its inhabitants were taken into captivity and exiled to distant and unknown lands. They disappeared without a trace.

Some Israelites managed to hide in the wild mountain valleys, and settlers from Babylon were brought in by the Assyrians. The former inhabitants and the new colonists mixed and gave rise to a new people—the Samaritans.

The Judeans despised the Samaritans—it was an ancient antagonism born during the existence of the two kingdoms, which had often waged fratricidal wars. But now, this old hatred found religious justification. Both sides considered themselves the only true worshippers of the God of Israel. However, of all the religious texts accepted by Judeans, the Samaritans recognized only *The Torah*—the first five books of the Old Testament attributed to Moses. They also celebrated distinct holidays and rituals.

During the reign of Alexander the Great, many Judean immigrants settled in Samaria, including a priest named Manasseh. He built a temple on Mount Gerizim, intending it to rival the Temple in Jerusalem. Later, when Palestine fell under the rule of the Seleucids, many Greeks settled in Samaria. Thus, over the centuries, the differences between the Samaritans and the Jews, their neighbors to the south, only increased.

Minor skirmishes between the two peoples occurred incessantly. Samaritans attacked caravans traveling from Galilee to Jerusalem, sparking bloody reprisals. It was said that the mutual hate was such that neither would give the other a cup of water if his life depended on it.

When Judea regained its independence under the Hasmoneans, Jewish forces quickly invaded Samaria. In 128 BC, they destroyed the temple on Mount Gerizim, and a quarter of a century later, after a year-long siege, they captured the city of Samaria. Samaria was incorporated into the Hasmonean kingdom, but the rule remained tenuous and spotty, and the population remained hostile.

Yet, Herod enjoyed support in Samaria, as he did in all the regions of Palestine unfriendly to Judea. To strengthen his power base in Samaria, he decided to build a new and magnificent city there. As he embarked on this plan, he had several goals in mind. First and foremost, he wanted to reward the loyalty of his veteran supporters, and they were to constitute the core of the city's settlers and receive the best plots of the surrounding agricultural land. Furthermore, the city commanded a strategically essential crossroads, where routes from Galilee to Judea and from the coastal plain to Scythopolis and the Jordan Valley crossed, and it was only a day's journey from Jerusalem. Finally, by building a new city, Herod wanted to pay a special tribute to the ruler of Rome, a tribute he would not dare to offer in Jerusalem.

Herod laid out the city's streets and fortifications where the ancient capital of King Omri once stood. Over the centuries, it had shrunk into a small village, but Herod allocated for its new construction a much larger area—larger even than it was in the glory days of the Kingdom of Israel. Herod planned on such a grand scale because the city was to be a living monument to his loyalty to the Emperor of Rome, and its name would enshrine it. The name of ancient Samaria was now changed to "Sebaste," a Greek word corresponding to the Latin "Augustus."

Augustus?

Yes. In the very year when the construction of the new Samaria-Sebaste began—27 BC—a significant event took place in Rome. Octavian, supposedly wishing to lay down the burden of power, reluctantly agreed, at the insistence of the Senate, to continue to protect the Republic for a while longer. Delighted by this, the Senate gave Octavian the honorable title "Augustus." The year 27 BC, when Octavian, in his boundless benevolence, agreed not to abandon the Republic to its fate, marked the formal beginning of the Roman Empire. As its first emperor, Octavian is remembered in history as "Augustus."

Over the succeeding years, Herod continued to beautify Samaria-Sebaste. New fortifications, collonades, and beautiful public buildings sprouted every year. Furthermore, at the very summit of the hill, where the castle of King Omri had once stood, Herod erected a great temple. Twenty-four monumental steps led up to it. This temple was dedicated to a deity previously unknown in Palestine, even to the Greeks, who constituted the majority of the inhabitants of Samaria-Sebaste. This deity was—Divine Augustus.

What remains today of the splendor of that city? An English traveler in 1958 described his impressions:

Samaria has shrunk to the size of a village suspended on the southeast slope of a high hill. The citadel has turned into an orchard of olive and fig trees. The forum now serves as a threshing floor. As we passed through there on a July afternoon, the entire village was working in the old forum, threshing and winnowing grain. The colonnaded avenue, which runs halfway up the southern slope, is now the main street of the village. Only the top of the hill has retained its former shape, crowned with the ruins of the temple once dedicated to Augustus. [48]

Archaeological excavations conducted here in the first half of the twentieth century have shed light on the former capital of Israel and its splendor under Herod. And though little more than a few fragments of columns and blocks of defensive walls remain of the proud work of the Idumean, yet, to this day, this poor Arab village bears the name *Sabastiyah*—the name of the first Roman emperor. Thus, it continues to testify to the exemplary loyalty of King Herod the Great.

The Palace

It's not possible to whitewash Herod of the charges of cruelty and murder, but no one can deny his attachment to the memory of those he had once loved. There was no act he would shrink from in order to acquire and retain power, but he also spared no means to exalt his family and friends—both in their lifetime and after their death. And thus, he built three magnificent monuments to three individuals closest to him. These were the three defensive towers of the new royal palace in Jerusalem.

He named them after a friend who perished years ago in the battle against the Parthians, a brother who took his life in captivity, and the wife he recently condemned to death: Hippicus, Phasael, and Mariamne. Such were the names of the three towers. They defended the northwest corner of the fortifications of Jerusalem and the nearby

---

[48] A. J. Toynbee, East to West: A Journey Round the World, 1958

massive gate where two critical roads converged: one leading to the sea, towards Joppa, and the other to the south, towards Bethlehem, Hebron, and Idumea. However, the towers also served as defenses and ornament of the new royal palace directly adjoining the city walls. Each of the three towers had a square plan and stood on a fundament of native rock faced with blocks of white marble. Similar blocks were used to construct the towers themselves. Looking up from below, one could see three giants towering overhead in the sky. Decorative alcoves and parapets crowned these impressive marble colossi.

In need, Hippicus could serve as a water reservoir since it housed cisterns for collecting rainwater. Mariamne, the lowest of the three, had beautifully furnished residential rooms. Meanwhile, the Tower of Phasael was the tallest and the most formidable. Today, only its mighty base remains, with a superstructure from much later times; the whole is called the Tower of David and has dominated the Old City of Jerusalem for centuries.

Herod likely began building the palace around 24 BC. The former residence of the Hasmoneans, also situated in the western district of Jerusalem but closer to the Tyropoeon Valley, was not sufficiently grand for the new king. He wanted his palace, the symbol of the new regime, to be equal in splendor to the religious center of Jerusalem—the Temple.

The vast quadrangle of the palace buildings was surrounded by a defensive wall fifteen meters high. At equal intervals, smaller towers reinforced the wall. From the west and north, the palace adjoined the city walls. The interior was dazzling. There were huge halls and courtyards, porticoes, and colonnades of various multicolored stone and marble. The two largest chambers were named Caesarion and Agrippa—Herod thereby honoring both the emperor and his closest friend, Marcus Agrippa. A splendid garden stretched among the buildings, planted with evergreen, fragrant trees. Streams of water flowed there, gushing forth from the mouths of bronze statues set up throughout the park.

The palace was still under construction in 23 BC when a wedding ceremony took place inside. Herod was bringing a new wife into his home, his third. She was a charming girl whose name, like that of her ill-fated predecessor, was also Mariamne. Her father, Simon, hailed from a priestly family settled for generations in Alexandria in Egypt. To make Mariamne worthy of becoming the king's wife, Herod appointed Simon as the High Priest, deposing Jesus, the son of Phobias, from office. To most Judeans, this was an unheard-of, impious degradation of the highest religious authority. But the gesture gained Herod the admiration of the Jews of Alexandria, one of the largest concentrations of Jews outside of Palestine at that time.

With what feelings did the young woman, elevated to the royal throne, gaze at the beautiful tower of the palace called Mariamne? Did she not fear the fate of her namesake?

Herodion

Then we went out onto a vast plain, in the midst of which rose a very tall and perfectly shaped mountain called the Frankish Tower or Bethulia, after the nearby village of the same name. Within an hour of leaving the Chariton Valley,[49] we stood at the foot of this high mountain, the ascent of which was difficult, but I managed to ride my horse up its rocky path. Local legend has it that after the Saracens captured Jerusalem, the Crusaders retreated to this peak and, having built a fortress here, defended themselves for forty years before finally fleeing to the mountains of Lebanon and merging with the Druze. No matter the authenticity of this legend, there had once undoubtedly been a Crusader fortress here, as the remnants of the walls date back to that period. The mountain is round and steep, and the summit appears to have been leveled by man, as the earth is somewhat different and there are almost no stones. In contrast, limestone makes up the rest of the mountain.

The top had once been enclosed by a double wall, with a circumference of over three hundred steps. At the four corners, four towers once stood, the most extensive of which was circular, while the other three were semi-circular. Today, only a few fragments of

---

[49] Wadi Khreitun, south of Bethlehem

the circular tower remain, and the rest lie in complete ruin, beneath which the beautifully and powerfully vaulted dungeons still remain. In the middle of the shapely circumference is a large pit; it is evident that there must have been living quarters there. The entire Dead Sea stretches out almost at your feet, and the pointed mountains of rocky Arabia close the view with their tall spires.

The southern slope of the Frankish Tower is less steep than the others, and it was once fortified with a high wall. The ruins of a church and other buildings remain at the bottom. The Arabs assert that the entrance to a subterranean passage to the castle is concealed beneath these ruins." [50]

The author of this description, Ignacy Hołowiński,[51] visited the Frankish Tower in the autumn of 1840. The mountain, also known as Jabal al-Fureidis, is located an hour and a half southeast of Bethlehem and about three hours south of Jerusalem. The description is accurate; among all the 19th-century accounts of Polish travelers in Palestine, Hołowiński's recollections stand out favorably for their skillful combination of erudition, keen observation, and vividness. However, the author makes one mistake regarding the history of the Frankish Tower. The ruins do not date to the Crusades, although the Crusaders, known as the "Franks," did indeed defend themselves there.

Herod had built this castle. He built it to commemorate a battle he had fought in this very place while fleeing from the Parthians in 40 BC. That's why he named it after himself—Herodion. He ordered the artificial raising of the mountain's summit, as ancient sources attest; Hołowiński observed this correctly. According to the same sources, the towers were round—just as the Polish traveler observed. However, all traces of the former splendor of the structure, so praised in ancient descriptions, have disappeared. There is no trace of the two hundred steps of white marble that once led to the top of

---

[50] I. Hołowiński, *Pielgrzymka do Ziemi Świętej* [A pilgrimage to the Holy Land], Petersburg, 1855, p.560.

[51] Ignacy Hołowiński (1807–1855) was a Polish Catholic cleric, and from 1851, the head of the Catholic Church in Russia; he was also the first Polish translator of Shakespeare.

the steep hill. The palace-like chambers have collapsed. Only a depression remains of the magnificent buildings at the foot of the castle hill. In Herod's time, an aqueduct brought water there from far away.

Herodion was one of the king's favorite palaces. It is easy to understand why as you look at the magnificent panorama: to the east, the dark-blue expanse of the sea, and in all other directions, wherever you look, rows and rows of rolling hills with small clusters of human settlements gleaming white.

Herodion was known as "the small fort." (The "Big Fort" was the massive fortress of Machaerus to the east of the Dead Sea, destroyed by the Romans and rebuilt by Herod).

The king gave the names of his family members to many of his towns and fortresses. On the fertile coastal plain, on the road from Joppa to Samaria, he founded Antipatris in honor of his father. He gave his mother's name, Kypros, to a splendid fortress built on a hill above Jericho. He channeled water from the local springs, transforming the entire area into a flourishing garden. Among the groves, plantations, and ponds, he erected beautiful buildings: two palaces, named "Caesar" and "Agrippa," like the palace chambers in Jerusalem; an amphitheater, a theater, and a hippodrome; and a large terrace for promenades.

North of Jericho, along the road running up the Jordan Valley, Herod founded a farming settlement called Phasaelis, another monument alongside the Phasael Tower, in honor of his tragically deceased brother.

Herod also established many farming settlements by making land grants to his veterans. One of these settlements, Gaba, was planted on the border of the great plain of Esdraelon and Galilee. There were many others, including some beyond the Jordan in Perea.

Caesarea

Thanks to the benevolence of Octavian, Herod's kingdom had broad access to the sea, from Gaza in the south right up to Dora in the north, though Dora itself fell within the borders of the province of Syria. But Herod needed a port that would meet the needs of the Jewish economy and his personal requirements for splendor. The population of Joppa, the largest coastal port in Herod's territory, had never been friendly to Herod. Moreover, Joppa's old and densely crowded buildings posed a great obstacle to grand urban planning.

Instead, Herod turned his attention to a small town called Strato's Tower. It lay three hours south of Dora, and Joppa was just a day's march away. In the hinterland of the settlement lay the northern part of the coastal plain of Sharon, and through it, one easily reached Samaria and the plain of Esdraelon. If Strato's Tower, despite its fortunate location, had not yet become a center of navigation and trade, it was due to its lack of a natural harbor. The coast ran in a straight line here: not even a tiny cove offered shelter to ships during a storm. However, there was plenty of space and a lot of unoccupied land. Nothing stood in the way of implementing a grand blueprint. For Herod, this was an excellent opportunity to showcase his organizational talents and impress the unwashed with the grandeur of a city that would owe its existence entirely to him.

Construction work began in 24 BC and continued for twelve years, with a tremendous expenditure of money and labor. Suitable stone had to be brought from distant locations. The most challenging task was the creation of an artificial harbor. Herod made enormous excavations to create the basin of the port and extended a broad causeway far into the sea to enclose it, its foundation made of giant boulders sunk into the water. A defensive wall, fortified with numerous towers, ran on the causeway halfway out into the sea. The tallest of these towers bore the name of Drusus—the stepson of Emperor Augustus, renowned for his conquests in Germany. On the inner side of this wall, accommodations for sailors were built.

This artificial basin opened to the north as the mildest winds blew from that direction. A mighty tower defended the entrance on one side, high rocks on the other. Colossal statues adorned the tower and the rocks, and a beautiful promenade ran alongside the quay. The houses of the city were built from noble, white stone, and a regular network of streets divided them into even blocks. There were market squares, a theater, and a hippodrome. Herod installed a highly sophisticated sewage system throughout the entire city.

In the center of town, on a small hill, stood a grand temple. Inside were enshrined the statues of two deities: Augustus and Roma. The former was modeled after the famous statue of Zeus at Olympia, which Phidias had sculpted centuries ago. The choice of patron deity was obvious since the whole city was dedicated to the ruler of Rome and named after him—Caesarea. Athletic games were held here in honor of its imperial patron every five years. The consecration of the temple took place on March 9th, 10 BC.

Augustus's best friend and closest companion, Marcus Agrippa, also had a port named after him, though a considerably smaller one. Herod built it near Gaza, on the site of the former town of Antedon, which was destroyed in the course of the wars. He named the new town Agrippias.

Caesarea quickly became the second most important city in Palestine after Jerusalem. It flourished for many centuries, well into the Middle Ages, until it was destroyed during the Crusades. Since then, it has become a small settlement again, much like it was before Herod's time. However, it still bears the proud name given to it by the great builder. It is called—*Keisaria*.

Our list of Herod's famous construction projects is already awe-inspiring, and yet, it is far from complete. The question inevitably arises: Where did the king of this small country obtain the means for such magnificent projects? How did he govern? How did he manage the economy?

HEROD THE RULER

Struggle against Nature

In 25 BC, at the command of Emperor Augustus, the Roman governor of Egypt, Aelius Gallus, led one of the most exotic expeditions ever undertaken by the Empire in its entire history. It was a military expedition to the southernmost part of the Arabian Peninsula.

In those days, fantastic and colorful tales circulated about the extraordinary wealth of this distant land. It was said to be the place where the most fragrant plants and most precious roots originated. Jewels and nuggets of gold were said to be as common as pebbles and sand. The land was commonly referred to as *Arabia Felix* or "Happy Arabia."

Of course, the tales of its riches were greatly exaggerated. The wealth of this land—modern-day Yemen—stemmed from its role in the maritime trade with distant India. But Greeks and Romans mistakenly believed that everything they received from southern Arabia originated there, and therefore, the emperor considered it of great importance to take control of that fortunate and wealthy land, hoping to replenish thereby the insatiable treasury of the Empire.

Gallus, entrusted with this honorable task, led Roman forces himself and demanded the support of the Palestinian rulers. Significant forces were contributed by the Nabateans. The king of Judea sent five hundred men.

But the expedition returned in 24 BC, having achieved nothing.

Although it got quite far south, it never reached the heart of Arabia Felix. Gallus blamed the expedition's guide, Syllaios, a Nabatean dignitary, for the failure. He claimed that Syllaios had tricked them and intentionally led the army by a circuitous route through the desert, which foiled the entire plan and resulted in significant loss of life. Perhaps Gallus was right. After all, Petra thrived on the caravan trade with Arabia Felix. Why, then, would its rulers assist the Romans in conquering it and thus help undermine the foundations of their own prosperity?

Herod's dispatch of a small unit was considered a commendable service.

In the meantime, dire calamities struck Judea. First came drought, poor harvests, and famine, and then came a plague. Tens of thousands of people died, and almost all the livestock perished.

Once again, as in previous similar situations, the populace was convinced that the king's immoral conduct was the cause of these disasters. They believed that his crimes and impious behavior provoked the wrath of heaven.

Herod found himself in an exceedingly difficult situation. The granaries and treasury were nearly empty. Extensive and costly construction work had just begun, but the moment the famine struck, no one cared about paying taxes.

The only salvation could come from Egypt. Its fertile fields were watered by the clockwork inundations of the Nile, which made it the bread basket of the Mediterranean. It was fortunate that after Gallus, Gaius Petronius[52] became the governor of Egypt. Herod had already met him in Octavian's entourage. Petronius, appreciative of Herod's loyalty and considering that the previous year, despite the dire economic situation of his kingdom, he had sent men on the Arabian expedition, was favorably disposed toward the request for grain. Yet the drought and the plague had affected not only Judea but also a significant part of Syria and Egyptian grain was in high demand. Naturally, even the most benevolent governor could not *give* Herod grain for free. Meanwhile, the king had almost no money at all.

Nevertheless, Herod managed to obtain it. He melted down every item of precious metal he could find in his palaces. He spared nothing, not even his tableware. Herod took charge of the distribution of the acquired grain himself. Tens of thousands of Jews owed their survival during those years solely to this relief. The king remembered to provide them not only with wheat but also flax and wool for

---

[52] No relation of the Petronius of *Quo Vadis*.

clothing, as there were difficulties with these as well. He cared for the elderly and sick as well, distributing baked bread to them.

Herod also managed to turn a profit on the Egyptian grain. He distributed part of his supplies to the neighboring cities and states in southern Syria on the condition that it be repaid with interest in a future year of plenty. He then sent thousands of his men to help harvest and transport the grain back to Judea. The result of all these energetic efforts was a significant increase in Herod's popularity in his kingdom.

He managed to turn a disaster into a success.

The Administration and the Army

Thanks to the generous land grants of the Roman emperor, Herod's kingdom became quite extensive. It encompassed an area nearly equal to the former Hasmonean state, and after 20 BC, following new grants from Augustus, it became only slightly smaller than the mythical kingdom of Solomon. It counted about three million inhabitants of various, often mutually hostile nationalities. Some lands were mountainous, others were semi-desert; the borders were highly irregular, and the country was open to attack on all sides. Managing and defending such a varied and ethnically diverse state was a challenging task.

Herod inherited a relatively well-developed administrative system when he assumed power. This system dated back to the time of the Hasmoneans, who, in turn, had inherited it from the great Hellenistic monarchies. Palestine had been under the rule of the Ptolemies in the 3rd century BC, and later, between 198 BC and the Maccabean Revolt, it was part of the Seleucid Empire. Of course, the administration of these extensive monarchies differed significantly in some aspects, though both were centralized and bureaucratic. Therefore, the system that took shape in Judea was not a replica of those administrative methods but a combination of various elements from both models. Likewise, in many other lands of the Middle East, similarly eclectic administrations emerged during that period. In this respect, Judea belonged to the great family of Hellenistic kingdoms.

Herod's undeniable achievement was a simplification and professionalization of the system; its extension to the annexed territories; the creation of new offices; the installation of a vigilant system of oversight to ensure that his officials performed their duties honestly and competently; and, above all, skillful recruitment of capable administrators. Even the most splendid scheme of a centralized state remains a mere lifeless model if there are no capable executors at every level of administration, subject to constant supervision.

The largest districts of the kingdom were called *merides* in Greek, which means "parts." These were Galilee, Samaria, Judea, Perea, and Idumea. In later years, after further grants from Augustus, several new *merides* were added in the northeast: Gaulanitis, Trachonitis, Auranitis, and Ulatha. High officials, known as *archons* or *meridiarchs*, supervised these districts. These were Greek titles, as were the titles of all other ranks in the bureaucracy, which was not surprising, considering that the entire system had Hellenistic origins.

The *merides* were further divided into smaller administrative units, equivalent to our counties, known as *toparchies*. For example, Herodion served as the capital of one of them. *Toparchs* held the highest authority in them. Each *toparchy* included a dozen or so rural communities, or *komai*, governed by *komarchs*.

Larger cities, like Jerusalem, Caesarea, and Joppa, and some cities beyond the Jordan, were not subject to *meridiarchs*. They were managed by *strategoi*, reporting directly to the king.

Officials known as *dioiketai* and *oiketai* maintained records of landed estates, harvests, and taxpayer lists in individual centers. The king appointed all higher and lower officials. They received compensation in the form of income from estates attached to their offices.

The chancellor, or what we would call the finance minister, bearing the title of "*dioiketes* of the kingdom," stood at the head of the entire bureaucratic hierarchy. This post, second in importance only to the king, was held for many years by a man named Ptolemy. The name was common in Palestine at the time, so it is uncertain whether he was Greek or Jewish. However, Diophantos, the king's secretary—or *grammateus*—was undoubtedly Greek. He also held this highly responsible position for many years.

The highest dignitaries constituted the royal council. Herod often sought the council's advice, and it handled the most important matters of national significance. This council replaced the old Sanhedrin, which had lost all influence even though it still existed formally. In this way, the king completed the total secularization of the administration.

Just as the royal council replaced the Sanhedrin, so did a new aristocracy—a creation of the king—replace the old noble families. In establishing this courtly and bureaucratic aristocracy, Herod followed the example of the Hellenistic monarchies. He adopted four degrees and categories of distinctions. The lowest title of the new aristocracy was "friend of the king." followed by "most honorable friend of the king," then "guardian of the person of the king," and finally, "a cousin of the king." These were, of course, only titles; they did not entail specific functions or incomes.

Herod intertwined the royal court with the state administration. He delighted in having a large, splendid, diverse entourage; both free and enslaved attendants always accompanied him. Herod wanted his palaces in Jerusalem, Jericho, and Herodion to serve as smaller but faithful copies of the opulent royal courts that had recently flourished in the royal residences of Alexandria, Antioch, and Pergamon. The ruler of Judea emulated the splendor and ceremonial of those courts.

As was the case everywhere in the East then, Herod's personal attendants and those of his family were mostly eunuchs. Through their hands passed the most crucial state matters, for only they had direct access to the king's private apartments. The most trusted among them held such important positions as the chamberlain or the master of the hunt. Others supervised the royal harem, for Herod soon married several wives.

The personal security of the ruler was guarded day and night by a bodyguard composed, as in all Hellenistic states, of foreign mercenaries and, therefore, men with no connection to the local population. Their fate depended solely on the king's favor, for his subjects despised them. In Herod's bodyguard, there were many Gauls and Germans, people brought from the opposite end of the then-known world.

The standing army, numbering several thousand infantry and cavalry during peacetime, also consisted of mercenaries, but some were of Palestinian origin. They were mostly Idumeans and Samaritans, but in times of war, Judeans were conscripted in large numbers. The organization of the army was Hellenistic; hence, the Greek names of the officer ranks, especially the higher ones: *taxisarchs*, commanders of formations, *hipparchs*, commanders of cavalry, and *chiliarchs*, commanders of a thousand.

The commanders of fortresses were called *frourarchoi*.[53] A network of these fortresses covered the entire kingdom; they guarded the borders and important communication routes and maintained peace in areas prone to disturbances. Light beacons provided long-distance communication between the fortresses.

Herod's troops were not subordinate to Rome. Nevertheless, among their ranks were Roman instructors who undoubtedly exercised some degree of political oversight.

Sources of Wealth

Shortly after the great drought, Herod reduced taxes imposed on the population by one-third and, ten years later, again by one-fourth. The financial regime was strict, and the levies were collected rigorously. A previously unknown tax was introduced in Judea: a percentage on the sale of real estate. Yet, for all the burden of taxation, the period of peace ushered in at the end of the last Roman civil war sparked a period of prosperity.

---

[53] From Greek *fruorio*, fortress

Still, the inhabitants of Palestinian cities and villages had to bear the enormous costs of constructing royal buildings, maintaining a magnificent court and an elaborate administrative apparatus, providing for the army, and equipping numerous mighty fortresses. How did it happen that, despite this significant burden, economic life did not stagnate but, on the contrary, flourished?

It's not easy to answer the question, as the clues in our sources are very scarce. Nevertheless, one can form a general picture of Herod's economic policy and understand how he accumulated wealth and balanced his budget.

Palestine was primarily an agricultural country, but crafts and trade also played a role, mainly intermediary between Egypt and Syria, Mesopotamia, and Asia Minor. The king's income largely came from a levy on agricultural produce paid by landowners and from cash taxes paid by merchants and artisans. There were also customs duties on goods imported and exported at the kingdom's borders.

Herod also had his vast personal fortune, partly inherited from his ancestors and partly acquired through confiscations soon after he took power. The king continually increased this fortune through various banking operations. He lent significant sums to nobles in neighboring countries, especially to Petra's rulers. Thanks to this, he had a substantial share in their profits from the lucrative caravan trade. Moreover, in later years, after 20 BC, Herod gained direct control over one of the important caravan routes leading to Damascus through the regions of Batanea and Trachonitis.

However, even the greatest wealth is meaningless if it is deployed unwisely. The income of the Parthian kings was probably a thousand times greater than all of Herod's. However, the economy of that great empire was slowly descending into chaos and ruin because they pursued the insane policy of hoarding: they stockpiled gold and silver in enormous treasuries but made almost no investments.

By contrast, Herod's city-building campaign proved to be a significant stimulus for the economy of Palestine. It entailed a vast expense but paid off relatively quickly because most of these cities and settlements were large agricultural colonies, such as Antipatris,

Phasaelis, Samaria, and even the fortress of Herodion. Thanks to these colonies, previously underutilized lands were put under cultivation, providing work for tens of thousands of people. Herod carried out extensive irrigation works in many areas and encouraged the adoption of new varieties of cultivated plants, such as the date palm, to increase agricultural yields.

The construction of the ports of Caesarea and Agrippias proved even more beneficial. Fees from incoming ships, customs duties, and taxes collected from merchants greatly enriched the king's treasury.

Even the construction of fortresses was not without economic benefits. They were built in areas constantly exposed to marauding raids, thus providing security for merchants, travelers, and the local population and promoting trade and agricultural production in those regions. Moreover, Herod punished robbers and thieves with draconian severity and sold captured criminals into slavery abroad. This was prohibited by ancient laws but proved highly lucrative.

The huge construction projects attracted many people from outside Palestine, both Greeks and Jews, which also enhanced the economic potential of the kingdom. Herod understood this and supported immigration.

So, Herod's actions were not the madness of an oriental despot who wanted to immortalize his greatness at any cost in useless stone colossi. Yes, he was not unaffected by the desire to impress with the grandeur of his buildings. He certainly wanted to pass into history as the creator of a new Palestine. However, he knew how to reconcile these ambitions with the practicality of a good manager.

Not all of Herod's subjects became rich, and not all equally so. The wealthy landowning aristocracy especially felt the burden of Idumean rule. Merchants, craftsmen, and peasants fared better. The latter, because—as we know—the king carried out irrigation works on a large scale, and the development of cities led to the inevitable rise in demand for agricultural products. And, by and large, instead of using slave labor, Herod hired wage workers. In this way, a part of the population of the overcrowded country found suitable employment and coin in hand.

Taxes were the chief complaint and were collected rigorously. Tax collectors probably abused the system in Herod's kingdom, as they did in most countries of the ancient world: treasury revenues were leased out to private individuals or companies who advanced the sums expected to the state and then collected from taxpayers dues increased by a profit margin. The taxpayers of Herod's kingdom must have felt bitter indignation at the splendor of the royal palaces, the phalanx of idle courtiers, and, above all, the ruler's generous donations to cities and peoples abroad.

Herod's person was the object of fierce hatred during his lifetime, and later, it became encrusted with a gloomy, bloody legend. This legend lives down to our day, and perhaps the praise I offer here for some of the king's achievements may seem an attempt at fashionable revisionism. But if it is, it isn't just mine. Just listen to one of the greatest experts on the Middle East in Roman times, A.H.M. Jones. He characterizes Herod's economy with these words:

> We do know that the annual revenue of the state treasury at [Herod's] death was about 1050 Jewish talents or one million and fifty thousand drachmas. However, this number is of little worth to us because we cannot determine either the purchasing power of the drachma or the ratio of this sum to the size of the economy of the kingdom. Nevertheless, a particular indication suggests that Herod's tax system was not oppressive. There is no mention of any significant changes—except for minor ones—in the tax rate in the fifty years after Herod's death, while his grandson Agrippa received a more considerable income—one million two hundred thousand drachmas—from his kingdom, which had roughly the same area.
>
> From this, we can draw the conclusion that the tax rate introduced by Herod not only did not devastate the country but also allowed for steady economic growth. There could be nothing fundamentally unhealthy in the finances of a country whose income remained at such a level. Given this, we should not attach too much importance

to the reports of constant demands for a tax reduction, particularly the abolition of the new sales tax. ([King] Archelaus faced these demands after Herod's death). But, such demands are a constant phenomenon accompanying the accession of all new rulers.

It is noteworthy that the Jewish delegation, which demanded from Augustus the abolition of the monarchy after Herod's death, said very little about financial oppression; they maintained—which was palpable falsehood—that at the beginning of Herod's reign, the kingdom had been flourishing, but now was brought to financial ruin; and specifically, they complained about confiscations, which destroyed the aristocracy but probably did not affect ordinary taxpayers. Perhaps more significant than these complaints of the rich were the widespread uprisings of the rural population after Herod's death, especially the burning of district offices, where tax records were kept. However, it is difficult to determine how much of this discontent stemmed from economic reasons and how much from political or religious agitation."[54]

The author concludes by citing the well-known fact of Herod twice lowering the tax rate—probably the land tax—and his efforts during the drought to show that Herod genuinely cared about the material well-being of the lower classes.

The Tomb of David

The splendor of Herod's rule amazed everyone in Judea. "Where does the king get his money?" people asked, astonished by the magnificent buildings rising everywhere in the country. People dismissed the explanation that the economic success of Herod's reign was due to ordinary prudence and good management as too prosaic. Soon, a different explanation emerged, which satisfied many, especially Herod's enemies: the godless king had plundered treasures hidden in an ancient tomb!

Of course, this was no ordinary tomb, but the most splendid

---

[54] A. H. M. Jones, *The Herods of Judaea*, Oxford 1938, p. 87

of the splendid and the holiest of the holy—the tomb of King David and his son Solomon. Those who claimed to be in the know whispered that Herod and his armed guard had broken into it secretly at night. The underground tomb was supposedly hewn deep into the rock and consisted of many chambers, cells, and passages. Herod promptly appropriated sacks of gold and silver vessels found in one of the chambers. However, money—which the king coveted the most—was nowhere to be found. He decided, therefore, to break into the deepest chamber, where the bodies of the two great kings lay buried. Then, a terrible thing happened: flames burst forth from the ground, and fire consumed two of the king's soldiers on the spot.

The story was what we would call an urban myth. The so-called Tomb of David had been plundered multiple times over the preceding ten centuries: how many foreign invaders had sacked Jerusalem during that time!—and treasures of tombs had always tempted the curious and the greedy. The comical aspect of the story was that it claimed that Herod decided to rob the tomb, encouraged by the example of the robbery of the same tomb by one of the Hasmoneans. That man was said to have taken silver worth three thousand talents from the tomb. There would have been very little left for Herod!

But what gave rise to this fantastic tale? Paradoxically, Herod's project to renovate and protect the tomb. Herod had erected, right next to a tomb believed to be the resting place of David and Solomon, a magnificent building of white marble, undoubtedly to demonstrate his respect for the memory of the great kings. After all, he considered himself their heir and desperately wanted others to see him as their equal.

Herod's enemies, unable to fight him openly, fought him with slander. They pointed to the marble monument and said:

"Why is the king raising this building at such a high cost? Certainly not without reason! Surely, he wants to appease the spirits of David and Solomon!"

Of such stuff, legends are born.

HEROD AND AUGUSTUS

The Question of Policy

The economy of Judea flourished under Herod's rule. However, prosperity is not everything; bread is just one of our needs, and despite economic well-being, the popular aversion to Herod never waned.

For his part, the king did much to deserve that hostility. He was suspicious. He expanded the system of internal espionage on a massive scale. Under the flimsiest of pretexts, he threw suspects into the dungeons of his fortresses, from which they rarely emerged alive; the fortress of Hyrcania was particularly infamous.

Still, Jews may have excused Herod for all of this. After all, a despotic system of government was neither an exception nor a novelty in the Middle East. On the contrary, it was practically the rule from which Herod's predecessors, the Hasmoneans, had by no means deviated. People grumbled and complained, but in reality, they regarded having a tyrant on the throne as the natural, perhaps even necessary, order of this world.

However, what genuinely pained Herod's subjects was his demonstrative submission and servility towards Rome. There he was: naming new cities after Augustus and Agrippa; raising wherever he could monuments to them and dedicating to them the most magnificent buildings; and, most importantly—and this bordered on blasphemy—building temples to the emperor and the goddess Roma on the sacred soil of Israel, thereby committing idolatry. He did so even though he considered himself a Jew and participated in Jewish religious ceremonies.

If anyone had dared to bring these accusations against Herod openly (although we can safely assume that no one ever did), the king would surely have countered them by appealing to common sense:

"What harm is there in naming a city after the ruler of a neighboring and friendly power? Even building a temple to him costs very little. Meanwhile, the benefits are enormous. It earns us the reputation of a loyal and sincerely devoted friend. This reputation, in turn, makes that friend more willing to make certain concessions and benevolent gestures, which—even if each is small in itself—when put together, can have great significance for the life of a small country."

Of course, Herod's arguments would not have been entirely honest. When he said "our country," he really meant himself and his family. *He* had gained power; *he* wanted to maintain it and pass it on to *his* descendants—that was Herod's entire political program. The realization of this program required skillful maneuvering between the avarice and suspicion of the mighty Empire and the uncompromising attitude of a small people fanatically attached to their distinctive identity.

Herod was a master maneuverer, but in this case, he took the path of least resistance: he revered the powerful and scorned the weak. He could do so all the more openly because his policy yielded good economic results. [55]

The Question of Succession

In 22 BC, Herod sent Aristobulus and Alexander, his sons by Mariamne I, to Rome for their studies. The young princes were received very hospitably in the capital of the world. They lived in the house of Asinius Pollio,[56] who had once been a leading politician and now lived in retirement, working on a history of the recent past. He belonged to the circle of the emperor's close friends.

Of course, the stay of Herod's sons in Rome served not only academic but also political purposes. The intention was to bring the princes closer to the emperor's entourage and familiarize them with

---

[55] This chapter, published in 1965 in Poland—just as a wave of discontentment was beginning to swell against the Russian-puppet regime in Warsaw, a regime unable to deliver good economic results—would have found a special resonance with Polish readers.

[56] Father of Asinius Gallus, for whose opposition to Tiberius and murder by the same see Jacek Bocheński's *Tiberius Caesar*, p. 156 nn.

the affairs of Rome, under whose protection they would rule after their father's death.

For here was one of the greatest triumphs of Herod's policy of subservience: the emperor had allowed the king of Judea to appoint his successor. Herod's kingdom became hereditary.

To understand the significance of this, we should remember that Rome usually pursued a completely different policy towards its client states. The dependence of a vassal king on Rome consisted precisely in the fact that his rule was *not* hereditary. The emperor and the Roman Senate granted him his royal title personally, and, though officially for life, in many cases, they deposed disobedient or distrusted kings without any regard for formalities. After the death of such a vassal-king, the legal status of his lands was reexamined, and either a successor was appointed or the kingdom was incorporated into a neighboring Roman province. And if there was a successor, he did not have to be someone from the king's family.

Thus, the privilege granted to Herod was exceptional. It provided stability to the dynasty, indirectly benefiting the entire country. After all, incorporating Judea directly into one of the Roman provinces would have meant a complete reorganization of the administration and Roman interference in all areas of life—a considerable shock to the population. That threat no longer hung over a country with a hereditary dynasty.

In most other respects, Herod's sovereignty was as limited as that of all the other rulers of small client states along the Roman borders. Without the consent of the Romans, he could neither wage war nor conclude treaties. He could mint coins in bronze but rarely in silver and never in gold. Only bronze coins of Herod survive: they bear symbols similar to those once used by the Hasmoneans. There is never a human image on them, so typical of Roman and Greek coins—an explicit concession by the king to the religious sensitivities of his subjects.

Trachonitis

Soon, Herod celebrated a new, splendid triumph. The Roman emperor, desiring to reward the loyalty of his vassal, enlarged his kingdom. He gave him lands to the east of Galilee: the fertile valley of Batanea, an extensive plateau of solidified lava, called Trachon or Trachonitis in Greek, and the vast mountain range of extinct volcanos, Auranitis.

Of course, this imperial favor had its specific reason. Until then, Prince Zenodorus ruled these lands. He caused a lot of trouble for his neighbors, secretly cooperating with bands of robbers who nested in the caves and the inaccessible labyrinth of gorges of wild Trachonitis. From there, the robbers carried out plundering raids as far as the vicinity of Damascus.

As was to be expected, Zenodorus immediately protested against this reduction of his domain. He traveled to Rome to lay his complaint before the emperor but to no avail. The emperor did not reverse his decision, even though the matter had by then become quite complicated for a new contender for Auranitis appeared—the Nabateans. They had recently bought this region from Zenodorus; it may have been a fictitious transaction intended to dissuade the Romans from the idea of giving the province to Herod. Now, to preserve their new acquisition, the Nabateans began a guerrilla war, sending well-equipped Jewish dissidents, enemies of Herod, into the disputed territory.

The emperor knew perfectly well what he was doing when he granted the King of the Jews the three territories on the Syrian-Nabatean border. Their pacification was necessary, as it was through this area that significant trade routes connected Damascus with Egypt and various centers of Arabia, and Herod was just the man to achieve it. This expectation proved correct. In a short time, Herod exterminated the robbers, repelled the Nabateans, and colonized the lands, putting them under cultivation. The settlements established by Herod in the new territories had a semi-military character. The settlers often had to turn into warriors and help suppress brigandry. In return, they received an exemption from various taxes.

Thus, thanks to the Roman decision and the energetic action of Herod's administration, extensive areas of the wild borderlands were integrated into the Jewish state. Its Jewish settlers came mainly from regions subject to Herod, especially from Idumea, but also from beyond the borders of the Roman Empire. In later years, a large group of Jewish exiles from Babylon settled in Trachonitis. Together with army units, they kept the native population in check. Where there once had been hideouts for ruffians and primitive nomadic encampments, now prosperous settled life flourished.

Ulatha and Paneas

In the winter of 22/21 BC, Herod set out on a long journey. He traveled to the beautiful island of Lesbos, to meet Marcus Agrippa. In recent years, Agrippa had become Octavian's co-ruler of the Empire. When Augustus was in the West, Agrippa dealt with Eastern affairs. Soon, he would become the emperor's son-in-law by marrying his only daughter, Julia.

Herod could not miss the opportunity to get to know better the man upon whom the fate of his small kingdom depended. The trip was a success, and from then on, the king of the Jews enjoyed the unfailing favor of his imperial friend.

Meanwhile, Zenodorus did not give up his efforts to regain his lost territory. Even before Herod's departure to Lesbos, he incited the inhabitants of the city of Gadara in the Decapolis region near the River Yarmouk. The city was populous and prosperous, and its territories extended to the Sea of Galilee. Since 30 BC, it had been ruled by Herod, although—as in other cities of this region—most inhabitants were Greek. Herod's stern rule had particularly affected the Gadarenes, as they had previously enjoyed complete autonomy. Therefore, Zenodorus quickly convinced them of the need to appeal to Augustus with a complaint about the ruthlessness of their new ruler. He thought that in this way, he would discredit Herod as a sovereign and regain the territories confiscated from him.

Soon, an excellent opportunity presented itself for the Gadarenes, for the emperor came to Syria in 20 BC on a tour of inspection of the East while Agrippa returned to Rome.

The foremost citizens of Gadara now traveled to Antioch, where the emperor was staying. They behaved haughtily and loudly, confident in Zenodorus's support and Augustus's well-known severity towards perpetrators of administrative abuses.

Besides, they were Greeks.

Naturally, Herod had promptly hastened to pay homage to the ruler of the world. He was received very cordially, for the emperor had had glowing reports of the state of affairs in Palestine. He highly valued the efficiency of Herod's rule and was not disposed to trust the accusations of his enemies. Thus, on the first day of the talks, the Gadarenes were disappointed. And on the second day—well, there was no second day. The Gadarenes did not turn up. It was said later that, afraid of being delivered into Herod's hands, they had all committed suicide.

Zenodorus, also present in Antioch, died at the same time, allegedly due to internal hemorrhage. The emperor promptly turned over his remaining possessions to Herod. These were the lands along the upper course and the sources of the Jordan: the land of Ulatha and the city of Paneas. Simultaneously, at the king's request, his younger—and now only—brother, Pheroras, was appointed *tetrarch* of the lands to the east of the lower Jordan—Perea.

Thus, Herod had every reason to bid the departing emperor farewell with great gratitude. Shortly afterward, he erected a magnificent temple to Augustus in Paneas at the source of the Jordan.

HEROD THE GREEK

The Pros and Cons of a Great Civilization

Herod not only bore a Greek name; he had also received a Greek education in his early youth. Greek had dominated almost all cities of the Middle East for three centuries. It served as a means of communication among the elites of the Eastern Mediterranean and played the role of an international language. Anyone aspiring to venture into the wider world, be he a politician, official, or merchant, needed to be proficient in Greek. Only the peasants in small Syrian or Egyptian villages were content with the language of their forefathers.

Jews living outside of Palestine—and in Alexandria alone, there were hundreds of thousands—spoke almost exclusively Greek. In Palestine itself, things were different. Hebrew, the language of their forefathers, was used primarily for prayer and interpretation of the Scriptures; only a very narrow group of religious specialists used Hebrew more extensively. A different language—Aramaic—prevailed in the daily life of Palestinian Jews: a Semitic language closely related to Hebrew. Nonetheless, Greek infiltrated Palestine from all directions. Greek was the chief language of communication in the coastal cities. Greek prevailed in Samaria and was dominant in the Decapolis. In fact, Meleager, one of the most famous Greek poets of the Hellenistic era, hails from the prosperous city of Gadara. He passed away sometime when Herod was a child. In one of his minor poems, Meleager spoke of himself:

> Now I live on the island of Tyre, but Gadara, the Athens of Syria, gave me birth... What is so strange about me being a Syrian? My friend, we all inhabit one homeland—the world! And one god begot all mortals—Chaos. [57]

---

[57] *Antologia Palatina* VII, 417

Lake Gennesaret at Tiberias

Certainly, Herod would have understood the sentiment of Meleager's poem. He was born and raised in Palestine but considered himself entitled to the riches of Greek culture. This great spiritual community, stretching from Iran to the western shores of the Mediterranean Sea, deeply impressed him. It was supra-political, supra-religious, and even supra-ethnic. Its membership was based on the command of the Greek language, familiarity with the magnificent works of ancient Greek literature, and the ability to relish the charms of the gymnasium and the theater. It was, in fact, irrelevant where one hailed from, in which country one lived, or which gods one worshipped. The Greeks themselves warmly welcomed foreign cults.

Why couldn't one be a member of the Greek cultural community and a Jew simultaneously? Herod saw no difficulty in this. Once he obtained political power, he openly expressed his Hellenic sympathies. Herod not only surrounded himself with Greeks and generously supported famous, ancient monuments of Greek culture—even in distant lands—but he also embarked on an ambitious study of Greek philosophy, rhetoric, and history. He practiced public speaking with a Greek scholar and engaged in philosophical discussions during his voyages abroad.

But Herod ruled a people determined to preserve their cultural distinctiveness. That Greek culture—with which Herod sympathized so deeply—was potentially more perilous to the survival of the tiny nation than all the brutal violence of all the foreign invaders or the Roman political supremacy. Just as many minor cultures of the Middle East had already assimilated into Hellenism, Hellenism could now swallow Judaism whole.

There were people in Judea who sensed this threat. To the best of their abilities, and sometimes with fanaticism, they tried to stem the tide of Greek influence. Although they probably could not articulate and justify their convictions well, they understood that maintaining a cultural distinctiveness was paramount for every nation.

But Herod did not understand it.

Nicholas of Damascus

The learned Greek who instructed Herod in rhetoric and engaged in philosophical discussions with him was named Nikolaos—the Greek origin of our "Nicholas." He hailed from Damascus and was somewhat younger than Herod. He was part of Herod's inner circle for nearly forty years, right up to the king's death. He likely participated in the dramatic flight from Jerusalem before the Parthian advance; after the victory, he received the honorary title of "friend of the king" and served as one of the king's secretaries. He also undertook complex and delicate diplomatic missions on Herod's behalf.

Nicholas was a scholar. He had very diverse interests: he delved into philosophy, contemplating specific questions of natural science; he studied rhetoric and wrote tragedies and comedies; but primarily, he devoted himself to the study of world history. Herod encouraged him in this work. The king understood that a good knowledge of the history of all humankind was useful for any politician wishing to look beyond the confines of his country and the pressing chaos of current affairs—even if only to see his own actions in an objective light.

Nicholas's work—the result of many years of study of the writings of numerous earlier historians—was an impressive work in 144 books. It provided an overview of the fortunes of all nations from the earliest times to Herod's death. Understandably, Nicholas represented his lord and benefactor in his work in great detail and in the most favorable light possible. This vast work has been lost—except for a few minor fragments. But the historians of the succeeding generations drew upon its material, and it is largely thanks to it that we can paint such a detailed picture of Herod's life.

Nicholas was not the only Greek scholar at the Jerusalem court. The king ensured that his sons received a solid Greek education and brought in the best tutors. He had many sons—ten!—from different wives. Some of them later pursued their studies in Rome.

Respect for scholarship and sponsorship of scholars were the most admirable traits of most Hellenistic monarchs. Jerusalem could not compete in this regard with Alexandria or Pergamon, but its king did quite a lot to ensure that Greek thought had its advocates there.

Patron of the Olympics

Herod emulated famous Hellenistic monarchs in another respect: he aided poor and struggling Greek cities in maintaining their heritage. Magnificent buildings funded by the King of the Jews adorned many Greek cities in neighboring Syria, Asia Minor, and mainland Greece.

You will remember that in 40 BC, as Herod the exile set sail for Rome in search of salvation, he generously assisted the inhabitants of Rhodes in rebuilding their devastated city, even though he was in dire straits himself and practically penniless at the time. Many years later, when a fire consumed the temple of Apollo on Rhodes, Herod, now king, rebuilt it from scratch at his own expense and on a much grander scale than before. He also contributed to the construction of the Rhodian navy—an important form of assistance, as maritime trade formed the basis of the island's economy.

The Greek cities of Tripoli and Ptolemais, located in Phoenicia, received beautiful gymnasiums from Herod. Byblos received its defensive walls, Berytos and Tyre—temples, market halls, and porticoes, and Sidon—a theater. The king carried out all of these construction projects at his own expense. Herod also generously bestowed gifts upon the famous cities of classical Greece: Athens, Sparta, and Samos.

The inhabitants of the island of Kos especially benefited from his support. He established a foundation, the proceeds of which were assigned to finance the operations of the *gymnasiarch*—the official responsible for overseeing the sports facilities on the island.

When he learned that the venerable Olympic games were at risk due to lack of funds, Herod offered a substantial sum to save them. In appreciation of his generous gift, he was inducted into the college of *hellanodikai*, also called *agonothetai*, who presided over the games when he stopped in Olympia during his journey to Rome in 12 BC.

The Olympic games were held that year for the 194th time, and one of their presiding officials was a king of the Jews.

The Savior of Troy

Marcus Agrippa, a friend and closest collaborator of Emperor Augustus, visited Herod's kingdom in the autumn of 15 BC. The reception was splendid, and he and the king quickly became fond of each other.

In the winter of the same year, Agrippa, already in Asia Minor by then, invited Herod to join a military expedition he was preparing. Its purpose was to assist Prince Polemon,[58] a Roman vassal fighting against the natives at the mouth of the Don River. In preparation for the war, Agrippa concentrated his fleet in Sinope, on the southern shore of the Black Sea.

Herod promptly prepared several ships and set sail from Caesarea in the spring of 14 BC. Both sons of the ill-fated Queen Mariamne I, Alexander and Aristobulus, accompanied him. They were nearing maturity, and the king wanted to start involving them in state affairs. The squadron first headed towards the islands of Rhodes and Kos and then had to stop for a few days off the coast of Chios as it encountered a strong contrary wind. And now the inhabitants of Chios owed to the king of Judea the reconstruction of a magnificent portico, which had lain in ruins for over half a century: Herod never missed an opportunity to show generosity to the Greeks. Here, on Chios, one of the royal sons remained behind to study rhetoric, while the other had stayed on Rhodes.

Herod had expected to meet up with Agrippa on the island of Lesbos, but now he learned that the Roman commander had gone to meet the fleet in Sinope. Herod's squadron, therefore, sailed through the Black Sea straits and quickly reached Sinope. But now it turned out

----

[58] Polemon I Pythodoros (died 8 BC) was the Roman client King of Cilicia, Pontus, Colchis and the Bosporan Kingdom.

that the entire expedition was no longer necessary: Prince Polemon had broken the rebels' resistance and had become the de facto ruler of the Bosporan Kingdom located in the eastern part of today's Crimea. Thus, a new vassal state came into the Roman fold on the north shores of the Black Sea.

From Herod's point of view, the expedition was a great success. He earned significant political credit at a very low cost: he had reinforced his image as that of an unwavering ally of Rome in general and of Agrippa in particular and suffered no losses. Soon, an opportunity would arise to harvest its benefits.

On the return journey, the two men traveled by land. They first traveled south from Sinope, through Paphlagonia and Cappadocia, and then west through Phrygia to Ephesus on the coast of the Aegean Sea. From there, they crossed to the island of Samos. Everywhere they went, Herod aroused popularity, not just the easy way—by gifts of money, although he spared no costs. Above all, the king took every opportunity to intercede with the Roman administration for the rights of the local Greeks. This won him general sympathy and satisfied his ambition—and it cost him little or nothing.

And now, the city of Troy became a beneficiary of Herod's benevolence. At the time, it was a small and impoverished town, but it still basked in the glory of centuries past and the halo of Homeric poetry. Every Greek child began their education with the *Iliad* and the *Odyssey*. The battles of the Greeks against Troy—the ten-year siege of Priam's stronghold by the forces of King Agamemnon—had been an inexhaustible source of motifs for generations of painters, sculptors, dramatists, and poets. Who has not heard of the heroism of Hector or of the terrible wrath of invincible Achilles? Even the gods took part in the battle of Troy—some defending the city, others trying to destroy it.

It is no wonder that many people who had read about the place or learned about it in school visited Troy, wanting to see it with their own eyes. A few months earlier, a very distinguished tourist paid a visit here—Julia, the only child of Emperor Augustus and wife of Marcus Agrippa. She had accompanied her husband on his journey to

Asia Minor. When he left for Sinope, Julia decided to visit the city from which, according to legend, her lineage had stemmed—the Julian clan. After the Greeks captured Priam's stronghold, the story went, Aeneas led the survivors of the massacre to Italy, and Julius, Aeneas' son, became the founder of the Julian line.

However, gods unfriendly to Troy were still on the prowl. On her way, near the city, Julia was surprised by a sudden storm and a flash flood of the River Scamander. The Trojans were—of course—innocent. They did not even know they were about to be honored by a visit of the emperor's daughter. But Agrippa was furious that his wife had found herself in such great danger. Since he could not punish the river or the rain, his wrath fell onto defenseless Troy. He imposed a high fine on the town, the payment of which exceeded the wherewithal of its citizens—for though they lived on top of magnificent treasures from a thousand years earlier buried underfoot, they did not know it. The treasures were to remain hidden for another two thousand years.

The dismayed descendants of Priam now turned to Herod, begging him for intercession. They were not disappointed. Still in Sinope, before leaving for Paphlagonia, the king negotiated with Agrippa to waive the penalty. Then, Nicholas of Damascus traveled by sea to Troy, carrying the joyful news and the official letter to the Roman governor. Grateful Trojans showered Herod with all the honors and accolades within their means; these were beautifully sounding resolutions of thanksgiving, praising the king like a living god. Even engraving the text of these resolutions in bronze and marble cost only a fraction of what the fine would have cost.

Once, Apollo and Aphrodite defended Ilion against the anger of other gods and the valor of Achilles. Now, the king of a small Levantine state averted the tide of misfortune. Then, the specter of a massacre and destruction stood before the city. This time—financial ruin. Times had changed and become prosaic. However, in both cases, the cause of Troy's misfortunes was a woman—then the beautiful and frivolous Helen, now the proud Julia.

The Greeks and the Jews

For all his well-known generosity towards Greeks and things Greek, when it came to a conflict between Greeks and Jews, Herod sided with the latter.

As Agrippa and Herod traveled back to the shores of Asia Minor, they entered a region called Ionia, whose central city was Miletus. Many Jews lived in Ionia alongside the Greeks, generally engaged in crafts and trade. Their legal status was peculiar: they were neither citizens of the cities—and thus had no say in the local government; nor were they Roman citizens. In essence, they were only tolerated guests.

Despite this, they managed to obtain from the Romans—like their brethren in other provinces—many valuable privileges, which gave them a position that was effectively more privileged than that of their Greek hosts. They received an exemption from military service, which would have compelled them to violate the Sabbath. They were excused from appearing in courts on the Sabbath and on Jewish holidays. Their communities enjoyed broad internal autonomy, including the right to collect and send contributions to the Temple in Jerusalem.

The local authorities of the cities in Ionia did not always wish to honor these privileges. They imposed on the Jews all kinds of dues and services, often maliciously. Therefore, as soon as Agrippa arrived in Miletus, Jews flocked to him in large numbers, bringing to him their complaints against the Greeks.

On the day when their complaints were to be heard, many distinguished Romans and several rulers of eastern states sat in the tribunal alongside Agrippa. Nicholas of Damascus spoke in defense of the Jews. He delivered a learned speech, revealing a brilliant command of classical rhetorical principles. He praised the benefits of Roman rule, cited the privileges granted to the Jews by Roman commanders, including Caesar, and emphasized the attachment of the Jews to their ancient laws and customs.

Nevertheless, even the most magnificent speech would have achieved little were it not for Herod's efforts. The Romans regarded him as the most competent and impartial person in the matter. His dedication to the Empire was well known, as was his goodwill towards the Greeks. Herod used all his influence, the verdict of the council proved favorable to the Jews, and their privileges were confirmed.

This verdict set a precedent for centuries to come. Henceforth, in all cases of conflict with local authorities in all provinces and regions subject to Rome, the Jews would invoke the Ruling in Miletus.

As Herod returned to Jerusalem, he could proudly address the council and the people, presenting his achievements during his journey to Asia Minor.

And in order to allow the Palestinian Jews to praise him sincerely and with a clear conscience, he announced a reduction of tax rates by a quarter.

TWO SANCTUARIES

The Temple of Jerusalem

Just as the walls of the grand Temple of Augustus began to rise towards the sky at the sources of the Jordan in Paneas, that is, in the year 20 BC, Herod undertook a colossal construction project in Jerusalem itself—the renovation and expansion of the Temple.

Herod's attitude towards religion was pragmatic and well-calculated. Religion was, for him, a tool of politics, a helpful aid in achieving certain specific goals. He dedicated to Caesar what was Caesar's, building many temples and monuments to him. He knew this caused widespread outrage in Judea, but it was difficult to explain to the Jews the real reasons for such ostentatious promotion of the imperial cult. Appealing to the fact that he, the King of Judea, owed to such actions the enlargement of his state and his people a period of stability and prosperity would certainly not appease the fanatics.

Herod also knew that his kindness to the Greeks and magnificent gifts to foreign cities caused envy and resentment. Political wisdom dictated that the king should do something towards at least a partial reconciliation with his people. Herod wanted to be able to say to all the dissidents:

"I am just! I bestow gifts upon foreigners, for such is my royal will. However, everything I have built abroad pales in comparison to my work in Jerusalem. I erect temples to foreign gods because I must. But to the Lord of Hosts, I will build a sanctuary that will outshine the temple of Solomon."

The people of Jerusalem initially received Herod's plan with great fear. The king proposed demolishing the existing buildings, and there were concerns about whether there would be enough resources to construct new ones—of the size and splendor that Herod intended. However, he approached the task with his usual energy and quickly convinced even the most skeptical of the feasibility of his idea.

He collected all the necessary construction materials in

advance. He gathered thousands of wagons to transport them. He assembled thousands of craftsmen. A thousand people from the priestly families undertook the task of demolishing the old temple and building the walls of the new one to ensure that the sacred walls would not suffer defilement. Herod provided them with clothing and trained them in the relevant crafts at his own expense. Preliminary work began at the beginning of 19 BC and was organized in such a way as not to interfere with the daily offering of sacrifices.

The first temple on the site had been built by King Solomon a thousand years earlier. It existed for nearly five hundred years and was demolished in 586 BC when the Babylonians captured Jerusalem. The Jews rebuilt it several decades later after returning from Babylonian captivity, but this second temple was not as magnificent. Moreover, it lacked its most extraordinary relic, destroyed or stolen by the Babylonians: the Ark of the Covenant.

King Antiochus of the Seleucid dynasty plundered the temple three centuries later, and he desecrated it by ordering the erection of a statue of Zeus within its walls. This became one of the reasons for the outbreak of the Maccabean uprising. When the victorious Judah Maccabee entered the holy precinct with his men, he found the courtyards overgrown with weeds, burnt gates, ruined buildings, and the altar profaned. His priests rebuilt the stone altars and made new tables, a new menorah, and new sacrificial vessels. Only then did they resume offering sacrifices.

In planning the expansion and enhancement of the Sanctuary, Herod set himself up on equal footing with the most revered figures of Jewish history. From then on, anyone speaking about the history of the Temple of Jerusalem had to mention his name alongside that of Solomon and Judah Maccabee.

Despite all the preparations and lavish expenditure, the construction of the Temple took about a year and a half. It took eight more years to construct the courtyards, defensive walls, and porticoes. Even then, the work was never finished. Minor adjustments and additions were made continuously for several decades until 64 AD; two years later, the Jewish uprising against the Romans broke out, ending in the destruction of the Temple—forever.

The work took that long in part due to the location of the Sanctuary. The top of the hill had to be widened and leveled, and since it was not flat but sloped slightly north to south and rocky bulges jutted out here and there, it took a lot of engineering. Likewise, the steep slopes of the hill, descending into the deep ravines, had to be reinforced. They were faced with gigantic boulders joined together with lead.

The whole formed an irregular quadrangle. The Fortress of Atonia occupied its north-western corner. The rest of the grounds rose in three successive platforms leading up to the main sanctuary. A great wall surrounded the entire complex. It had four gates facing west and two facing south. After passing through these gates, one entered a spacious courtyard—the first platform. It was called the Court of the Gentiles because anyone could enter it. It was surrounded by large double colonnades running along the external wall. The collonades were thirty cubits wide—about ten meters—and were covered with flat cedar roofs. The eastern colonnade ran alongside a wall, which descended perpendicularly into the gorge of the Kidron Valley, giving the impression of being suspended over an abyss. The southern colonnade, known as the Royal, was distinguished by its grandeur. It had four rows of mighty columns with rich Corinthian capitals; each column was so thick that three men could hardly embrace it. This colonnade contained a hundred and sixty-two columns, with the last row embedded in the outer wall, the whole creating three great corridors.

The entire space of the Court of the Gentiles was paved with stone slabs, forming beautiful patterns. There was always bustle and traffic here. Sacrificial animals were sold here—pigeons, oxen, and sheep. There were tables of money changers, where Jews arriving from all over the world exchanged foreign currencies for coin acceptable to the Temple. (All Temple dues were payable in Tyrian drachma). Public debates among scholars of the Scripture took place here.

From the Court of the Gentiles, one ascended fourteen steps to a narrow terrace enclosed by a stone balustrade. Greek and Latin inscriptions were placed on the columns near this balustrade, prohibiting further entry to all non-Jews.

From this terrace, five steps led to the gates in the wall surrounding the courtyard called the Court of the Israelites. This had four gates on the north and south sides, while on the east side, there was a double gate. These gates were splendidly decorated with gold, silver, and Corinthian bronze.

The eastern gate led to the so-called Court of Women because women were allowed to enter it—but could proceed no further. From this courtyard, fifteen steps led higher, towards a large and high gate, behind which lay a courtyard accessible only to men. Above it, behind a stone wall, stretched the highest courtyard, which only priests were allowed to enter; even the king had no right to enter it except on certain holidays.

The Sanctuary stood in the middle of the Court of Priests. It was erected on a high foundation and in white stone adorned with gilding. Its roof bristled with an entire forest of gilded spikes: they served to protect the sanctuary from pollution by birds.

A traveler approaching Jerusalem could see from afar what seemed like a cloud of dazzling white rising high above the city, shimmering with gold in the sunlight: the most magnificent of all works of Herod.

In 70 AD, the Romans burned and demolished this sanctuary. Some sixty years later, after suppressing yet another Jewish uprising, Emperor Hadrian erected a new temple on the site—a sanctuary dedicated to Capitoline Jupiter—and placed his own statue within it. If Herod were still alive at that time, he would have asked the fanatics: had it not made more sense to build imperial temples and statues all around Palestine and, in return, make sure that the Jerusalem sanctuary remained unviolated?

In the 7th century AD, when the Arabs took control of Palestine, the large platform of the former courtyards and temple buildings became one of the most revered places of worship in the Islamic world, and it remains so to this day: Haram el-Sharif, the second holiest site after Mecca. The seven-sided mosque of the Domeof-the-Rock occupies the center of the immense space, built above the rock which once, centuries ago, served as the base for the stone altar of burnt sacrifices.

The site is not accessible to Jews. No one enters the sacred precinct, fearing to tread accidentally the place which once only the High Priest had the right to enter. The Jews gather instead at the wall built by Herod centuries ago, at the base of the temple's outer western wall, overlooking the Tyropoeon Valley. There, praying, they remember Herod's great temple.

They pray at Herod's wall.

The Temple in Hebron

Sara lived for one hundred and twenty-seven years. She died in the city of Hebron. Her husband Abraham came to mourn the death of his wife. Then he asked the sons of Heth, who owned Hebron at that time: "I am a stranger and a sojourner among you. Give me a piece of land for a burial place among you, that I may bury my dead." The sons of Heth answered him: " In the choicest of our burial places, bury your dead. None of us will withhold from you this burial place." However, Abraham insisted that Ephron, son of Zohar, sell him the cave that he had at the far end of his field. Abraham weighed out four hundred shekels of silver to Ephron and bought the field with the cave and all the trees upon it. In the cave, Abraham buried his wife, Sarah. Later, he was buried there himself, followed by his son Isaac and his wife Rebecca, and then Isaac's son Jacob and his wife Leah.

This narrative appears in chapter 23 of the *Book of Genesis*, one of the oldest books in the Bible. The cave, considered the patriarchs' tomb, became one of the holiest places in Palestine, just as Hebron was one of its main cities. It was the capital of southern Judea, and it lay at the crossroads of the main routes from Jerusalem to Gaza and from the coastal plain to the Dead Sea. When, in the 6th century, the Edomites conquered southern Judea and Hebron, they treated the tomb with the same reverence because Esau, from whom they claimed descent, had been the son of Isaac and Rebecca. Likewise, the Arabs, who ruled over Palestine following the conquest of the 7th century AD, revered the tomb.

To this day, an impressive structure stands in Hebron; a massive wall encloses a rectangular area, a field with the cave that Abraham is said to have bought from Ephron. The lower parts of the wall, up to the height of several meters, are constructed from gigantic, tightly fitted, and well-smoothed stones—the building technique used for the walls of the Jerusalem Temple and the harbor in Caesarea. There seems to be little doubt that the sanctuary in Hebron was the work of Herod. Perhaps Herod intended to remind Jews and Idumeans that according to the Scriptures and tradition, they shared the same ancestors—Abraham and Isaac.

Part Three
THE SHADOWS OF TWILIGHT

A PROLOGUE TO THE TRAGEDY

Ecclesiastes

> I made me great works; I builded me houses; I planted me vineyards;
> I made me gardens and orchards, and I planted trees in them of all
> kind of fruits; I made me pools of water, to water therewith the
> wood that bringeth forth trees: I got me servants and maidens, and
> had servants born in my house; I had great possessions of great and
> small cattle above all that were in Jerusalem before me. I gathered
> me also silver and gold, and the peculiar treasure of kings and of the
> provinces. I gat me men singers and women singers, and the delights
> of the sons of men, as musical instruments, and that of all sorts. So
> I was great, and increased more than all that were before me in
> Jerusalem: also my wisdom remained with me. And whatsoever
> mine eyes desired I kept not from them, I withheld not my heart
> from any joy; for my heart rejoiced in all my labor: and this was my
> portion of all my labor.
> Then I looked on all the works that my hands had wrought, and on
> the labor that I had labored to do: and, behold, all was vanity and
> vexation of spirit, and there was no profit under the sun.[59]

Tradition ascribes these words to King Solomon. In reality, this book
of sadness was composed no more than two centuries before Herod.
Its Hebrew title is *Kohelet*, meaning "The Preacher." It quickly gained
popularity and is still one of the best-known books of the Bible,
perhaps because in every person's life, there comes a moment when she

---

[59] Ecclesiastes 2:4-11

or he will agree with the words of The Preacher: "Oh, vanity of vanities! And all is vanity!"

Herod probably heard this chapter often: it seemed written for him. Who knows if, upon hearing it, the king did not object: Why should I consider my deeds vain and futile? Here they are! They will last forever!

Yet, his time was coming to an end.

The Sons of Mariamne

Herod saw with horror that the sons of Mariamne I—the wife he had loved and murdered—were drifting further and further away from him. He had spared no effort to secure a splendid future for them. With them in mind, he sought the emperor's approval for his succession plan. He sent them to Rome to present themselves at the world's capital, become familiar with it, and facilitate their rule in the future. In 18 BC, he traveled to Italy to bring the boys back to Judea— two of them, Alexander and Aristobulus, for the third had passed away.

Alas, shortly after returning to their homeland, relations between Herod and the two princes deteriorated. In the spring of 14 BC, they traveled with their father to Asia Minor when Agrippa had summoned the king. Then, for a while, they continued their studies in Greece, where the famous schools of rhetoric were flourishing at that time. But after Herod's triumphant return from Asia Minor—where he had acted as a savior of the Trojans and as the defender of the Jews of Miletus—a sharp quarrel arose between the father and his sons.

Alexander and Aristobulus were very accomplished young men. Handsome, educated, and well-read in Greek and Latin, they were also forthright and outspoken. They were also proud: through their mother, Mariamne, they were Hasmoneans. Their names were dynastic names of the royal lineage. They felt more connected to their Hasmonean mother than to their Idumean father. The tragic fate of Mariamne weighed heavily on their conscience: the shadow of their murdered mother lay between them and their father.

Resentment and misunderstanding grew in the hearts of both the father and his sons. Herod could not forget that in the veins of Alexander and Aristobulus flowed the blood of the Hasmoneans— the family from whom he had stolen the throne of Judea; and whose members he had murdered: Hyrcanus, Antigonus, Aristobulus.

> Yea, I hated all my labor which I had taken under the sun: because I should leave it unto the man that shall be after me. And who knoweth whether he shall be a wise man or a fool? Yet shall he have rule over all my labor wherein I have labored, and wherein I have showed myself wise under the sun. This is also vanity.[60]

And Herod may have added: "And I do not know whether they will not hate me. Is there anything more wretched?"

Though mutual suspicions greatly hindered reconciliation, none of these things had to lead to an open conflict. The fatal role was played by women.

Herod's Harem

According to a custom common among wealthy Jews of the day, Herod had many wives. He divorced his first wife, Doris. She lived away from the palace with her son Antipater. His second wife was Mariamne, the mother of the heirs to the throne. Mariamne II's son was named Herod Philip. A Samaritan named Malthace[61] gave birth to Herod Antipas and Herod Archelaus. Cleopatra, a Jewess from Jerusalem, was the mother of Herod and Philip, and Pallas was the mother of Phasael. Of the remaining wives, two gave birth to daughters, and two were childless. Each of these women thought about her children's future and was ready to do anything to elevate them above others. The court constantly buzzed with conflict and

---

[60] *Ecclesiastes* 2:18-19
[61] Malthace (Greek: Μαλθάκη, romanized: *Malthákē*)

intrigue.

Soon, more women arrived at court, as Herod gave wives to his sons after their return from Rome. Aristobulus was given Berenice, the daughter of Salome, Herod's sister. Alexander was assigned Glafira, the daughter of Archelaus, the ruler of Cappadocia in Asia Minor. The two princesses came to live in Herod's palace and quickly developed a venomous distaste for each other.

Glafira constantly boasted of her lineage, claiming to carry the blood of both the founders of the Macedonian dynasty and King Darius of Persia. She showed her contempt for the lowly Jews at every step, not only towards her sister-in-law but also towards Herod.

Once, in an argument, Aristobulus criticized his wife, Berenice, saying that she and her mother were of inferior birth, being Idumeans of low status and, therefore, not worthy of the royal blood of the Hasmoneans. The girl, with tears in her eyes, complained to her mother. Perhaps motivated by her humiliation, she said that the two brothers were already preparing changes at court to take effect the day they took power: that all the wives and daughters of Herod would have to go to work with the slaves and his other sons—the stepbrothers of the two princes—would at best serve as village scribes.

Her daughter's complaints riled Salome. She had long feared that the moment they put on the royal diadems, the sons of Mariamne I would take her life in retribution for her role in the murder of their mother: it was no secret to anyone in Judea that Salome had been the primary driver of their mother's downfall. Salome now did everything she could to distance the aging king—Herod was already sixty—from the two young men.

By marrying Aristobulus to Salome's daughter, Herod had hoped to end the long-standing dispute that had divided his house and family for years. In reality, he only inflamed the unhealed wounds.

Salome spared no effort to sow new suspicions in her naturally suspicious brother's heart. She seized upon every careless word Aristobulus uttered in Berenice's presence. The latter, as many young wives do, in her naivety, repeated everything to her mother.

In her intrigues against the two princes, Salome had a staunch ally in her younger brother Pheroras. Envy motivated him: why shouldn't he, the blood of Antipater, Phasael, and Herod, be next in line for the throne?

Pheroras and Salome did not hesitate to use any means to fuel the king's suspicions; they even resorted to provocation. Bribed individuals from the entourage of both princes engaged them in conversations about Mariamne and the circumstances of her death. They seized upon and amplified every word spoken by the princes and fabricated many others. Soon, rumors circulated throughout Jerusalem that Alexander and Aristobulus were out to avenge their mother's death. Of course, Salome and Pheroras promptly informed Herod of all of this.

Then, the king learned from the same source that Alexander was planning to escape. Supposedly, he intended to go to his father-in-law, Archelaus, and, with his help, reach Rome to accuse formally his father of killing Mariamne.

This seared Herod. He feared Augustus more than he feared anything. Nevertheless, he did not take rash action; perhaps he also harbored suspicions about the source of the information. He decided to give his two heirs a lesson.

Antipater, Son of Doris

For over twenty years, Herod's firstborn son, Antipater, had only been allowed to appear in Jerusalem on major holidays to offer the prescribed sacrifices in the Temple. By marrying Mariamne, his father had effectively banished him from the capital, condemning him to exile. But now, suddenly, at the end of 14 BC, Antipater was summoned to court, warmly welcomed, and treated with all the honors due to a royal son. He was assigned permanent quarters in the palace, befitting his princely dignity.

Herod believed that in this way, he would check the rebellious ideas of Mariamne's sons: they would suddenly realize that another heir was available to take the throne. Alas, Antipater's arrival only worsened the already complicated situation. Herod's first-born, Antiater, a talented man, had no scruples whatsoever. He had no intention of settling for the minor role assigned to him in his father's plans, and he immediately set a far more ambitious goal for himself. After all, he was the firstborn: what did it matter that he had come into the world before Herod became king? What did it matter that his mother, Doris, did not come from a royal clan? Ultimately, Herod himself had shown that even an ordinary commoner could seize the throne if he were prepared to pursue it by any means necessary.

Indeed, Antipater was his father's true son.

Of course, Antipater was too sensible to confront his half-brothers directly. He understood the situation at court—who sided with whom—and deemed it best to cooperate with Salome and Pheroras. The three intensified the work of their informers and provocateurs. Antipater exploited every careless remark made by the two princes but never made any critical comments about them in the presence of Herod. On the contrary, he always defended them—even against accusations he had originated himself. Thanks to such behavior, he quickly gained the reputation of a completely impartial, noble, and devoted family man.

As the importance of Antipater grew and his father's affection for him became apparent, the resentment of Mariamne's sons also increased, and this provided the informers with a constant supply of useful material. Soon, Antipater's mother, Doris, arrived at the Jerusalem court. This led to a violent quarrel, as the proud descendants of the Hasmoneans considered it beneath them to live under the same roof with a woman of such low birth.

In time, the combined efforts of Salome, Pheroras, and Antipater and the proud recklessness of the young princes bore fruit. At the beginning of 13 BC, Herod annulled his will and declared Antipater his sole heir and successor.

Agrippa's stay in Asia Minor was coming to an end. Herod traveled to bid him farewell, taking Antipater with him. He entrusted his firstborn to Agrippa and asked him to present him to the emperor in Rome as the future king of Judea.

Herod and Agrippa said their goodbyes, never to see each other again. Agrippa passed away a few months later.

Aquilea

In 12 BC, in the Italian city of Aquilea, on the northern shores of the Adriatic Sea, a shocking confrontation took place.

Before Emperor Augustus and his closest advisors, a father accused his two sons of conspiring against his life. The father was Herod, and the sons were Alexander and Aristobulus. Antipater was "in attendance."

Perhaps, by then, the mind of the King of Judea was not as sharp as it had once been. Herod had always been suspicious—usually with good reason. After all, the courts of Eastern rulers witnessed many heinous crimes and dark and slippery intrigues. He himself had come to the throne through plots and murder, so only naturally, he was ready to suspect others of treachery. With age, this trait of the king's character intensified. His suspicions—skillfully fueled by Salome and Antipater, who, even from Rome, kept a close watch on the developments at the Jerusalem court—turned into a morbid obsession and finally erupted in an explosion of hatred towards Mariamne's sons.

But the old king retained enough common sense not to want to decide anything regarding Alexander and Aristobulus on his own. Perhaps he had a vague feeling that something was amiss and desired a broader and more impartial forum to consider the matter. Or perhaps he feared the consequences of murdering two youths well-known to the emperor and many influential figures in Rome. Both considerations likely played some role in his decision to travel to Italy with Mariamne's sons and to place his complaint against them before Augustus.

The emperor listened attentively to Herod's accusatory speech and questioned the two princes. They had had their suspicions regarding the purpose of their joint journey to Italy. Their father's hostile attitude towards them did not escape their notice. Still, genuine astonishment and terror filled them now when the illustrious Imperial tribunal accused them of planning patricide, and the full horror of the whole vile intrigue against them unfolded before their eyes.

Augustus was too astute a judge of people for this to escape his notice. Moreover, Herod's entire speech sounded limp and unconvincing. The king was unable to present any facts, or witnesses, or evidence.

Therefore, when Alexander, who was allowed to speak after his father, pointed out the gaps and contradictions in his arguments, he effectively dismantled the case. The young prince was an excellent speaker and knew well which arguments to use before the distinguished assembly and what sentiments to appeal to. He skillfully refuted all the charges in words that sounded sincere because they were. He appealed to the mercy of both the emperor and his father. He and his brother, he said, were prepared to accept any punishment if even the slightest hint existed that they had plotted patricide.

Augustus took a cautious stance. To preserve Herod's dignity, he emphasized that the princes had behaved too haughtily towards their father, which could have given some basis for speculation and gossip. However, he had an unwavering hope that the king would generously overlook these minor transgressions. Of course, any serious talk of planned patricide was out of the question. Mutual understanding would quickly restore complete harmony within the family.

Herod immediately realized that the emperor was leaning towards the two princes. Therefore, when they knelt at his feet to ask for forgiveness, he embraced them tenderly and, shedding tears, hugged them. Emotion filled the hall.

The epilogue of the trial took place a few months later in Jerusalem, where huge crowds gathered in the Temple courtyard. There were priests, courtiers, and prominent citizens. The king stood before them, with both of Mariamne's sons and Antipater by his side. He delivered a speech that was partly a report on his distant journey, partly a justification of the accusations he made in Aquileia, and partly

The Oasis of Ein Gedi near Qumran

a proclamation of the future order of the dynasty. After Herod's death, Antipater would become the king of Judea, but the sons of Mariamne would receive separate principalities under his suzerainty. However, the king emphasized that, for now, he alone was the ruler, and soldiers and citizens owed their obedience to him. The heir to the throne had the right only to royal attire and honors, but he had no power to give any orders.

Herod concluded his speech by calling on his sons to embrace each other in true brotherly love, reminding them of the reconciliation made before Augustus in Aquileia. However, the experienced ruler and politician likely realized that the promised division of the kingdom would lead to even fiercer competition between his sons.

Repta

The brigands of Trachonitis took advantage of Herod's trip to Italy and his slow return, interrupted as it was by extended stays in Olympia and Cappadocia. The half-nomadic natives of the rocky desert, whom the king had forced into a settled way of life, had borne the "benefits of peace and agriculture" with great reluctance. And now, during Herod's prolonged absence, the rumor suddenly spread—undoubtedly spread by someone—that the king had died abroad. The old banditry of Trachonitis revived immediately and raids on the borderlands of Syria and Palestine resumed. The royal governors of Trachonitis, working in tandem with the king's settlers, suppressed the unrest as best they could, but many rebels managed to escape. They sought refuge in the Nabatean territory, where a friendly reception awaited them. The all-powerful minister of the King of Petra, Syllaios, welcomed the refugees with open arms. It was the same Syllaios who, a few years earlier, had so cunningly thwarted the Roman attempt to conquer Arabia Felix.

As before, the grounds for supporting the bandits was the dispute over Trachonitis and control of its profitable trade route. But Syllaios also had a personal reason to hate Herod. Sometime earlier, he had asked for the hand of Salome, the sister of the Jewish king. In the ambitious plans of the Nabatean magnate, a marital connection with the ruler of Judea would have been an important step up.

But Herod took a dim view of the matter. He ostensibly agreed to the marriage but on the condition that Syllaios should convert to Judaism. Of course, he knew perfectly well that this was impossible since Syllaios would immediately lose all respect and all political influence among the Nabateans as a consequence. Salome, who had been receptive to Syllaios's plans originally, married Alexas, a dignitary at Herod's court.

And now, Syllaios welcomed the Trachonites and gave them

226

refuge in Repta, a Nabatean fortress located near the border. From there, they conducted raids both into Judea and Syria. Herod was powerless. He could not enter Nabatean territory, as it would mean starting a war, something the emperor would categorically oppose. Rome was on the verge of a great campaign to conquer Germany—the land between the Rhine and the Elbe. Roman legions had waged persistent campaigns there year after year. In such a situation, an armed conflict in the Middle East was highly undesirable.

Unable to find any other way to deal with the Trachonites, Herod ordered the capture and execution of their families in Trachonitis, and he brought more Jewish settlers into the province, mainly from Idumea. This provoked terrible rage among the men in Repta. From then on, they fought not only for plunder but also for revenge. They ravaged the lands of Judea and murdered its inhabitants. Due to the influx of Trachontite fugitives, their numbers continued to grow.

Herod attempted to exert pressure on the rulers of Petra. He demanded the return of the money he had once lent them, but Syllaios denied any debts were due. Finally, under pressure from the Roman governor of Syria, Saturninus, the Nabateans agreed to pay their debts to the king of Judea within thirty days and to carry out a mutual extradition of fugitives. But the deadline passed, and they had not fulfilled their obligations. Meanwhile, Syllaios traveled to Rome to further his intrigue, both against King Herod and his own ruler, Obodas. He had long since planned to depose him as the king of Petra and take the diadem for himself.

The king of Judea was unable to compel the Roman governor of Syria to undertake a punitive action against Nabatea, but he did obtain his promise that Saturninus would look the other way and not interfere in case of a conflict. Herod immediately gathered his best units. He crossed the border and took Repta by surprise. He captured the entire garrison and leveled the fortress walls. It was the beginning of 9 BC.

Almost immediately after this success, Herod went to Caesarea. After nearly ten years of uninterrupted work, he had completed its most important buildings, and now he staged splendid festivities to celebrate the achievement. Gladiators and wild beasts engaged in combat during the circus games. There were chariot races and athletic performances. The games were staged in honor of Augustus and were to be repeated every five years. The emperor himself contributed to the cost of the celebrations.

Imperial Displeasure

Almost immediately after these grand festivities, bad news arrived from Rome, news which could spell complete ruin of all of Herod's work.

His implacable enemy, Syllaios, was still in the capital of the world. Meanwhile, King Obodas, a powerless tool in the hands of his minister and the subject of his intrigues, had died and was replaced by his son, Aretas. This did not affect Syllaios's plans. He was as happy to replace Aretas as he had been to replace Obodas. The example of Herod, who, twenty-some years earlier, had replaced the Hasmonean dynasty, was Syllaios's guiding light. Like Herod, Syllaios sought to realize his plan with the help of the Romans.

And he achieved a great deal in a short time. Thanks to his generosity—both public and private—he managed to gain favor with influential individuals at the court of Augustus, and when an embassy from Aretas arrived with a request to recognize Aretas as king, it was dismissed. Herod's envoys, who had been sent to Rome to justify the expedition against Repta, were refused an interview. Syllaios, informed by his supporters in Petra about Herod's raid, presented the entire event to Augustus in a light favorable to him: the Nabateans were innocent victims of a bandit assault by the king of Judea, who devastated their land with fire and sword, leaving over two and a half thousand peaceful inhabitants dead. Syllaios did not fail to point out that, had he been present and in charge, no such thing would have ever happened.

The situation incensed Augustus. A war between his vassals

without his knowledge and consent! The emperor now recalled the conference in Aquileia and began to think that Herod was perhaps losing his mind.

Sharply worded letters were sent to the East—to Herod and to the Roman governor of Syria. Syllaios made sure that the content of these letters quickly became public knowledge: Herod had fallen out of favor. Augustus refused to receive his envoys, refused to accept Herod's gifts, and severed their friendship! At the same time, Syllaios informed his people in Petra that things were going well and encouraged them to take action. He had a specific goal in mind. An escalation of the Judean-Nabatean conflict would cause the Romans to want a man they knew and trusted to rule Petra—namely, Syllaios.

Enemy forces crossed into Judea, and the native population of Trachonitis took up arms again. Soon, complete anarchy prevailed on the border. The attackers committed the most terrible excesses, but Herod, terrified by the turn of events and for fear of losing everything, did not dare to defend his people. He lived in fear that the emperor might strip him of his throne and he smelled treason, intrigue, and disloyalty everywhere. Above all, he suspected the sons of Mariamne. Old grievances suppressed in Aquileia returned and were renewed by the dramatic events.

Now, it was noticed that Alexander had established unusually close ties with three eunuchs in Herod's personal service. Taken in hand by Antipater's skillful torturers, the eunuchs confessed everything they were instructed to confess. Words allegedly spoken by Alexander to one of them deeply affected Herod:

"You should not place your hopes in the king! Surely you do not think this old man will become young again just because he dyes his hair? Put your faith in me instead. I will one day be king, even against Herod's will. Then my friends will reap their rewards."

Arrests, interrogations, and torture began immediately. Many otherwise honorable people became informants out of fear of false accusations. Others settled personal scores as the opportunity arose. How easy it was to destroy an inconvenient person by whispering just a few words to the right people! And while some preferred to die by their own hand rather than incriminate their innocent friends, Antipater expected that most of the arrested would remain true to human nature. Honest and noble they may have been, but the sight of the instruments of torture quickly had the desired effect. The invented conspiracy found many witnesses: the princes had intended to assassinate the king during a hunt; or were preparing to flee to Rome; or both.

In those terrible days, Herod seemed to lose his mind. He suffered from hallucinations and raged in hatred and disgust towards everyone around him.

Finally, one of the tortured individuals testified that he knew of a letter from Alexander to his high-ranking acquaintances in Rome; in it, the prince accused the king of engaging in secret negotiations with the Parthians.

Though the evidence was a blatant fabrication, Herod believed it. He ordered the imprisonment of both sons of Mariamne. The older of the two, Alexander, behaved very shrewdly. He immediately prepared a massive memorial in which he admitted to plotting against his father's life and provided the names of the co-conspirators. He listed Salome and Pheroras in the first place and then all the king's closest friends. In this way, he reduced the accusation to an obvious absurdity.

And everything would have perhaps gone differently if not for the arrival in Jerusalem of Prince Archelaus, Alexander's father-in-law. The ruler of Cappadocia quickly realized how suspicious Herod was and he decided to employ a cunning tactic. He launched a violent attack on his son-in-law and his criminal nature, thus gaining the king's trust. Here was a man who understood Herod's loneliness and the family tragedy! Then Archelaus announced that he considered it necessary to annul his daughter's marriage and take her back to Cappadocia.

Ambition stirred in Herod. He began to persuade Archelaus that Alexander's guilt was not yet proven, and even if it was, he, the father, had the right to forgive him.

The princes were released, and Archelaus departed with

generous gifts. But the relations at the Jerusalem court were never normal again. Shortly afterwards, imperial disfavor fell upon Herod, rekindling old resentments. Possessed by suspicion, the ruler of Judea asked himself: maybe Augustus intends to take the crown from me and give it to my sons? Perhaps secret negotiations have already begun?

Eurycles

Misfortune had it that at that moment, Alexander committed an act of folly: he confided his aversion for his father to a certain Eurycles. Eurycles was an aristocrat from Sparta who had spent years wandering through the courts of the East, entertaining himself with their intrigues—always, of course, with a view to personal gain. When he arrived in Jerusalem, he did not miss the chance to boast to Alexander and Glafira that he knew Archelaus. On this account, both received him with more trust than they should have. They complained about their strained relations with Herod, whose suspicious nature made their life unbearable.

Meanwhile, Eurycles realized that the future belonged to Antipater and that *his* favor was where the money was. At the first opportunity, he related to Antipater everything he had heard from Alexander, making it clear whose side he was on. Antipater seized his chance. He suggested to Eurycles that the Spartan should speak to the king. Shortly afterward, Herod learned shocking things from the mouth of a distinguished guest from a distant land—a person who, therefore, was obviously entirely impartial and trustworthy: the sons of Mariamne hated their father; they wanted to avenge the death of their mother and their great-grandfather, Hyrcanus. They already had secured the support of both Archelaus and Augustus. After assassinating their father, they were going to declare him a criminal and condemn his memory.

As a reward for conveying this priceless information, the Spartan received the vast sum of fifty talents from Herod. Reportedly, he left straight for Cappadocia, where he obtained more gifts from

Archelaus for "affecting a reconciliation between Herod and his sons."

Meanwhile, terror raged at the Jerusalem court. Under torture, two attendants of Alexander gave the testimonies required of them. They testified that the princes had urged them to kill the king during a hunt.

The commander of the fortress in Alexandrion was accused of planning to surrender the fortress and its treasury to the two princes. An incriminating letter turned up.

Given the evidence, Alexander and his brother were imprisoned again. This time, they were put in chains. Fear deprived them of reason. They wrote a confession saying that although they had planned to escape from Palestine, they had never conspired against their father. In the presence of the representatives of Archelaus, Alexander stated that he had only intended to flee to Cappadocia and, from there, with the help of his father-in-law, go to Rome. He repeated the same during a confrontation with his wife, Glafira. He probably thought that such a testimony would clear him of the main charge—the plot to murder the king. He did not understand that an appeal to Augustus was precisely what Herod feared the most in the current situation.

The Mission of Nicholas

Although matters had already gone far, Herod did not dare to resort to the ultimate step without the emperor's knowledge and at least his tacit approval. He sent envoys to Rome with an extensive memorandum about the alleged conspiracy of the sons of Mariamne. However, it could only be delivered if Augustus first changed his view concerning the Jewish-Nabatean conflict.

Misfortune had it that a change of heart had taken place in Rome. Based on independent reports, many decision-makers in Rome concluded that the Nabateans were taking advantage of Herod's helplessness and had intentionally caused anarchy on the Palestinian border. Naturally, this situation had to concern the emperor and his advisors. Alarming reports from Roman commanders in Syria confirmed them in the belief that they had acted too hastily in condemning Herod's expedition against Repta. And now, unwittingly, the Nabateans helped Herod's case: a new set of envoys of King Aretas arrived in Rome to renew his plea for an official recognition of his royal dignity. These envoys went out of their way to present Syllaios in the worst possible light as a schemer, slanderer, and troublemaker. They even managed to sway some of his former supporters in Rome to their side.

In a somewhat paradoxical way, two mutually hostile sides—Herod and Aretas—joined forces to bring down their common enemy.

At this very moment, the secretary and one of Herod's most trusted advisors, Nicholas of Damascus, arrived in Rome. The king had sent him, hoping that the learned and thoughtful Greek would find a way out of the situation. Nicholas did not disappoint. He presented the nature of the Trachonitis conflict in a persuasive manner. And since Syllaios was now vilified by his own compatriots, Augustus agreed to receive Herod's envoys and study the king's memorandum regarding the sons of Mariamne. The emperor did not pronounce in the matter of their guilt. He decided that further course of events should be left up to Herod's discretion but advised the king to leave the matter in the hands of the most impartial team he could assemble, a team composed of eminent Romans and people from his own entourage.

Trial in Beirut

A jury of one hundred and fifty officials sat in a tribunal assembled in Beirut to determine whether Alexander and Aristobulus were guilty of planned patricide. The tribunal was heavily biased in its composition: it included Pheroras and Salome but did not include Archelaus. Herod brought the charges himself. He delivered his speech with unheard-of vehemence, not hiding his anger and hatred. The princes were not even brought into the room.

The tribunal could not deny the king the right to punish his sons, for in the ancient world, this practice was sanctioned by the customs and laws of most nations. And since Herod had personally selected the judges, they delivered the anticipated verdict: the guilt of the sons of Mariamne had been proven, and they deserved death. Only the Romans—Saturninus and his three legates—expressed their doubts, saying that such a punishment would be too severe.

Of course, this verdict was not binding on the king. It was really just a justification for whatever final decision he would make. He now hesitated. Perhaps he was influenced in his delay by the report of Nicholas of Damascus, who had returned from Rome. The scholar informed the king that Roman public opinion was against him and that even his Roman friends thought it was enough to exercise strict supervision over the princes.

The fate of the sons of Mariamne was decided in Caesarea. Herod stopped in the city on his way back from Beirut. Here, an old soldier named Tyron came to see the king; his son had once belonged to Alexander's entourage. Confident in his past merits, Tyron boldly criticized Herod's behavior towards both princes and stated clearly that the people and the army were outraged by it. Herod flew into a fury; he commanded the immediate imprisonment of Tyron and of all the commanders he had named.

The case had further and far more dangerous consequences. The royal barber, a certain Tryphon, now suffered—it seems—a fit of madness. He shouted at the top of his voice that Tyron had incited him to cut Herod's throat while shaving him.

Both men were tortured, but it proved impossible to extract from them any sensible information. Tyron's son, who had once served Alexander, was brought to the torture chamber. The sight of his father's suffering terrified the young man. He knew he was next. Hoping to save his father from torture and to distance himself from the case, he testified that Alexander had asked Tyron to murder the king.

All the prisoners—there were over three hundred in all—were

brought before the crowd gathered in the main square of Caesarea. The multinational throng of the port city now assumed the role of a high tribunal, and again, like recently in Beirut, Herod was the accuser. However, the king had an easy task here, for the judges immediately became executioners. The enraged crowd beat the alleged conspirators with sticks and stones.

All three hundred were murdered.

The king, terrified by the possibility of defections in the army, which Tyron had suggested, no longer hesitated about the fate of the sons of Mariamne. They were strangled in the dungeons of the castle of Sebaste, and their bodies were buried in the fortress of Alexandrion.

But their role in history was not over. The descendants of both brothers were destined to play a significant role in the history of Judea.

THE FATE OF THE FIRSTBORN

Herod, the Guardian of Orphans

"Grim fate took away my sons, the fathers of these children, for whom I wish to care. I was an unhappy father but will be a completely devoted grandfather. I will ensure that these children receive the most careful upbringing and that, when I close my eyes, my closest friends will take them under their care. I pray to God that these orphans will one day show me more gratitude than their fathers ever did."

The king spoke sincerely. He had tears in his eyes and embraced the little children with genuine tenderness, and then he joined their hands. He intended their betrothals to bring love, unity, and peace to the entire family, now very numerous, and announced them publicly and solemnly before his friends and court dignitaries.

Alexander's children were indeed complete orphans. Right after the execution of their father, Herod sent Glafira back to her father's home, to Archelaus in Cappadocia, returning her dowry. Now, the king betrothed one of Alexander's sons to the daughter of his brother, Pheroras; one daughter of Aristobulus, Mariamne, he promised to the son of Antipater, and the other, Herodiade, he gave to his own son by Mariamne II.

He announced these betrothals but soon made changes to these plans. The proposed marriages did not align with the intentions of Antipater, who had, in the meantime, become very powerful at court. He managed to pressure Herod into giving him Aristobulus' daughter, Mariamne. He also arranged for his own son to marry Pheroras' daughter.

The deaths of both his half-brothers practically assured Antipater of the throne. Yet, he feared that the king might transfer his affections to the orphaned grandsons and assign them certain regions from the state, which Antipater already considered his own. In the current situation, the speediest possible death of the king would be the most beneficial outcome for the heir presumptive. It was probably possible to hasten that happy event, though, in light of Herod's suspicions, it was a dangerous proposition. For now, Antipater limited himself to gaining as many allies as possible, both in Palestine and in the neighboring countries, and especially in Rome. With that in mind, he distributed generous gifts, favors, and aid.

Pheroras

However, the all-important business was at court which was a veritable snake pit of plots and double-dealing. Here, Antipater's position could be shored up by winning the support of influential people. While seeking allies, the heir to the throne concentrated on Herod's brother, Pheroras. The brothers had been at odds for some time, as Pheroras had married his own slave. Herod saw his subsequent refusal to divorce her in order to enter into a prestigious marriage with one of the royal princesses as a contemptuous slight. In his isolation, Antipater extended to Pheroras a hand of friendship.

In addition to Pheroras, Herod's wife, Mariamne II, also decided to support the current heir to the throne. For a while, the three became the most potent faction at the Jerusalem court. The only significant opposition came from the king's sister, Salome. Since she reported everything to Herod, Antipater pretended that he had fallen out with Pheroras. This might have deceived the king but not Salome. She decided to reveal to Herod the connection between Pheroras' wife and the Pharisees.

Despite Herod's efforts to sway this influential faction, the Pharisees viewed his policies with increasing aversion. Their recent act of civil disobedience—refusal to swear allegiance to the Emperor—was a demonstration of this. Herod did not dare to act too harshly against them, as he feared disturbances. However, to preserve his authority, he imposed a large fine on the six thousand members of the Pharisees for their disobedience. Pheroras's wife provided the money out of her own funds, and Salome discovered the fact.

At the same time, Herod's informers reported to him that

rumors of the imminent end of his rule were spreading at court and among the people. The Pharisees disseminated these prophecies in various versions tailored to the preferences of different audiences. One of the alleged prophecies proclaimed that after Herod, Pheroras would ascend the throne of Judea.

Many Pharisees paid for these prophecies with their lives. Along with them, several courtiers of the king also lost their heads. Herod did not dare and did not want to deal with Pheroras in the same harsh manner, but he demanded that he make a drastic choice between his love for his brother and his love for his wife. He accused him of supporting the Pharisees, plotting against his daughters, and being a poisoner. To all of this, Pheroras responded boldly, stating that he would rather part with his life than with his wife.

Soon, Antipater set out for Rome on his father's orders. He had two critical missions. First, he was to present to the emperor his father's new will, in which he named Antipater as his successor, or, if for any reason, the choice of Antipater did not please Augustus, then Herod Junior, a son of Mariamne II. Secondly, Antipater was to bring before the emperor a new accusation against Syllaios, who was also on his way to Rome. Antipater was to present evidence that Syllaios had been plotting against Herod's life by bribing people in the king's bodyguard.

Antipater left for Rome at the beginning of 5 BC. Pheroras, who firmly refused to divorce his ex-slave wife, left Jerusalem and permanently relocated to his principality in Perea, beyond the Jordan. In a fit of pique, he had sworn that he would not return to Judea as long as his brother lived. And when Herod fell seriously ill and begged his brother to return, Pheroras refused.

We must acknowledge that Herod now behaved with dignity. When, a few months later, Pheroras himself became seriously ill, the king immediately hurried to Perea. He stayed by his brother's bedside for several days until his death.

The splendid funeral of Pheroras took place in Jerusalem. At least his body returned to Judea while Herod was still alive.

The Catastrophe

Antipater learned of Pheroras' death on his way back from Rome in Tarentum, a city in southern Italy. Some weeks later, as he arrived in Cilicia, in Asia Minor, he received a warm letter from his father urging him to return quickly. But at the same time, he received a confidential message from one of his informers that accusations against his mother surfaced at court concerning a new plot against the king.

Suspecting nothing, Antipater continued on his way. Where else could he have gone? Where else could he live? What other fate could he possibly have hoped for? He assumed that nothing terrible had happened in Judea. Herod had uncovered—how many plots against his life? Forty-seven? Fifty? Even if the confidential report turned out to be true and Herod were to treat him with suspicion, Antipater felt confident he could find a way to clear his name.

He had to. He had nothing to hide.

However, as soon as Antipater set foot on Palestinian soil, he immediately realized that the matter was far more serious than he had imagined. Massive crowds had bid him farewell in Caesarea only seven months earlier. Now, no one greeted him. Everyone avoided meeting the prince and his retinue. On his way to Jerusalem, he and his entourage passed through nearly deserted streets of towns and settlements. Gloomy thoughts troubled the heir to the throne; evil forebodings seized his mind and froze his heart.

Nevertheless, he boldly pressed on, head held high. There was no turning back in any case.

In Jerusalem, royal guards stopped Antipater's men right in front of the royal palace gate and escorted them away. He entered alone, though still fully armed. The guards immediately admitted him to the king's chambers. He approached his father to kiss him. At that moment, Herod spread out his arms, turned away his cheek, and shouted in a terrifying voice:

"This, too, proves that you are devious! You kiss me, knowing what you are accused of! Perish, accursed one! You will not touch me until you clear yourself of these charges. Tomorrow, you will stand before the tribunal. Prepare your defense. One night is all you have."

Antipater was unable to utter a word. Only now did he learn from his wife what had happened during his absence.

Poison

Immediately after Pheroras's magnificent funeral, two freedmen approached Herod and informed him that someone had poisoned their master: his wife had served him a poisoned dish. She had allegedly purchased this poison with her mother from a certain Nabatean woman, supposedly as a love potion. Tortured slave girls did not reveal anything: the accusation was most likely a fabrication concocted by Salome to harm the woman she despised. But during the investigation, the king learned that Antipater had been meeting with Pheroras and his wife. During one of these meetings, someone supposedly uttered the following words:

"After Alexander and Aristobulus, we will be Herod's next victims."

On another occasion, Antipater supposedly told his mother:

"I will ascend the throne as a gray-haired man—if I do not die before my father."

From these reports, Herod concluded that Salome had been right in warning him about Antipater. He directed his anger towards Antipater's mother, Doris, again banishing her from Jerusalem. Then he subjected some of Antipater's friends and courtiers to torture. One of them testified that his master had bought Egyptian poison, which he then passed on to Pheroras, who gave it to his wife. The poison was to kill the king during Antipater's absence—to divert all suspicions from his person. Summoned, Pheroras' wife admitted that she indeed possessed some poison. To retrieve it, she went to her chambers. Suddenly, a noise and a scream came from her rooms—the unfortunate woman attempted to kill herself by jumping out of the window. Alas, she only succeeded in breaking both her legs. When she came to and was brought before the king, terrified of the threat of torture, she immediately began to talk: her husband had indeed received poison from Antipater and entrusted it to her for safekeeping. However, when Herod visited him during his illness, filled with remorse and already preparing for his own death, Pheroras threw the poison into the fire; he kept only a little portion for himself in case he ever needed to commit suicide.

The individuals involved in supplying the poison confessed. Mariamne II's involvement in this affair came to light. Herod immediately expelled her from the palace and amended his will, removing the paragraph naming her son as the second in succession after Antipater. He stripped Mariamne's father of the office of High Priest.

In the meantime, letters from various influential individuals began to arrive from Rome warning Herod about his two sons by the Samaritan woman Malthace—Archelaus and Antipas. They had been studying in the capital for some time, and the reports stated that the two princes slandered their father and lamented the fate of their half-brothers, the sons of Mariamne I. It took little effort to establish that the reports had been concocted on Antipater's initiative.

Trial in Jerusalem

When Antipater was brought into the courtroom the day after arriving in Jerusalem, he saw Publius Quintilius Varus, the new governor of Syria, standing beside his father. Also present were many royal council members and the leading Romans from Varus's entourage. They were assembled to repeat the scene of the trial in Beirut: the king and governor presiding, distinguished judges sitting in the tribunal, and a son of Herod's as the accused. The course of the trial was also similar, especially its first part, in which, in a passionate prosecutorial speech, Herod once again lamented his wretched fate as the father of degenerate sons.

However, unlike in Beirut, where Mariamne's sons were not

given the opportunity to defend themselves, Antipater began to speak immediately. Herod, weary and perhaps moved by his son's words, interrupted Antipater and gave the floor to Nicholas of Damascus. Antipater's defense had been brilliant and moved everyone, allegedly even the Roman governor. However, his beautiful words about filial love and his desperate plea for mercy faded away like melted snow when Nicholas of Damascus began to speak—not because of his extraordinary eloquence but because of the chain of irrefutable evidence the scholar was able to present, each link exposing a different crime or machination of Antipater. Witnesses were called, and testimonies were read. The most dramatic moment of the trial came when the poison discovered in the possession of Pheroras' wife was tested. It was given to a convict right in front of the court. The man dropped dead on the spot.

Antipater was thrown into prison, where he was to remain until the emperor's response came from Rome, for Herod, as prudent and as loyal as ever, did not fail to send envoys with the appropriate letter to Augustus immediately after the trial. Shortly after their departure, Herod's agents intercepted letters indicating a new intrigue by Antipater, this time directed against Salome. During his stay in Rome, he had persuaded a certain Jewish woman, a slave of the emperor's daughter Julia, to inform Herod that Salome was planning to marry Syllaios.

ULTIMATE THINGS[62]

The Golden Eagle

Above the main entrance of one of the temple courtyards, Herod affixed the statue of a golden eagle with outstretched wings, the symbol that the Roman legions carried before them into battle. By doing so, the ruler threw a challenge in his subjects' faces: a challenge that doubly offended them, for it hurt both their religious sentiments and their national pride. Yes, the Law prohibited the making of images of living creatures, but how offensive it was to place such an image within the confines of the Temple—as if to remind everyone of their downfall and subjugation.

Indeed, it is not easy to fathom what prompted Herod to take such a step. Throughout his reign, he had diligently avoided offending the religious sentiments of the Jews. If he built temples for Augustus and erected his statues, he did it only outside of the province of Judea. And he had the Temple rebuilt on a magnificent scale precisely to make up for those transgressions and to demonstrate to Judeans that he was a faithful Jew.

Perhaps the king, entirely dependent on the emperor's favor and fearing its loss due to family quarrels, desired to manifest his absolute loyalty to Rome. Perhaps the message of the eagle was for the emperor: everything in Herod's realm was subject to the Roman eagle, even the Temple of Jerusalem.

Or perhaps this decision arose from some senile delusion? Herod was ill. He now resided mainly in Jericho, his favorite city. He realized that his life was drawing to a close, and he set about composing a new will. Antipater's downfall nullified the king's last testament. He

---

[62] The Polish title of this chapter uses the term of the Catholic catechism usually rendered in English as *Eschata*: the fundamental Catholic beliefs about the "end of days": the second coming of Christ, resurrection of the dead, and the Last Judgment.

appointed his youngest son, the second son of his wife Malthace—
Herod Antipas—as his successor, bypassing two older sons: the first
son of Malthace, Archelaus, and Cleopatra's son, Philip. (Antipater's
machinations in Rome had accomplished this much). Nevertheless,
the king bequeathed substantial legacies to them, as well as to other
members of the family and friends. The most generous bequests went
to the emperor, his wife Livia, and the king's sister, Salome.

It was not going to be his last will.

The entire country knew that the man who had directed its fate for
several decades was dying. New hopes were kindled, old ambitions
revived, and the resistance movements, once broken and suppressed
by the iron hand of the tyrant, stirred again.

At the beginning of March 4 BC, a crowd tore down and broke
the golden eagle into pieces. The commander of Fortress Antonia
immediately intervened. The crowd dispersed at the sight of the
soldiers, but about forty of the most fanatical young men remained in
the courtyard: men who considered it an honor to suffer martyrdom
for the sacred cause, students of Judas and Matthias, the two most
prominent Pharisees of that time. All were imprisoned, including their
two teachers. During the interrogation before the king, they all
proudly confessed to the deed and appeared to await death with
genuine joy.

Herod summoned the leading citizens of Judean society to
Jericho and instructed them to assemble in the amphitheater. The king
was carried in in a litter, for he was already so weak that he could
neither walk nor stand. He spoke with great bitterness, enumerating
all his good deeds for the people and the country and, above all,
expounding on the splendor of the Temple, which, after all, was his
work. He cried out:

"And what gratitude do I receive for all this? Behold,
blasphemers and desecrators raise their hands against my gifts! They
think that in this way, they insult me. Never! In reality, it is a crime
against the Temple!"

Of course, the entire amphitheater broke out in unanimous indignation. Everyone shouted that the perpetrators of the crime deserved exemplary punishment. This display by the assembled throng mitigated the king's anger. He replaced the High Priest (again), blaming him for failing to keep the peace at the Temple, but everyone left Jericho free, if with a heavy heart.

A different fate befell the destroyers of the eagle. They and their leaders were sentenced to death and burned alive. It happened on the night of March 13, a night of a lunar eclipse.

The Hippodrome of Jericho

A few weeks later, representatives from all the cities and villages of Palestine were summoned to Jericho again. This time, Herod ordered them into the hippodrome. Guards stationed at all its entrances did not let anyone out.

The summoned crowd camped in the hippodrome for days in anticipation and dread. Among the detained, sinister rumors circulated, linking their fate with the king's life. Everyone knew that Herod was on his deathbed. He suffered pains, ulcers, and—write the historians—"putrefaction of the intestines and the lower abdomen." Doctors had advised the king to take baths in the thermal springs of Callirrhoë, beyond the Jordan, and he nearly breathed his last there. He returned to Jericho and gave the order to bring in his most distinguished subjects to the hippodrome. People guessed that he had once again changed his mind about the succession plan. Others, more fearful, thought that they were simply hostages and guarantors of peace; if incidents like the tearing down of the eagle were to happen again, they would pay for it with their lives.

As is usual in such situations, among those confined in the hippodrome were people who seemed to know everything—even such words as had been whispered by the dying king in most profound secrecy to his sister, Salome. He had instructed her, they said, that as soon as he closed his eyes, his soldiers should kill everyone in the hippodrome. "They all hate me and await my death. Let us give each town and each settlement a reason to cry at my demise."

The rumor was taken more seriously when the news came that Antipater, held until then in the palace dungeon, had been executed. He was killed immediately after the king received a letter from Augustus in which the emperor left his loyal subject a free hand in deciding his son's fate.

Of course, those who knew everything embellished this event with dramatic details. In a fit of pain, Herod attempted to kill himself with a fruit knife. However, one of his friends intervened, stopping his hand at the last moment. When moaning and lamenting rang throughout the palace, Antipater, believing the king had already died, tried to convince his guards to set him free. Upon receiving this report, Herod promptly dispatched men to execute him.

For five long days following Antipater's death, the people in the hippodrome were kept locked up, uncertain of their fate.

Herod's Last Journey

Now Salome and her husband Alexas arrived at the hippodrome. They did not come to order the general massacre, as was feared at first, but, on the contrary, to release all those detained inside.

Exhausted by anticipation and uncertainty, the people immediately dispersed in all directions. In this joyful moment of liberation, who had the time or inclination to question the reasons for their detention over the past few weeks? Rushing to their families in various regions of Palestine, they already knew the most important thing: the king was dead.

The official announcement of the king's death came a few hours later at a grand assembly of the army and the population of Jericho in the city's amphitheater. First, the king's last address to his soldiers was read aloud. In it, the king thanked them for their faithful service and requested that they show the same loyalty and dedication to his successor. Then, the royal chancellor Ptolemy presented Herod's final testament: Archelaus, the son of Malthace, was to be the king of Judea; his younger brother, Herod Antipas, received Galilee and Perea; while Philip, the son of Cleopatra, got the lands of Trachonitis, Batanea, and Auranitis. Salome received three cities: Jamnia, Phasaelis, and Azotus,[63] along with five hundred thousand drachmas. The will also left substantial legacies for all the king's relatives and friends, with the largest cash legacy going to Augustus and his wife.

The soldiers immediately acclaimed Archelaus as king. Nevertheless, everyone wondered: would the emperor approve the final will of his loyal vassal?

The king's body was now transported to Jerusalem; from there, a magnificent funeral procession headed south towards Herodium, along the same path along which the king had fled the Parthians thirty-six years earlier.

The monarch's remains, draped in royal purple and adorned with symbols of power, lay on a bier covered with scarlet carpets and studded with sparkling jewels. Behind the bier walked the surviving sons and relatives, the highest dignitaries, the units of the royal guard, and soldiers clad in armor shining with silver and gold. Five hundred slaves swung censers in the air, raising a thick cloud of fragrant smoke.

Thus, they approached the high castle hill to place the remains of the king in his tomb. They approached the steep hill slowly, then ascended the two hundred steps of white marble. With each step, a more expansive view unfolded before them. Far away, among the ranges of hills to the right, beyond the broad valley, the white houses of a small settlement gleamed, almost hidden in the dark green of dense orchards.

The settlement was called Bethlehem.

Who among those following the bier of the king could have foreseen that the fame of this inconsequential village would live on even after the marble and mighty boulders of the mighty fortress of Herodion

---

[63] Jamnith, Fasayil, Ashdod

turned into a heap of ruins? Who could have guessed that Herod's name would remain familiar across the world only because of a tale that would link it to that humble town?

Let us drop in on Bethlehem.

The Legend of Herod

And it came to pass in those days that there went out a decree from Caesar Augustus that all the world should be taxed. (And this taxing was first made when Cyrenius was governor of Syria). And all went to be taxed, every one into his own city. And Joseph also went up from Galilee, out of the city of Nazareth, into Judaea, unto the city of David, which is called Bethlehem; (because he was of the house and lineage of David).

The Gospel attributed to Luke says this in its second chapter. The second chapter of the Gospel attributed to Matthew says a little more:

Now when Jesus was born in Bethlehem of Judæa in the days of Herod the king, behold, there came wise men from the east to Jerusalem, saying, Where is he that is born King of the Jews? for we have seen his star in the east, and are come to worship him. When Herod the king had heard these things, he was troubled, and all Jerusalem with him. And when he had gathered all the chief priests and scribes of the people together, he demanded of them where Christ should be born. And they said unto him, In Bethlehem of Judæa: for thus it is written by the prophet,

And thou Bethlehem, in the land of Juda, art not the least among the princes of Juda: for out of thee shall come a Governor, that shall rule my people Israel.

Then Herod, when he had privily called the wise men, enquired of them diligently what time the star appeared. And he sent them to Bethlehem, and said, Go and search diligently for the young child; and when ye have found him, bring me word again, that I may come and worship him also.

When they had heard the king, they departed; and, lo, the star, which they saw in the east, went before them, till it came and stood over where the young child was. When they saw the star, they rejoiced with exceeding great joy. And when they were come into the house, they saw the young child with Mary, his mother, and fell down, and worshipped him: and when they had opened their treasures, they presented unto him gifts; gold, and frankincense, and myrrh. And being warned of God in a dream that they should not return to Herod, they departed into their own country another way. And when they were departed, behold, the angel of the Lord appeareth to Joseph in a dream, saying, Arise, and take the young child and his mother, and flee into Egypt, and be thou there until I bring thee word: for Herod will seek the young child to destroy him. When he arose, he took the young child and his mother by night, and departed into Egypt: and was there until the death of Herod: that it might be fulfilled which was spoken of the Lord by the prophet, saying,

Out of Egypt have I called my son.

Then Herod, when he saw that he was mocked of the wise men, was exceeding wroth, and sent forth, and slew all the children that were in Bethlehem, and in all the coasts thereof, from two years old and under, according to the time which he had diligently enquired of the wise men.

These two accounts raise some interesting questions. And, surely, the first of them is: when was Jesus actually born?

The Beginning of the New Era

Herod died in the early spring of 4 BC. All sources clearly and unambiguously attest to this. Of course, the ancients did not use our system of reckoning time, so this year was designated differently: 750th year since the founding of the city of Rome; the first year of the 194th

Olympiad; the year in which Gaius Calvisius and Lucius Passienus held the office of consul in Rome; the 23rd year since the Senate granted the title of Augustus to the emperor—or some other way. However, when converted to our system, all these dates always signify the same thing: 4 BC.

Yet, the Gospels tell us that Herod was still alive when Jesus was born in Bethlehem. Since Christians maintain that they count their era from the birth of Jesus, there is a contradiction here. How can we reconcile this discrepancy?

The first generations of Christians saw Jesus as the Messiah who heralded the coming of the kingdom of righteousness and the rule of his chosen believers. And for them, it was sufficient to hear what the Gospels said: that Jesus was born when Herod was king of Judea and Augustus was the emperor of Rome. Since they expected a global catastrophe, the end of the world, the day of judgment, and the return of the living, triumphant Christ at any moment, it didn't seem worth pondering to them in which year Jesus had come into the world.

However, as centuries passed, and the return of Christ was delayed again and again, Christianity gradually turned its focus from the impatient expectation of the future to the remembrance of its past. Gradually, educated individuals who wished to emulate the examples of ancient literature and scholarship embraced the faith. Thus, the history of the Church was born, and like any history, it needed a chronology and a starting point.

In the 6th century AD, a Roman monk, Dionysius, known as Exiguus, or "the Lesser," presented a system of counting years based on "the incarnation of our Lord Jesus Christ." To determine when that happened, Dionysius had the same data that we have today: the statement in the Gospels that when Jesus was born, Herod was still alive. This clue is not very specific because, by its lights, Jesus could have been born some years, perhaps even a dozen years, before the king's death. The Gospels do not tell us how long the holy family stayed in Egypt, whether months or years. Perhaps to simplify things, Dionysius assumed that Jesus's birth occurred in the year of Herod's death.

But in establishing the year of Herod's death, Dionysius made a mistake. It is difficult today to determine whether he did this due to a simple oversight or because he consciously aligned the incarnation date with some idea of cycles of years. Whatever the cause, he stated that Herod had died in the year 754 since the foundation of Rome, when, in fact, he died in the year 750.

In the following centuries, the system introduced by Dionysius became widespread and known as the "Christian" or "Common" Era, taking as its starting point the year 754 from the founding of Rome.

Until not so long ago, it was common to use the terms "Before Christ" (BC) or "Anno Domini" (AD) to designate whether a given year belonged to the series of years before or after that initial point, which has its age-old tradition, but is entirely unfounded from the scholarly point of view. After all, even the most devout Christian, one who desires to uphold all the details of the story of the events in Bethlehem, must acknowledge the truth of the following statement: Christ was born several years Before Christ.

Then, there is the question of the day of birth. As late as the 3rd century AD, Christians gave different dates, including May 20th. The oldest mention of December 25th as the feast of the Nativity of Christ dates back only to the year 336 AD. Why was that date chosen? The answer seems simple. December 25th coincided with the pagan holiday of the sun (*Natalis Solis Invicti*—the Birth of the Unconquered Sun). The church wished to give a Christian character to celebrations that the broad masses of the empire had cherished for centuries.

The foregoing might lead you to object that I overlooked a particular chronological detail clearly attested to in the Gospels: that when Jesus was born, Cyrenius (the correct spelling is Quirinius) was governor of Syria, and, on the orders of Augustus, a census of the entire world took place. Why not use this information to determine the year of Jesus's birth?

So, let us address this issue as well.

Quirinius and the Census

Publius Sulpicius Quirinius, for such was his full name, is a figure well-known in history. Various ancient sources mention him, not only the Gospels.

He hailed from humble origins but, through courage and ability, rose to the highest offices of state and became one of the closest collaborators of Emperor Augustus. In 12 BC, he held the office of consul and later served as the proconsul of the senatorial province of Asia, which corresponds to the western part of present-day Turkey. A few years later, he became the imperial legate (*legatus Augusti pro praetore*) of the provinces of Pamphylia and Galatia, also in present-day Turkey. In this position, he distinguished himself by subduing the people of Homana.[64] Finally, in the year 6 AD, he received the office of imperial legate for the second time, this time over the province of Syria.

That year, in Rome, Augustus made an important decision regarding Palestine. Herod's last will had given the largest part of his kingdom—Judea, Idumea, and Samaria—to his son Archelaus to rule as an *ethnarch*—an *ethnarch* because Archelaus never received the royal title from the Emperor. However, Archelaus, while he had inherited his father's faults, had not inherited his virtues. Endless complaints of the oppressed population finally had their effect. The Emperor deposed Archelaus, exiled him to Vienna[65] in southern Gaul, and annexed his possessions to the province of Syria. He entrusted Quirinius with the implementation of this last task.

One of the first steps in assuming control over the new territory was to conduct a census of the population, a land survey, and a thorough accounting of all private property of Archelaus—this last because Rome decided to confiscate it, too. Judea's population was henceforth to be subjected, like the population of all Roman

---

[64] Southwest of Lake Trogitis, Seydişehir, Konya Province, Turkey.
[65] Today Vienne, in the department of Isère.

provinces, to direct Roman taxation.

The news of the impending census stirred violent opposition among the Jews. It only eased after the intervention of the High Priest. Yet some continued to call for armed resistance, and among these last, the Zealots played the leading role.

Our sources attest that the census was conducted in the 37th year after Octavian's victory at Actium, corresponding to the year 6/7 AD. It left a lasting impression on the memory of the inhabitants of Judea: it was the tangible proof of the transition to direct Roman rule, it affected every person in the country, and it almost led to an outbreak of rebellion.

These are the facts. The conclusion that emerges from them is clear. If we try to determine the birth date of Jesus based on the mention of Quirinius' governorship and the population census, we must thereby reject the Gospel account of Herod—because the king had already been dead for ten years by then. Instead, we would have to propose that Jesus was born in 6 or 7 AD.

Some apologists try to find a way out of this difficulty by maintaining that Quirinius was the governor of Syria twice. They point to an inscription found in the Roman suburb of Tibur (modern-day Tivoli), which states that Quirinius held the office of imperial legate twice. However, more recent studies have shown that the inscription does not say that he served as governor of Syria twice, but rather that he twice held the office of imperial legate. Which we already know: he held it once in Pamphylia and Galatia and then again in Syria. Furthermore, we do not know of any case in the early Empire where the same person served twice as the imperial legate of the same province.

But even if Quirinius had governed Syria twice, the difficulty is not resolved, for the issue is not how many times Quirinius governed Syria but whether he held this position during the reign of King Herod. And it so happens that we know the names of the Roman governors of Syria during the last years of Herod's reign. They were Gaius Sentius Saturninus (9-6 BC) and Publius Quintilius Varus (6-4 BC). The latter governed Syria until the summer of 4 BC—several months *after* Herod's death (spring of 4 BC). Where could Quirinius fit into this?

Some even propose that Quirinius conducted the census not as the governor of Syria but as a special envoy of the Emperor with specific powers while Saturninus was the legate of Syria, but that is a rather strained construct: after all, the Gospel explicitly names Quirinius as the governor of Syria. The Greek term *hegemon* cannot be interpreted in any other way. Equally importantly, the census in the Roman Empire always fell within the jurisdiction of the governor of the province. The authorities never sent special envoys for this purpose. Such an office did not exist.

Furthermore, whoever was the governor of Syria during Herod's lifetime would not have had the right to conduct a census in his kingdom because it formally constituted a separate, independent state. The Emperor's decrees had no legal basis within the borders of Judea. The fact that the news of Quirinius' census provoked outrage and resistance among the Jews demonstrates this clearly. Moreover, other circumstances of the census mentioned in the Gospel raise doubts. In Rome, censuses of citizens had been conducted systematically for centuries. Later, starting with the rule of Augustus, censuses were also taken of the inhabitants of individual provinces. However, we know nothing about any census ever encompassing the entire Empire—all Roman citizens and all "provincials."

The Gospel also asserts that the census required each person to go to the city of their "ancestral origin." But such a requirement would serve no purpose, for what would be the use of counting people where they did not live? Roman censuses never imposed such a requirement.

In fact, this detail reveals the motives that the author of the Gospel had in mind when mentioning the census. He wanted to demonstrate that Jesus, although raised among the Galileans, was born in Judea. In the eighth century BC, the prophet Micah, speaking of an imaginary leader who would one day defeat the Assyrians, had said that the leader would come from Bethlehem, and he probably said this because David, the conqueror of the Philistines, had come from that city. But how to bring a family of Galileans to a small town in southern

Judea? And for a short time, too: only for the time of birth of Jesus?

For the author of the Gospel, who likely wrote during the reign of Emperor Nero (54-68 AD), the memory of the great census conducted several decades earlier came to the rescue. The census shook the country and perhaps did require some inhabitants to travel since everyone had to register *in the place of their residence.* Thus, it seemed reasonable to suggest that Joseph's family temporarily relocated to Bethlehem. After two generations, the census was still remembered—as was the name of the man who had imposed it: Quirinius. But no one remembered the exact chronology or circumstances, and who would even know whether the famous King Herod was still alive then? By the time the Gospels were written, the Romans had governed a significant part of Palestine for many years. It must have seemed natural to the authors, born and raised under Roman rule, that by the time Jesus was born, the Roman Emperor's and his governor's commands applied in Judea. Such retrojection of contemporary relations into the past is very common, even among people with a certain level of historical education.

The evangelist also thought it self-evident that the census, which took place only in Judea and Syria, encompassed the entire world.

The Wise Men and the Star

The Greek text of the Gospel states that *the Magi* paid homage to the Child in Bethlehem. The Magi were Zoroastrian priests. In modern translations, they are often called "Wise men." It is interesting to trace how the legend of the Wise Men developed and transformed over the centuries.

It seems that the story was included in the Gospel in order to add greater splendor to the birth of Jesus. In the first few centuries of Christianity, the tradition of the homage of the Magi made no mention of any royal dignity associated with them. The oldest extant artifacts of Christian art confirm it. It was only in the 6th century that the belief that the three Magi were *kings* became widespread. It found its root in Psalm 72:

> He shall have dominion also from sea to sea, and from the river unto the ends of the earth. They that dwell in the wilderness shall bow before him; and his enemies shall lick the dust of his feet. The kings of Tarshish and of the isles shall bring presents: the kings of Sheba and Seba shall offer gifts. Yea, all kings shall fall down before him: all nations shall serve him. [66]

This psalm had been composed many centuries before the new era and described a powerful, long-awaited king of Israel. Later tradition assumed it referred to the Messiah.

The depiction of kings paying homage in Bethlehem appears in medieval art from the 10th century onwards. And yet, even on a reliquary from Cluny dated to the 12th century, only two out of the three figures bearing gifts wear crowns.

The Gospel does not specify the number of Wise Men. In the 3rd century, artists often depicted two Wise Men paying homage, while in the 6th century, they portrayed as many as four. The Eastern Christian churches believed that there were twelve. Eventually, the belief that there had been three Magi-kings prevailed because the Gospel states that they offered three gifts: gold, frankincense, and myrrh, leading people to imagine that each Wise Man gave something different.

There was also no consensus regarding the three Wise Men's names. As late as the 7th century, they were named Larvandad, Gushnasaph, and Hormisdas. Today, the three bodies enshrined at the Cologne Cathedral bear the names of Melchior, Caspar, and Balthasar. [67]

---

[66] *Psalms* 72:8-11

[67] The *Shrine of the Three Kings* at Cologne Cathedral, according to tradition, contains the bones of the Three Wise Men. Reputedly they were first discovered by Helena of Constantinople on her famous pilgrimage to Palestine and the Holy Lands. She took their remains to the church of Hagia Sophia in Constantinople; they were later moved to Milan (some sources say by the city's

The Guiding Star of the Wise Men deserves a separate chapter in the history of the Bethlehem legend. Over the centuries, people have proposed numerous bizarre hypotheses on this matter. Some have said that the star might have been a comet, a planet, a planetary conjunction, and even—a spaceship. Gathering all these speculations together would make for one fat book, even longer than the one you have before you. Such a book would be a great monument to the history of human naivety.

In reality, the matter is simple and not even very interesting. But some understanding of the the beliefs of that era when the Gospels were written is necessary. It was an era in which astrology held immense significance—the belief that stars influenced everything that happened on Earth. It is difficult for a modern person to imagine how widespread and deeply ingrained this superstition was then. Many believe this even today. But to understand a person from antiquity, we must always remember that more or less everyone at the time adhered to this superstition, not only ordinary people but even philosophers. Therefore, anyone describing the life of an outstanding individual felt it his sacred duty to emphasize that some extraordinary celestial phenomena accompanied the hero's birth, deeds, and death. Such claims bestowed a celestial glow upon the individual, and readers fully believed them; after all, they, too, patronized astrologers.

The Star of Bethlehem does not seem to have anything to do with any real phenomenon anyone has been able to document. It most likely reflects the beliefs and convictions that dominated the human mind then—and to some extent still do today.

The Massacre of the Innocents

For generations, the people of Judea retained the memory of a ruthless

____

bishop, Eustorgius I), before being sent to their current resting place by the Holy Roman Emperor Frederick I in 1164. The Milanese celebrate their part in the tradition by holding a medieval costume parade every 6 January.

king who spared not even his children, not even his firstborn son. They also remembered the messianic prophecies that spread in the last years of his rule, which met with severe repression from the king.

These obscure, exaggerated, distorted reports and echoes of the past served as a basis for the evangelist to craft a colorful narrative. It has a fairy-tale character: a cruel and suspicious king; a mortal danger unwittingly brought upon the newborn Child by strangers from distant lands; a miraculous rescue at the eleventh hour; and the king's wrath vented on the innocent.

Of course, the author needed to take the opportunity to demonstrate that, in this case, once again, what the prophets had foretold for centuries came to pass. So, when he speaks of the flight to Egypt, he cites the words of Hosea: "Out of Egypt have I called my son." Yet, he prudently does not quote the beginning of this sentence, which reads, "When Israel was a child, then I loved him, and called my son out of Egypt." Thus, Hosea referred to the legendary exodus of the Jews from Egypt under the leadership of Moses—not to the promised Messiah. The practice of quoting words out of context has not been invented by modern media.

It is unnecessary to argue that the massacre of the innocents in Bethlehem is purely legendary. Our sources allow for a relatively accurate reconstruction of Herod's history and meticulously record all his crimes but never mention this one. Herod was undoubtedly a ruthless tyrant, a murderer of his own family, but he was not insane.

In many ancient peoples, we encounter this fairy-tale motif: a king learns that a newly born child will bring about his doom, so he tries to find it and kill it. In this connection, it is worthwhile to recall what some said about the birth of the Roman emperor Augustus. Just a few months before his birth, a soothsayer prophesied: "This year, a child will be born who will become the king of Rome." The terrified Senate proposed a law to execute all newborns, but this decree was not carried out, as senators with expecting wives defeated it.

Herod and Solomon

The Massacre of the Innocents—a massacre that never happened—became a symbol of cruelty for ages. Artists used it as the subject for many magnificent works. And it was this crime—the crime he did not commit—that gave Herod his grim reputation. It is not an exaggeration to say that, due to the Gospel story, the ruthless king of Judea is more widely known today than all the great rulers of antiquity who shaped the course of history. The radiant stars of Alexander the Great, Julius Caesar, and Emperor Augustus pale next to the bloody halo surrounding Herod's name.

Indeed, one could argue that this ill fame is a just comeuppance for all those terrible crimes of the killer of his wife and his three sons. However, upon reflection, the fairness of the judgment of posterity is questionable. Not only because, as an administrator, Herod presents himself in a relatively favorable light. For even though he gained power and held onto it by various questionable means, he ensured relative independence for his country—the only sort achievable at the time—internal peace and economic prosperity. He constantly navigated the ship of his nation between the Scylla of Roman greed and the Charybdis of Jewish fanaticism, yet he guided it safely into a haven of great economic prosperity. He felt closely connected to the global culture of the time but also understood the traditions of the people he ruled.

The assessment of Herod's character and deeds also lacks fairness because people generally apply different criteria to different historical figures. No one reminds us constantly that Alexander the Great personally killed several of his closest friends—including one who saved his life in battle. Who would emphasize that Emperor Augustus sentenced his only daughter to lifelong exile and, later, his granddaughter? That he ordered the immediate execution of his great-grandson at birth? That, citing the "reason of state," he condemned his last grandson to exile—and perhaps even death? Furthermore, who reproaches Cleopatra for the murder of her brother and sister and her readiness to get rid of her husband and benefactor, Antony, after their joint defeat?

From a certain point of view, considering such facts does have some value. Of course, this is not a matter of simplistic weighing of merits and faults or of naive pondering over who was better or worse. A broader approach to the matter is possible. For instance, we can compare different figures and inquire why posterity celebrates one while condemning another.

Let us stick with the history of ancient Jews and compare two rulers who became symbols for later generations: the wise king and the tyrant, the just judge, and the cruel monster. The juxtaposition of the names Herod and Solomon may seem shocking. But let us recall some facts.

After David's death, the throne of Israel was supposed to go to his eldest living son, Adonijah. However, things turned out differently. The aging king succumbed to the intrigues of the faction hostile to Adonijah and brought his younger half-brother Solomon to the throne. David's eldest son knew his brother's character well and sought refuge in the Temple. Only after Solomon solemnly swore that no harm would come to Adonijah did the rightful heir to the throne leave the holy place. However, the king proved to be a perjurer. Adonijah was soon put to death on Solomon's orders.

Not only Adonijah, by the way. David's eldest son had had many supporters and friends at court and among the priests. Solomon dealt with all of them with absolute ruthlessness. Abiathar, the famous priest of David, was banished; he faced death if he ever returned to Jerusalem. The eminent and deserving commander Joab, conqueror of the Edomites, like Adonijah before him, sought sanctuary in the Temple. This did not save him, for on Solomon's orders, he was killed at the altar. Another nobleman, Shimei, had been ordered not to leave Jerusalem, and when he briefly crossed the Kidron while chasing a fugitive slave—he was put to death.

Thus, Solomon ascended to the throne through treachery and bloodshed. And how did he rule? His reign came at a fortunate time when no great power existed in the Middle East. Babylon and Assyria had weakened; Solomon even managed to marry one of the pharaoh's daughters. The Philistines and Edomites, defeated by David and Joab, posed no threat. Maintaining peaceful relations with the neighboring small states was easy.

However, Solomon, a king supposedly wise and magnificent, could not even retain the entirety of his father's legacy. Edom broke away, and a strong state with its center in Damascus arose along the northern borders.

Solomon was more preoccupied with his court, construction, and extravagant living. He built a palace and a temple, several settlements, and fortresses. To cover the costs of these works, he gave Hiram, the King of Tyre, twenty cities in Galilee; for construction material—cedar and fir from Lebanon—he paid the same king twenty thousand measures of wheat and twenty thousand measures of olive oil annually. Solomon forced thousands of Israelites to work felling forests and transporting timber: all construction work was carried out by corvée.

The whole country was divided into twelve districts, each supporting the court for one month. And the court was expensive. Seven wives, scores of concubines, entire armies of servants. Each day, they ate thirty measures of fine flour and sixty measures of ordinary flour, ten fat oxen, twenty pasture-fed oxen, a hundred sheep, and an abundance of game and birds. All the wealth of the country was unable to support the expense of the court: together with Hiram, Solomon organized trading expeditions to distant lands to gather treasures and luxury items.

This heavy burden fell on the shoulders of the tribes of Israel. The burden was made even heavier because Solomon did not distribute it evenly. Solomon favored the population of Jerusalem and its surroundings, that is, Judea, and this caused bitterness among the other tribes and revived the scarcely healed antagonisms between the regions.

The consequences of this shortsighted policy were catastrophic. Soon after Solomon's death, the kingdom split into two parts: Judah and Israel. It led to subsequent wars and disasters and the downfall of the whole people.

So, given these clear and undeniable facts, whence comes the legend of Solomon as the wisest and most magnificent of kings? The answer is simple. Solomon's policies won over the Judeans and the priests—the sector of the society which, after the destruction of Israel, became the exclusive bearer of the memory and tradition of the nation.

And the reader of this book knows that Herod treated these groups of the population of Palestine worst of all.

The lesson here is this: if you wish to secure for yourself a good reputation in history, you must win over those who will pass down your image to posterity.

CODA

Rabbi Hillel

This book tells a tale of blood and hatred, fanaticism and lust for power, heroism and betrayal.

It is perhaps fitting to close with the story of a man who witnessed those grim events as a contemporary of Herod and a resident of Jerusalem. He was as famous and honored as the king, though he lived in poverty, modestly and quietly, shying away from worldly glory.

Hillel hailed from a Jewish family settled in Babylon. He may have come to Jerusalem in the company of Hyrcanus when the Hasmonean returned from Parthian captivity. He came to study the Mosaic Law at the renowned school of Shemaiah. He earned his living through manual labor. He gave a portion of his meager daily earnings to the school's porter, who would let him in, for Hillel could not afford the regular school fee. One winter day, he earned so little that he could not pay anything. To avoid missing a day of learning, he climbed onto the flat roof of the school building and listened to the teachers' words from there. Meanwhile, snow and frost came; only on the second day was Hillel found, stiff and half-frozen from the cold.

By the time Herod, following the defeat of Cleopatra and the extensive favors granted to him by Octavian, finally solidified his grip on power, Hillel was already the most famous scholar of the Scriptures. People turned to him to resolve all manner of disputes, and his answers were treated as solemn verdicts, even though no political force backed his decisions. To what did Hillel owe his universally recognized authority?

Not only to his outstanding mental qualities, broad knowledge, and keen wit: at least equal admiration attached to his kindness to all, crystal-clear integrity, and a serene gentleness that nothing could ever disturb. Hillel's teachings always aimed to mitigate the strictest demands of the Law. In this, he differed from the austere school of Shemaiah. Hillel developed a system of interpreting the Law and adapting the ancient commandments to the constantly changing requirements of modern life. Hillel drew his system from the spirit of Greek philosophy and logic. Elaborated and improved by generations of later scholars of the Scriptures, it became the basis of the Talmud.

We are curious to know if Herod ever met Hillel. He had certainly heard about him. It speaks well of the King of Judea that he tolerated in his capital a man who enjoyed such great authority and respect among the people; it is evidence that where politics were not involved, Herod was not petty.

The destinies of Herod and Hillel took strange paths. The descendants of the former continued to rule parts of Palestine and even other lands in the Middle East for four generations, but by the end of the 1st century AD, the Herodian line died out.

But the school of Hillel endured. From generation to generation, its leaders bore the title of *nasi*,[68] and according to tradition, they were all descendants of Hillel himself. The destruction of the Temple of Jerusalem in 70 AD and of the city in 135 AD did not put an end to the school; from then on, it conducted its teaching in small towns of Palestine, where significant concentrations of Jews still survived. *Nasi* became the spiritual leaders of the entire Jewish community, living scattered in all the lands of the world. They were the visible symbol of the survival of a people who, though deprived of a state and even homeland, refused to die out. The magnificent fortresses built by Herod—Alexandrion, Masada, Herodium— turned into piles of rubble, but Hillel's school lived on.

What was the most essential teaching of Hillel's school? Rabbi Hillel himself answered this when a stranger asked him sarcastically:

---

[68] The noun *nasi* (including its grammatical variations), occurs 132 times in the Masoretic Text of the Hebrew Bible, and in English is usually translated "prince," occasionally, "captain." During the period of the Second Temple, the president of the Sanhedrin bore the title of *nasi*. The title was later applied to those who held high offices in the Jewish community, and Jews who held prominence in the courts of non-Jewish rulers. Today it refers to the President of Israel.

"Explain the Law to me, but briefly, so briefly as I can stand on one leg."

The Rabbi answered him:

"Do not do unto your neighbor anything that is hateful to you. This is the whole Law. Everything else is just commentary."

Sources

Herod's memoirs have not survived. A similar fate befell the work of his court historiographer and secretary, Nicholas of Damascus. Although it had covered the entire history of humanity, it devoted a considerable amount of space to the rule of Herod. The autobiography of Nicholas has also been lost.

While we do not possess these primary sources in their original, we are well acquainted with their content, especially the work of Nicholas, particularly the sections concerning Herod. This is thanks to the later writings of the Jewish historian Josephus, known as Flavius.

He was born in 37/38 AD, hailing from an aristocratic priestly family. When the great Jewish uprising against the Romans erupted in 66 AD, he became one of its leaders in Galilee but soon fell into Roman hands. The Roman commander Vespasian Flavius, who later became emperor, released him. Hence, Josephus acquired the epithet "Flavius." For the remainder of his life, and following the final suppression of the Jewish rebellion in 70 AD, he resided in Rome, consistently enjoying the favor of Vespasian and later of his sons, Titus and Domitian. He wrote extensively, primarily in Greek, often with the assistance of Greek scribes or scholars.

Josephus' principal works include:

The Jewish War. This work, in seven books, recounts the struggle of the Jews against the Romans, covering the events of 66-70 AD. However, Book I, which is a prologue to these events, discusses the Maccabean uprisings, the Hasmoneans' reign, and Herod's rule.

Jewish Antiquities, in twenty books, recounts the history of the Jews from ancient times to 66 AD. The initial dozen or so books are essentially paraphrases of the Bible. The books dedicated to the time of Herod are Books XIV-XVII.

In both works, the period of Herod is presented almost identically, with some passages even using identical wording. Differences are generally inconsequential, as both works rely heavily and faithfully on the same sources. Chief among these was the work of

Nicholas of Damascus. Additionally, Josephus used the memoirs of Herod. Given that these sources displayed excessive favoritism toward the king, Josephus occasionally incorporated alternative accounts with opposing perspectives because Josephus was a staunch enemy of Herod, partly due to his own family ties to the Hasmoneans.

Consequently, both of Josephus's works sometimes feature contradictions and inconsistencies in portraying and evaluating the king and his actions. There are also chronological discrepancies and occasional repetitions or mistakes. Nonetheless, Josephus remains an invaluable source for us due to his copious, generally reliable, and often unique accounts of many events.

Naturally, Josephus's reports should be cross-checked and supplemented based on other sources whenever possible. In cases where classical authors reference Palestine and the Jews, directly linking the history of Judea to events in the Greek and Roman worlds, one can achieve this kind of broad understanding.

The Talmud is a crucial source for understanding the religious customs of ancient Jews. While it does not directly address Herod and his reign, it provides extensive insights into the contemporaneous scholars of the Scriptures and their views.

The manuscripts from the Dead Sea Scrolls, recently highly acclaimed, are silent on the subject of Herod. However, they shed much light on the way of life and religious teachings of the Essene sect, which held great significance in those times.

Palestine has been a terrain of intensive archaeological research for many years. While the primary focus is on earlier epochs, Herod's times, which left behind numerous splendid monuments, have not been neglected. Archaeologists have recently conducted significant excavations in the ancient Caesarea Maritima; in Samaria; and in Jericho. William F. Albright's book, "The Archaeology of Palestine," published in 1960, provides a solid orientation in the intricate matters of the archaeology of this land from ancient times through the Greco-Roman and Herodian periods.

Newer literature dedicated to Herod and his times is vibrant and diverse.

FROM YOUR TRANSLATOR
Translating and publishing this book has been a labor of love for me.
I grew up reading it, and I have always wanted to be able
to share it with my American friends. And so here it is.
It will not make me rich, but if you liked the book, would you please
recommend it to a friend?
And give it an Amazon review?
https://www.amazon.com/dp/2919820494

THANK YOU!

ABOUT MONDRALA PRESS

Mondrala Press publishes English translations of great
Polish books—books with a track record of international
critical and commercial success but which, for political
reasons, have never been published in English.
To see our newest titles or to subscribe
to our mailing list, please visit
www.mondrala.com
The Greatest Books You Have Never Heard of

Seven Against Thebes

Before the Trojan War, there was the Theban War. Who fought it? Why? What does archeology tell us, and what has survived of ancient the epics?

The Last Olympiad

Serapeum destroyed! Emperor murdered! Pagans raise a revolt! Read leading lights of their time (389-395 AD) as they debate everything from bathing to demon possession.

A Meeting in Oea

Meet Apuleius, Rome's all-time best-selling author, a Platonic scholar, a part-time magician, and a dowry-hunter, as he works on his treatise on Plato at night and schemes to marry a rich African widow by day.

Titus and Berenice

The last vestiges of the kingdom of Judah hung for a while on the outcome of the love affair between the elderly Jewish queen Berenice, granddaughter of Herod the Great, and the 12 years younger son of Vespasian, the emperor of Rome.

Jacek Bocheński

Tiberius Caesar

Terror is normal.
The horrifying tale of Tiberius Caesar, the second emperor of Rome:
the man who normalized political terror. A moral, intellectual,
emotional zero whose only skill in life was to grab and hang onto
power. At any cost. A dizzying look into
the great void of an empty soul.

Joe Alex

The Ships of Minos 1-5

A Bronze Age Saga.
1600 BC. A Minoan ship sails to the ends of the earth in search of the
sources of amber. Days without night, water turning to stone,
monsters of the deep, peoples who sacrifice their kings to their gods
and build great stone circles to worship the sun. And god's face upon
the waters.
One of the greatest exploration sagas ever written.

Witold Makowiecki

Out of the Lion's Maw

570 B.C. They slip their jailors in Carthage and rush across the Mediterranean pursued by enemy agents and assassins: a mysterious oriental priest and his Greek apprentice. Their mission: to prevent the outbreak of a civil war in Egypt.Their opponents: the Great Phoenician Council and the entire state apparatus of Eternal Egypt. Their resources: the old man's wit and the young man's courage.

Wind from the Hospitable Sea

Greece 562 BC. For insolvent debtors, the price of bankruptcy is slavery. When his mother and siblings are seized for unpaid debts, little Diossos must run to fetch help. He must cross mountains, forests, and stormy seas, brave wild animals, slave catchers, pirates, and... the law. He has one month to achieve his quest but only days to grow up.

Arkady Fiedler

The White Jaguar 1-5

AD 1726. An uninhabited Caribbean island off the Spanish Main. A
Virginian renegade. Pirates, Runaway slaves. Cannibals.
The great saga of the mysterious White Jaguar, a white man named
John who became a war leader of the Orinoco Indians in their wars
against the Spanish.

Maria Rodziewiczówna

A Summer of the Forest Folk

The most beautiful book you will read this year.
Turn of the nineteenth century. Three women spend their summers
in a remote cottage deep in the last virgin forest in Europe. This
summer, their teenage big-city nephew joins them. A heart-warming,
feel-good tale of love and friendship, of coming of age, and of the
healing power of nature. This is a book like nothing you have ever
read, a phenomenon, a genre of its own.